🌿 *The Creek*

To MAC AND GERT

Best Wishes

J.V. Johnson

6 - 7 - 06

University Press of Florida

Gainesville *Tallahassee* *Tampa*

Boca Raton *Pensacola* *Orlando*

Miami *Jacksonville*

The
CREEK

J. T. GLISSON

07 06 05 04 03 02 C 7 6 5 4 5 4
07 06 05 04 03 02 P 11 10 9 8 7 6

Library of Congress Cataloging-in-Publication Data
Glisson, James T.
The creek / James T. Glisson.
p. cm.
Includes index.
ISBN 0-8130-1184-1 (alk. paper).—ISBN 0-8130-1185-X
(pbk.: alk. paper)
1. Cross Creek (Fla.)—History. I. Title.
F319.C86G57   1993
975.9´79—dc20   92-32537

Cover illustration and interior art by J. T. Glisson.

Book design by Louise OFarrell.

The University Press of Florida is the scholarly publishing
agency for the State University System of Florida, comprised
of Florida A&M University, Florida Atlantic University,
Florida International University, Florida State University,
University of Central Florida, University of Florida, University of North Florida, University of South Florida, University
of West Florida.

University Press of Florida
15 Northwest 15th Street
Gainesville, Florida 32611
http://www.upf.com

❦ *This book is dedicated to my wife, Pat, my sons Nick and Tom, and my parents, Tom and Pearlee Glisson, who made it all possible.*

Contents

Foreword

by Rip Torn

I HAD BEEN rehearsing a film for television in Char-
lotte, North Carolina. I had a few days off before I was needed to act
on camera, so I flew down to Gainesville, Florida. The flight arrived
early, but J. T. was waiting for me beyond the security door.

He's "Jake" to his family and friends, but Tom Glisson's boy, J. T.,
now is in his season, a patriarch at Cross Creek. People come to him
when they have a problem they can't solve themselves. And that's how
I met this remarkable man, by asking his advice about a problem I
couldn't solve myself on a job of acting in a film shot near his ancestral
home at the Creek.

J. T. Glisson is over six feet, strongly built, a man in his sixties. He
has a full shock of almost white hair and a gray-eyed penetrating look
that was softened by a shy boyish grin when he saw me. As we picked
up my fishing rods at the baggage claim, he said, "We're just past full
moon and a cold front is moving in from the North, but knowing how
you love to fish, I'm determined to git you some."

"I've just come down to finish up this foreword to your book," I
replied.

J. T. pointed out, "You can do that tonight after supper. Here come
your poles." He grinned as if to say, *Don't kid a kidder, Rip, we know your
priorities.*

Driving out of town, we caught up on family and friends. I'm a few years younger than J. T. and honored to be a friend of this artist, author, aviator, and explorer who grew up in the magical land between Lochloosa and Orange Lake called "The Creek."

We passed a seafood market. "Do they still sell cooter, gator, and frog legs there?" I asked.

"In season," J. T. replied. People who grow up in rural areas have a relationship to the land of their heritage and the play of the seasons that is biblical.

J. T. Glisson has been commissioned to paint and sculpt all over the world. He and his beautiful wife, Pat, have been given the seat of honor at the tables of nobility, celebrity, and wealth. Their manner is cultured and gracious. You could say Pat has it because of her Italian parentage but Jake gets it from the people who raised him—a style of honesty, warmth and dignity that comes from the subjects of these stories, the pioneer families who homesteaded the Creek.

Some years ago I was flown to Los Angeles to talk to producer Robert Radnitz and director Martin Ritt about playing an important role in a movie called *Cross Creek,* based on the book by Marjorie Kinnan Rawlings about how she came to fall in love with rural Florida and settle down there. I entered the Radnitz office carrying my script. After a spell of negotiating, Bob gave me a grin and a hug. "You're on board, kiddo. And I'll do something for you if you accept my offer. You can stay on the lake near the set and fish when you're not working."

I flew to Orlando, rented a car, drove to Ocala, and checked into the Ramada Inn, where I met Mary Steenburgen, Peter Coyote, Alfre Woodard, and Dana Hill (whose father I played).

I reminded Bob of his promise. He puffed on his pipe. "Don't you want to stay here in Ocala while we rehearse? I meant while we shoot on location at Cross Creek—hell, man, it's thirty miles away. The Teamsters can't take you out there today." But Bob relented and gave me the directions to find the manager of the grove where we were to film.

So I started living at the Creek right on Orange Lake. In the two weeks of rehearsal in Ocala, Marty and Bob commented that my accent was improving, that I sounded more southern and less Texan. My character in the film was Marsh Turner, who farmed, raised cattle, broke horses, and to make ends meet trapped fish to sell and ran a moonshine still. Many of my major scenes in the movie took place in a fishing boat.

Before and after driving to Ocala to rehearse I would try to get into character by borrowing a boat to fish the lake, and every day I would walk through the backwoods and orange groves to the point on Orange Lake called Cane Hammock, where the set was being built. One day I found myself looking at two giant rattlers the construction crew had killed when they couldn't run them off. These snakes were about six feet long, big as my arm, with beautifully marked diamond backs and rattlers as big as my thumbs.

The night I met J. T. I told him that I had a handle on the role and was rehearsing and had bought a double-barreled Parker. I had a good horse to ride, a big quarter horse with a walking-horse gait. I said that many of my major scenes in the movie took place in a fishing boat but the boat selected wasn't proper for the period and had an outboard motor. Although the era was the 1930s the boat was a 1956-vintage plywood runabout with an outboard transom.

J. T. said, "Well, you've a right to be concerned. A person running fish traps would not use an outboard. That would be a dead giveaway to game wardens."

I drew a sketch of a small bateau like the boat my grandfather and I built. Jake studied it and said, "You fished rivers, didn't you? The bow swept up . . . like this? And why did you use tin—you pulled it up on gravel banks, right? Ours were different." And he sketched one. "I'm not promising you anything but I would like to see the house they've built on the Cane Hammock movie set, if the film people aren't around."

I said, "Everyone's off tomorrow. I've got an okay from the producer and the security guard has been alerted to expect us."

After church J. T. picked me up and we drove to the set. He was taken with the construction of the main set of the movie, a Cracker home with a porch and dog trot. Movie sets are constructed so that the walls can be removed and replaced for lighting and camera purposes. The house faced Orange Lake, a stone's throw away, and there tied to a small dock was the boat I was to use in the film. J. T. laughed. "This movie takes place in the thirties? This is like a 1956 *Popular Mechanics* design made of plywood. We didn't have plywood down here till after World War Two, and we sure didn't have gasoline motors till then. We've got a problem all right," he went on. "It needs to be built of cypress and that's going to be hard to find. We would need boards one by fourteen by fourteen inches. You won't find an old boat. We've looked and I've made a few calls. The kind my dad and I used to make are long gone."

How J. T. decided to build a new boat, how he persuaded a small sawmill owner at Eureka to sell him the cypress and plane it, is another story. It was built in three days and nights of intensive labor without plans, just Jake eyeballing it and shaping it.

Bull Gator, as we named our craft, was a gem. A Teamster from the movie came over, looked at it, and smiled. He returned with Bob Radnitz, who said, "It's a beauty. I know a good craft when I see it." He leased it from us, and it's all through the movie *Cross Creek.*

During the filming a storm blew in from the Gulf. It rained a little over thirteen inches. The lake came up over a foot and Silver Springs Run, where another set was built, backed up over two feet. The land around the sets was under water. Scenes that were meant to be played on foot were played in that authentic Orange Lake boat. Marty Ritt told me we could never have used our original boat in that shallow flooded water—"that little boat Mr. Glisson and you built saved us." When Jake visited the set, I had the pleasure of seeing movie executives rush up to pump his hand and thank him.

I don't believe any of the movie people have ever been back to the Creek, except me. A while back J. T. gave me a manuscript and said, "Rip, read this when you have time and tell what you think." He couldn't have asked a more enjoyable favor. *The Creek* is an intimate view of a special place in America, and a first-person visit with J. T.'s neighbors, Marjorie Kinnan Rawlings, Henry Fountain, Charley Fields, and all those remarkable people that made Cross Creek a part of the American scene during the first half of this century.

I get down here as often as I can to hunt and fish and just to visit. I always stay at the Glissons' wonderful house filled with paintings and sculpture and projects. We love to catch up on family and—like this morning—to hear and watch hundreds of sandhill cranes yodel and cry and dance as they glide in to land in the pasture behind the house.

Acknowledgments

I WANT to thank especially the survivors of the Cross Creek families, whom I contacted when this manuscript was finished: Elsie Belvin, Tom Morrison's daughter; Alfred Bass and his mother, Theresa Bass; John-Henry Bauknight and his nephew Virgil Bauknight; Danny Calton, C. J. Calton's son; W. C. Calton; Mr. Gillis's daughter Mary Lou Gillis Cochrane; Marcel Ferguson's son Julian; Zemilla Mickens Fountain, Henry Fountain's wife; Hazel Griggs's daughter, Frances Underwood; Hoyt Haymans, Jr.; Lillie Mae Hill, Murray Zetrouer's sister; W. D. Howard, son of Oni Howard; Sigsbee Scruggs's son Lee Scruggs; Snow Slater and his wife, Ella Mae; Christine Townsend Polk; Marvin Townsend; Dorsey Townsend; and Virginia Perkins, daughter of B. K. Wheeler, the agriculture teacher who gave me my hog Blue.

For checking facts I relied on several resources: the Rawlings Collection at the University of Florida Library; *Selected Letters of Marjorie Kinnan Rawlings,* edited by Gordon E. Bigelow and Laura V. Monti (University Presses of Florida, 1983); *Invasion of Privacy,* by Patricia Nassif Acton (University Presses of Florida, 1988); *Marjorie Kinnan Rawlings: Sojourn at Cross Creek,* by Elizabeth Silverthorne (Overlook Press, 1988); *The Yearling* and *Cross Creek,* by Marjorie Kinnan Rawlings (Charles Scribner's Sons, 1938 and 1942 respectively).

It is impossible to thank all of my friends and neighbors who encouraged me and helped me complete this book. I am especially grateful to Patricia Acton, Norton Baskin, Marguerite Deaderick, Annie Lou Fields and her son, Marcus, my sister, Marjorie Glisson Aldora, my brother, Carlton Glisson, Nick Lyons, Kay and Jim Ponder, Steve Mudra, David Seybold, Nancy Richardson, Jack Roberts and his lovely wife, Stephanie, my buddy Rip Torn and my dear friend Ed Richardson.

J. T. Glisson

🌿 *The Creek*

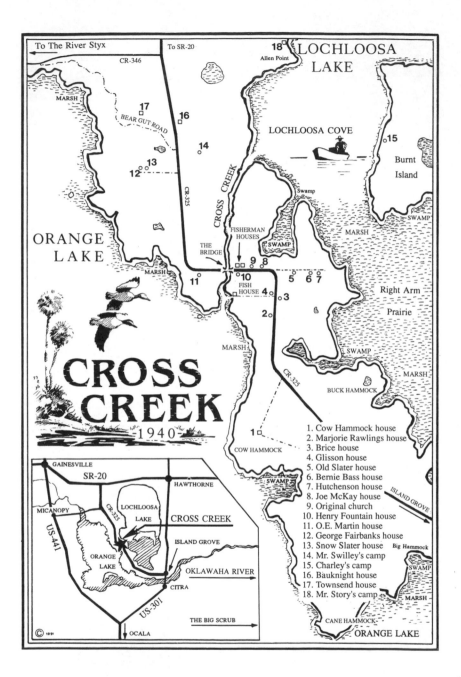

To The River Styx
CR-346
To SR-20
18 LOCHLOOSA LAKE
Allen Point
LOCHLOOSA COVE

MARSH
17
BEAR GUT ROAD
16
15
Burnt
14
Island
13
12
Swamp
SWAMP
CROSS CREEK
FISHERMAN HOUSES
MARSH
SWAMP
THE BRIDGE
SWAMP
ORANGE LAKE
9 8
MARSH
11
10
FISH HOUSE
5 6 7
4
3
Right Arm
2
Prairie
SWAMP
MARSH
BUCK HAMMOCK

CROSS CREEK
1940

1
COW HAMMOCK

1. Cow Hammock house
2. Marjorie Rawlings house
3. Brice house
4. Glisson house
5. Old Slater house
6. Bernie Bass house
7. Hutcheson house
8. Joe McKay house
9. Original church
10. Henry Fountain house
11. O.E. Martin house
12. George Fairbanks house
13. Snow Slater house
14. Mr. Swilley's camp
15. Charley's camp
16. Bauknight house
17. Townsend house
18. Mr. Story's camp

SWAMP
ISLAND GROVE
Big Hammock
SWAMP
MARSH
CANE HAMMOCK
ORANGE LAKE

GAINESVILLE
SR-20
HAWTHORNE
MICANOPY
LOCHLOOSA LAKE
CROSS CREEK
ISLAND GROVE
ORANGE LAKE
OKLAWAHA RIVER
CITRA
THE BIG SCRUB
OCALA
© 1991

Introduction

ENRY FOUNTAIN said, "Truth is something everybody can afford, and truth ain't necessarily in the believing." Therein lies the difficulty in telling about Cross Creek.

My father told me, "If any man calls you a liar and you don't knock hell out of him, I'll kick your behind even if I am a hundred years old and you're seventy-five." Faced with that predicament, I am careful about what I say or write. Even as children all of us that grew up at the Creek learned to be cautious of what we said around outsiders.

And I had another problem. If one grows up next door to Ernest Hemingway, he should write about the sea only after prudent consideration. And if one grows up next door to Marjorie Kinnan Rawlings, he should think hard before writing about Cross Creek. That is the dilemma I faced ten years ago when I first started writing about the Creek. I wrestled with the idea while I wrote notes for my personal enjoyment—some on airlines, some in hotels, and some in the Argentine Andes when I was homesick. As the volume grew my friends asked, "Why don't you publish your version of life at the Creek?" Finally my wife said, "If you asked Mrs. Rawlings, should I publish what I wrote, what would she say?" I had to answer that she would probably say, "Do it, J.T., do it!"

When I started I had not read *Cross Creek* in over twenty years and avoided it out of fear of unconsciously plagiarizing. Early on I adopted two objectives: to try to tell the truth and to write about the Creek as I remembered it. After I finished my manuscript, I reread *Cross Creek* and was pleasantly surprised when I came to the passages about specific individuals I had also written about. My childhood memories and theirs were the same, with only a few exceptions.

When I was a young'un, Cross Creek was a small island of humanity in a sea of forests. We were a handful of independent, ornery Cracker families (white natives of Georgia and Florida) with the exception of a writer from up north and one extended black family. Thanks to the swamps and hammocks of north central Florida we were able to maintain our isolation for a half-century after motels and signboards spread across the rest of the state.

The name of the creek and the area surrounding it was Cross Creek, but we simply referred to both as the Creek. It is still impossible for me to separate the place from the people who lived there because surviving necessitated taking on the ways of nature. The Creek folks were like the lakes. They could lay quiet and calm for weeks, basking in the subtropical sun, and then suddenly break loose and kick up all hell before settling back as if nothing had happened.

There was no electricity, telephones, or central heat. With the exception of our resident writer, Marjorie Kinnan Rawlings, the entire community derived some or all of its living from fishing (illegally, in the opinion of outsiders) and hunting frogs and alligators. We made our own rules and settled our differences within the community.

Marjorie Kinnan Rawlings created a second Cross Creek when she wrote a book by that name that described her vision of us in our world. Her book is beautifully and eloquently written, and in my view could not be improved upon. I am truly grateful for her gift of *Cross Creek* as well as her novels that preserve her view of the time and place that is still my image of home.

There is a third Cross Creek. It is the beautifully dramatized and visually rich movie *Cross Creek*, which is based on Mrs. Rawlings's books.

A fourth version of the Creek has evolved from a combination of the book and movie. This Cross Creek is in the imaginations of a new generation of commuting residents who live there now in air-conditioned houses with modern appliances while they attempt to create a link with a mythical time that is no more.

It is the purpose of this book to share the first Cross Creek with those who would enjoy my unpolished view of that world. It is about the way the Creek existed day-to-day starting in the late twenties and continuing through the early fifties; about a time when isolation and the abundant mosquitoes and snakes were our only claim to fame; when we mixed frontier justice and tolerance of one another with the ability to endure hardship and still see the beauty of the world around us.

Everyone is a character if they have the room and opportunity to be one. And most certainly the Creek was the perfect spot for characters. Everyone had one or more titles: "meanest," "nicest," "best catfisherman," "laziest," "most pregnant," "most profane," "stingiest." None of the titles were meant to hurt. They represented the distinction we associated with idiosyncrasies, local humor, and respect for individuality. To some degree there was family love involved, as in, "He may be a son-of-a-bitch, but he is my brother." We were family.

Any event, good or bad, anything that affected one of us at the Creek, ultimately affected everyone. Things didn't happen in an orderly, chronological manner. Some of the occurrences that caused the greatest impact on our way of life spanned several years, while others came about suddenly and were soon over and done with. There were times in Cross Creek when all hell was breaking loose in several unrelated events while other, more subtle happenings were taking place simultaneously. It was precisely for that reason that when I set out to write about Cross Creek I found it necessary to do it in the way we pass on our heritage to our children: a series of vignettes, not always in chronological order, strung on a common thread and leading to a collective conclusion. It has been necessary to quote my friends more than is usual, but that is the way we relate to one another. I have tried to be accurate and repeat the words as closely as they were told to me or as I heard them.

Telling a true story is remembering, and there is nothing I enjoy more than remembering Cross Creek.

One. A Place Called Cross Creek

*T*HE Creek folks perceived the world in three dimensions: the outside world, the celestial world, and the place called Cross Creek.

The Creek was an S-shaped strip of land less than a mile wide lying between two Florida lakes connected by a slow-moving stream. The smaller of the two lakes, lying to the northeast, Lochloosa was a sand-bottomed jewel surrounded by live oak hammocks and bald cypress that were old when Ponce de León came to the shores of Florida. Orange Lake, lying to the south and west, formed a twenty-mile crescent barrier that was both beautiful and primitive. It had hardly changed since prehistoric mammals roamed the rising Florida peninsula.

The outside world began at the perimeter of the Creek's lakes and forest, starting with the villages of Island Grove to the east and Micanopy to the west. It extended outward through Gainesville, where we paid our taxes, to Ocala, where we bought our supplies, and on to Georgia, where most Creek families originally had migrated from.

The celestial world determined the beginning and end of all sustenance at the Creek. We studied the night sky before making decisions. Although we knew little of the causes of the heavenly influence on our world, we were acutely aware of its effects. Fish lay dormant or swam into our traps as if they were controlled by the cycles of the moon. Aunt Martha Mickens, the wise old matriarch of the Creek's only black family, said, "Even folks and varmints is born 'pending on the times of the moon." The subtlety of sunrises and sunsets and the clarity of stars foreshadowed conditions that affected every aspect of our daily lives. My dad once philosophized, "A man needs to predict his own weather, if for no other reason but to cause him to look up and see how little he is." The cycles so apparent in nature and the stars were a constant reminder of our mortality and even of the temporary existence of the Creek itself.

Cross Creek is located about halfway between Tampa and Jacksonville in north central Florida, sixty miles east of Cedar Key on the Gulf and sixty miles west of St. Augustine on the Atlantic. A clerk at Fisherman's Supply in Jacksonville once asked my dad, "Tom, where is Cross Creek?" Dad said, "It's about seventy-five miles south of here." The man said, "How do you get there from here?" My dad pretended to study on it, then said, "I don't know how to get there from the outside, but anybody at the Creek could tell you how to get out if you were there." The clerk took this as an insult, when none was intended.

The Cracker families (such as my parents) who moved to the Creek in the twenties were not the first settlers. Potsherds and arrowheads are found there in abundance. Several Timucuan ceremonial and burial mounds are scattered through the hammocks west of the Cross Creek bridge, evidence that a large number of these pre-Columbian Indians lived there thousands of years ago. Although the Timucuans proved themselves equal to Florida's climate and terrain, they fell victim to the invading Spanish. All were killed or died from European diseases.

By 1720 north Florida and Cross Creek were deserted. The area was vacant only a short time before the Creek Indians (part of the Cherokee tribe, later called Seminoles) migrated from Georgia and Alabama into Florida. When I learned about them at school, I told Dad with authority that Cross Creek's first inhabitants were Creek Indians. He said, "It figures, Cross Creek being named after a bunch of mean Indians" ("mean" being my dad's pun on "cross").

By 1750 they occupied the area. Their tenure lasted three-quarters of a century. Historians describe them as farmers. They have my sympathy. Without tractors and snake boots they didn't need any harassment from governments and outsiders. In 1823 these Creek Indians were driven south, leaving north central Florida open for resettlement. A few Crackers seeking isolation and land of their own moved as far south as Ocala, and two families, the Johnsons and the Bauknights, moved into the general proximity of Cross Creek. Anything less than a five-mile separation was considered crowding your neighbor then. The Crackers were in no hurry to tame and civilize the area. They were tough and skilled in the art of living off the land. They did only what farming was necessary for survival.

Henry Plant, the railroad pioneer, opened central Florida from Jacksonville to Tampa in 1880. This railroad also made Cross Creek accessible, if the word is construed to mean reachable any way possible no matter how miserable. The railroad cut through Alachua and Marion counties following the west shore of Orange Lake and passed only six miles as a crow flies from Cross Creek and near double that distance by the only land route.

The first attempt to civilize Cross Creek came as a result of the railroad. In true Florida fashion the developers arrived before the right of way was cleared. When the railroad was completed they were ready to sell acreage and building lots in Evinston, McIntosh, and Cross Creek. The developers advertised their Florida real estate as the land of sun and opportunity; a garden spot where citrus was easily grown and harvested; property that guaranteed the good life to northerners willing to invest and settle here. The developer who laid out Cross Creek named it Forest Grove. The name, like these early investors, did not last, and it exists today only on old deeds and abstracts.

Tracing the migration of those first white settlers is difficult and sketchy. My friend Woodard Coleman, a black man, knew them when he was growing up. Woodard was born on the west side of the River Styx more than one hundred years ago and lived there until his death in 1980. His father owned a stable and transported most of the new settlers across the Styx as they arrived on the last leg of their journey to Cross Creek.

Woodard said they all arrived tired, overdressed, and expecting a paradise. To reach the Creek, his father drove them in his mule-drawn wagon, fording the River Styx swamp and following a road that was really no more than a trail through several miles of dense hammock. He said, "Them poor folks didn't see the sun from the time they left the swamp till they got to the Cross Creek Bridge. Course they was kept busy slappin' skeeters and deer flies." He laughed. "Most jest turned around and come back to the railroad with my pa. It was them ladies what was pitiful, with their white skin and not knowin' nothing about the backwoods."

Woodard came to know the ones that stayed. When it was necessary to purchase supplies not available in Micanopy, they came by wagon or horseback, penned their horses in his father's stable, and traveled to and from Gainesville and Jacksonville on the train. His father hauled building materials shipped by rail from the railhead to the Creek for their houses and utility buildings.

Armed with ignorance and optimism, some of the purchasers of the newly opened property set out to tame the half-mile strip along the east side of the creek. They built houses, cleared land with primitive tools, and set out orange groves. As the trees matured, the northerners built a packinghouse and a tram road to a dock on the edge of the creek, where they could load their crops for shipment across Orange Lake to the railroad at Boardman. The final touch was a church to solidify their community. All of this was abandoned following the devastating freezes that wiped out the citrus across the state at the turn of the century. Only the old Cracker families who took their living directly from whatever nature provided stayed on.

During the time I was growing up I found remnants of these pioneer lives, like the shadows of a community that had deliberately erased its existence. They intrigued me then and they do today. After a rain I would find a piece of china or an ornate button uncovered by the plowing in an orange grove. On other occasions I was surprised by a domestic plant growing deep in the hammock that seemed to have clung to life only to confirm the passing of those settlers, blossoming again and again with no one to smell its fragrance and admire its beauty.

The only record of these settlers as individuals today is a name on an old deed or a shipping address written on the backside of a board in a barn. The coming and going of that small group of families opened the door for my parents' generation at Cross Creek.

For many years the only road to the north from the Creek was the one Woodard's dad used to transport the northern settlers from the railroad. That road continued on to the old Indian town called Micanopy. Appropriately named Bear Gut, it was passable only on horseback except during the driest season.

For reasons no one remembered, the state in 1928 cut and graded a sand road from the bridge nine miles north to Phifer Station and then on to the old Gainesville–St. Augustine highway. The road was never serviced, and anyone willing to tackle it risked getting stuck alternately in wet and dry sand on the same trip. On the rare occasions when two vehicles met, it was almost impossible for either one to escape from the deep ruts. This often necessitated one car backing an unbelievable distance to find a spot where the other could pass. Everyone at the Creek agreed the road's drawbacks exceeded its benefits. My friend Bernie Bass said, "That old road is all right exceptin' all the bugs, and dust, and bog holes." He laughed, "It's so rough a feller's got to keep the windows rolled up to keep from throwing his young'uns out."

For the first eight years my parents lived at the Creek, the only road leading southeast to the village of Island Grove consisted of sand ruts that cut back and forth between marshes and lakes. Like most roads then, it followed the course that offered the least resistance to mules pulling a wagon. The present road was cut and paved in 1929, and although it has been widened several times, it is today much the same as it was in the thirties and forties. The original narrow finished surface was bedded with lime rock, shot with asphalt, and finished with slag imported from steel mills in Alabama.

As in most things, the State and the Creek folks didn't see eye to eye on how the road should be at Cross Creek. Property owners freely donated land for the right of way from Island Grove to the bridge.

However, clearing land was far more expensive than the land itself, so they balked when it came to giving up more citrus trees than were necessary for vehicles to pass. The State compromised by accepting the land and allowing the citrus growers to retain ownership of the trees growing on the shoulders of the road.

We had two categories of houses at the Creek: those built by settlers in the 1880s and 1890s and those built by Crackers who could not find any old settler houses vacant and therefore built shanties. From the turn of the century until the late 1930s, only two conventional houses were built at the Creek: the house that finally became my family's home and a tenant house at Cow Hammock.

The abandoned settlers' houses coupled features brought from the North with the builder's personal ideas of how a Florida house should be designed, limited by the amount of money builders had or were willing to spend. On the practical side they were built with local pine framing and siding and roofed with cypress shingles. All of them had open porches to shade the walls on the south and west sides, plus tall windows and many exterior doors for ventilation. In addition, a hodgepodge of impractical features alien to Florida included roofs capable of carrying substantial snow loads. When the roofs deteriorated, those who could afford it replaced the shingles with galvanized tin that conducted unbearable amounts of heat in the summers. The ultimate convenience for those lucky enough to purchase or squat in any of these houses consisted of a shallow well with a hand pump on the back porch. Womenfolk didn't brag openly, but they enjoyed a certain dignity associated with having a two-holer outhouse built with lumber that matched the original dwelling.

The kitchen's wood stove and a small fireplace were considered sufficient for our mild winters. We had only a few cold snaps; nevertheless, when the temperature fell into the low thirties accompanied with high humidity, as it did every winter, it could be downright miserable.

On one occasion when I was a kid I spent the night with a family who lived in one of those old structures. I slept in the same bed with three of the children. Shortly after we all piled in between sheets that smelled of having been dried in the sun, a thunderstorm passed over, followed by a soft rain that continued through the night. The bed was strategically located in the only place in the room that was not leaking. Shortly after it began to rain, the mother came in with a beeswax candle on a jar lid and placed it on the dresser. A few minutes later she returned and distributed containers about the room to catch the leaking rainwater. She put pots and buckets in places that had not yet started to leak. Obviously she knew that when the old roof became saturated it would leak there too. When she was finished, she went around the bed tucking and patting its occupants. She saw me peeping and puckered her lips in my direction as she left the room. It was a perfect good-night kiss, not slobbery. I lay there trying not to sleep, listening to the water dripping into various pots, tin cans, and buckets, savoring the sound. To this day I am convinced nothing soothes the human soul like the sound of rain on a lichen-covered cypress-shingle roof, especially added to the various sounds created by water dripping into assorted containers. When I returned home, I could not understand why my family laughed when I told them I wished we had a leaking roof that sounded like someone playing a xylophone.

Only a few of the old houses had been built with screened windows and doors, and those screens were generally in a perpetual state of disrepair. The parents and girls usually slept under mosquito nets made of cheesecloth, suspended from the ceiling. The boys, who were considered tougher, smoked their rooms with rags and green moss or slept with their heads and ears covered.

The single men who drifted to the Creek usually picked a spot bordering the lake and built their shelters casually when fish weren't biting. Sand floors were of no consequence, as privacy and the convenience of the location were the first priorities. Charley Fields lived in his thatched hut of palmetto fans. Mr. Story and several others lived in houses made of poultry wire stretched over wood poles and covered with tar paper. Mr. Swilley (the Creek's only Native American Indian) and George Fairbanks lived in shanties constructed of blackened tin salvaged from the ashes of houses that had burned.

This is not to say we were the unfortunate victims of impoverished

circumstance. Settlers came to the Creek for different reasons, and all encountered the same inexplicable phenomena: a natural bonding with the fundamental elements of nature and an honest feeling of kinship with their dissimilar neighbors.

In contrast to our houses and the general haphazardness of the Creek we had a single landmark that served the community and was the epitome of proper construction: the Bridge. The Bridge was an integral part of our lives. We took it for granted, as if it were created at the same time as the giant cypress trees that shadowed it and Cross Creek itself. It would have been a formidable bridge in any setting: extremely sturdy, constructed with heavy steel I-beams utilizing engineered triangular bracing connected with bolts and giant rivets. Two huge parallel trusses wrong. Like his wife, he stared in amazement. Orange trees and tangerine trees loaded with golden fruit surrounded the houses. The white sand yards were edged with flowers blooming as if they didn't know it was winter. This was the Florida they were looking for.

The local grocer told Tom, "There's a man at a place called Cross Creek was here yesterday. Armstrong is his name . . . said he's looking for a man to care for his grove." He leaned over the counter, intimating that he was speaking only in strict confidence. "I doubt y'all want to live out there though, the place is wild and them people is all peculiar."

Tom laughed. "That sounds like the kind of place we're looking for. How do you get to Cross Creek?"

The storekeeper seemed disappointed. "You cross the railroad yonder an jes' keep trying to go west. It's out there locked in betwixt two big lakes that's connected by Cross Creek. Most say that is where the place gets its name. Course if you ask me—I say it's named for the temper of them Crackers that lives out there." Tom thanked him and joined Pearlee at the door. The grocer called after them: "It's about five miles not counting the kinks in the road."

When they were in the truck, Pearlee said, "That was not much of a recommendation for Cross Creek." Tom laughed and replied, "Everybody in Alabama said the same thing about the people over in Georgia." He patted his wife's knee. "Now, ain't you glad I didn't listen?" He didn't get a response and continued, "I always figure a man's got to see for hisself and then make up his own mind."

A quarter of a mile west of the railroad the village ended. Thin yellow pines shaded thick patches of scrub palmettos. Titis and gall berries provided the rest of the ground cover. Cat faces, cuts made in the pines to extract turpentine, extended two feet above the dense ground foliage. Pearlee thought they looked like Oriental masks peeking above the palmettos.

Around a turn in the narrow road a young man stood waving a blue handkerchief, indicating he wanted the truck to stop. Tom brought Moses to a halt parallel to the young Cracker. They all said howdy. The man, who was barely grown, removed his tired sweat-stained straw hat when he saw Pearlee. "I'm Pete Johnson, I live to Cow Hammock."

Tom introduced himself and his family, adding, "We're from Georgia."

Pete grinned. "Just about everybody is." They all laughed. "How far you folks goin'?"

"To a place called Cross Creek—if we can find it."

The young Floridian looked at the overloaded truck. "If it won't be puttin' you folks out any, I would be obliged if you could give me a ride. I could show you the way."

"The only space we got left is the running board," Tom replied. "You're welcome to stand on it and I'll try to keep the bushes from wipin' you off."

Pete climbed onto the side of the truck and immediately assumed the role of local guide. He shouted above the engine, perilously releasing one hand to point out landmarks. "That's Right Arm Prairie over yonder to the north and Pee Gee Marsh on this side. This ain't nothing along in here but piney woods. All the good hammock land is at the Creek."

A small herd of half-breed cows scurried from where they had been feeding on wild grass, acting as if they had never seen an automobile. The cows leaped the narrow ditch and crashed through palmettos, behaving more like a herd of wild deer than cows. Pearlee asked, "Are they wild?"

Pete responded, "No, ma'am. Them's Hoyt Haymans' cows. He's my boss and owns Cow Hammock. The reason I was over here this mornin' was to run 'em back this-a-way. They was gettin' too close to the railroad."

Tom asked, "Does your boss own all this land?"

Pete looked around. It was obvious he had never thought of who owned the flat woods. "Could be nobody owns it, or maybe the turpentine company." They had driven more than a half-mile before he stuck his head into the cab and said, "I hear most folks that owns land like this gets it if they pay the taxes. It's all open range. A feller don't have to own land to own cows. Cows is as free as panthers or bears, rested on massive piers set on both sides of the creek, clear spanning more than eighty feet. Its rusted steel blended into the surroundings as well as a rigid steel bridge could be expected to. No one claimed to know when or how we became the recipient of such a magnificent structure, and no one cared. It was the Cross Creek Bridge, and we considered it ours free of taxes or titles.

The Bridge was the common meeting place. It was really the capitol of Cross Creek, and we only grudgingly recognized the state and national capitols in Tallahassee and Washington. In our thinking the proud old structure was a point of beginning, with everything at the Creek lying to the east or west, making it a sort of Greenwich in our world.

The Creek folks could not afford what we called a "falling out" between two neighbors, since unity was necessary to survive the constant threat of the elements and fear of encroaching government. When disagreements arose and could not be settled, the offended party told his adversary, "I will meet you on the Bridge." This was the supreme challenge. The challenged accepted the invitation and met the challenger at the prescribed time or was marked a coward for life.

The rules were simple. When the parties met, there were no guns or knives and in no case were the participants to leave the Bridge until the matter was settled and they had shaken hands. Normally the disagreements were settled with words in a face-to-face confrontation, but in some instances words failed and bare knuckles, boots, and choke holds clarified the disputed points. There was one other rule: The dispute once settled on the Bridge was not to be mentioned again.

It is natural that without lawyers to collect the fruits of our labor, settling nothing and dividing us, peace generally prevailed over the Creek. In addition to being a center of justice, on rare occasions we gathered at the Bridge to negotiate new rules with the game wardens or territories in the lakes.

Cars crossing the Bridge caused a rattling of the steel railings against the trusses as the tires bumped across the uneven fat lighter-wood flooring (pronounced "lighterd" by all Crackers). The rather pleasant sound vibrated through the surrounding hammocks and alerted everyone that a car was crossing the Bridge. We all speculated whether it was a friend or possibly a stranger, because it was important that everyone know if there was an outsider in our midst. On most days the only car to cross was the mailman from Hawthorne.

Many hours of my growing up years were spent on the Bridge. For young'uns it was a super-sized set of monkey bars that would challenge the most sophisticated gymnast. Walking the high and low banisters and trusses while watching one's reflection mirrored below was not for the timid.

Today people ask me what Cross Creek was like back then. That question has always been difficult to answer. To tell them what they want to hear, I have to skip over the humid heat, the insects, and our occasional internal rows. The remaining description, though true, would sound like advertising copy for a south Florida subdivision. I would have to say, "Cross Creek was a special place where the efforts of human beings fused harmoniously with the grandeur of nature; a place where stately sabal palms swayed above emerald green citrus groves; a place where live oaks, sweet gum, and magnolias bedecked with soft gray curtains of Spanish moss separated the intimacy of the interior from the glitter of pristine freshwater lakes lying just out of sight; a garden where great white herons glided silently over lush forest and bald eagles soared high in a subtropical cerulean sky; an enchanted island where yellow jasmine, orange blossom, and the delicate fragrance of magnolia each took their seasonal turn, tinting the air with an indescribable ethereal bouquet." I would have to tell them the Garden of Eden could not have been more beautiful. They would be uncomfortable with such an answer, and I would be embarrassed to give it. So I tell them, "It sure was purty."

Beauty is the bait nature uses to attract us into perpetuating her scheme of things. The strategy doesn't always work. But I'm thankful it lured Tom and Pearlee Glisson like mosquitoes to a light, or I would have missed everything that happened in that special time and place.

Two. A Better Life

CHARLIE JOSEY had eleven pairs of mules, two horses, three sons, and seven daughters. He personally saw to the feeding and tending of the mules and horses. He expected his sons and daughters to share in the work on his farm and attend church at least once on Sunday. Some said the reason Mr. Josey set aside five acres of good farm land directly in front of his house for a racetrack and a ball field was not a sense of civic responsibility. They said it was because he wanted to sit on his front porch and watch over the honor of his daughters when boys came courting.

The Josey farm was on the east side of the Chattahoochee River in southwest Georgia. Farmers on that side of the river believed everything was better on their side and consequently had little or no contact with their neighbors across the river in Alabama. The Joseys and their friends were thus surprised when a young man from the Alabama side unexpectedly appeared one Sunday afternoon. He introduced himself as Tom Glisson and joined in the activities. His clothes reflected good taste and a distinct pride in his appearance although he clearly was too tall for his trousers. In fact he was taller than anyone there. What he lacked in style, he made up in skill. He outran and outrode the other young men with little effort.

When the afternoon was over, young Tom Glisson sought out Charlie's daughter Pearlee. He said he wanted to thank her for a pleasant afternoon. Then, with little more than a flicker of one eye, he winked and said, "I'll be back. I think we will have something to talk about." Before she could think of a response he was gone.

Pearlee's sisters joked and teased, telling her the Alabaman definitely had his eye on her. She snapped back, "He looks like Fido in our first reader to me." In truth, the only man she was interested in was a professor at her alma mater, the Cyrene Institute of Higher Learning.

The following Sunday Tom was back. He made two home runs in the baseball game and came in a tactful second in a race that included Mr. Josey's horse. When the sun moved close to the horizon and the games ended, Tom approached Pearlee with an air of calm self-assurance.

Curiosity is a powerful force, and the Josey girl had more than her share. During the week she had decided to ignore Tom. On Sunday afternoon she changed her mind, telling herself she did not want to be rude. She would simply tell him she was not interested in whatever it was he wanted to say. At the last moment, when she saw him coming toward her, she scrapped all of her plans and greeted him with a warm smile and a pleasant hello.

Tom walked her away from her chattering young friends. He came directly to the point. He explained he had seen her at a distance on several occasions and found her unbearably attractive. Speaking as if he was sharing a great confidence, he told her, "I am going to ask you to marry me." He held up his hand to restrain her from speaking, a useless gesture in that she was already speechless. "But, before you even think about it," he continued, "there is a condition. If you say yes, we will work until we have enough cash to move to a place where we can accumulate land and amount to something. I won't have my family wondering where their next meal is coming from." He paused. "I love you. Think about it." He turned and walked to his horse and was gone.

Pearlee was infuriated, and amused, and interested. The audacity of presuming she would even consider such a proposal! Nevertheless, she was attracted to her suitor from Alabama and began to see him regularly. They decided to be married in August.

Charlie Josey was not receptive to losing his daughter or to gaining

a son-in-law from Alabama. He told Pearlee she was only seventeen and her boyfriend barely eighteen—too young. When Tom approached him directly for his blessing, Mr. Josey repeated his objection
and questioned Tom's ability to provide for his daughter. Then he
attempted to close the discussion with "I forbid it!"

Tom Glisson was most certainly not the boy he appeared to be. He
spoke clearly and simply: "Mr. Josey, I am the second oldest of seven
children. Our mama died before I was eight. Now, I was forced to quit
school in the fifth grade because me and my older brother had to
support our family. In his grief my dad drank away everything we had.
When we could not make a living on the farm me and my older
brother went into town and fought each other for nickels and dimes.
The town sports pitched coins to us for beating hell out of each other. I
have a stepmother who is a living saint on this earth. She taught us if
we didn't respect ourselves, no one else would." He stepped closer to
his intended father-in-law. "You see, sir, I have already been support-
ing a family, so I know I am qualified." He paused. "Mr. Josey, I am
going to marry your daughter. I did not come here to ask your permission, only for you to give Pearlee your blessing, but I don't need either
one. My respect for you as her father is the only reason I came."

Tom and Pearlee were married on August 6, 1916.

Tom Glisson worked at a local sawmill "from can to can't" (from
the time in the dawn when you could see until twilight faded into
darkness and you couldn't see) for the next four years. Pearlee grew a
garden, milked a cow, and made their clothes. On weekends Tom
bought and sold livestock for profit. He told Pearlee, "You kept the
books for your dad, so I am putting you in charge of money." It was a
good decision. During the next five years they saved more than half of
the money Tom earned. Finally, with the addition of two children,
Carlton and Marjorie, they were ready to set out to complete their
original goal: to go to a place where Tom could make a living, own
land, pay poll tax, and vote (only property owners could vote in
Georgia at that time).

Tom asked drummers (traveling salesmen) if they knew of a frontier that had been bypassed in the rush to settle the country. They all

pointed toward Florida. A harness salesman told him, "Some might say out west, but three-fourths of the Southwest is so damn dry it won't grow trees. The Northwest is too damn cold. Florida—that's the place with a future."

They bought a used T-model Ford truck. Tom named it Moses and told his wife, "You're looking at the mechanical mule that is going to deliver us out of the wilderness into the Promised Land." Roads back then were often poorly drained and hence frequently flooded; therefore, Tom said, it was going to be up to Moses to part the Red Sea. On February 12, 1921, they loaded their possessions onto the truck and headed south.

For three days the family zigzagged out of Georgia and down north Florida's unpaved roads through flooded creeks and sand beds. More than once Pearlee got out and persuaded Moses onward, using a pry pole to wrestle the wheels from the deep ruts.

After three days they agreed everything still looked like Georgia, only the land was poorer. The Florida they were looking for had orange trees. On their fourth day they were forced to detour farther east because numerous bridges were being rebuilt to accommodate the growing popularity of automobiles. In the late afternoon they missed the road and continued driving south until long after dark, hoping to make up for lost time. Ten miles after passing through a small town they came to the village of Island Grove. Tom saw a lamp burning in the back of a general store. Leaving Pearlee and the children in the truck, he went to the door and knocked but got no response. He went to the side window and called. Eventually someone answered. They talked through the screen for several minutes, while Pearlee and the children became acquainted with their first Florida mosquitoes. He returned to the truck. "Pearlee," he announced, "I guess we've got to where we're going. We're at the end of the damn road."

The Glissons spent the night in a local boardinghouse and slept late the following morning. Pearlee awoke startled to see the sun shining brilliantly through the second-story screened window. She slipped from the bed and peered out. She whispered in a tone of disbelief, "Tom—get up and come here!" He rushed to the window thinking something was

wrong. Like his wife, he stared in amazement. Orange trees and tangerine trees loaded with golden fruit surrounded the houses. The white
sand yards were edged with flowers blooming as if they didn't know it
was winter. This was the Florida they were looking for.

The local grocer told Tom, "There's a man at a place called Cross
Creek was here yesterday. Armstrong is his name . . . said he's looking for a man to care for his grove." He leaned over the counter,
intimating that he was speaking only in strict confidence. "I doubt y'all
want to live out there though, the place is wild and them people is all
peculiar."

Tom laughed. "That sounds like the kind of place we're looking for.
How do you get to Cross Creek?"

The storekeeper seemed disappointed. "You cross the railroad
yonder an jes' keep trying to go west. It's out there locked in betwixt
two big lakes that's connected by Cross Creek. Most say that is where
the place gets its name. Course if you ask me—I say it's named for the
temper of them Crackers that lives out there." Tom thanked him and
joined Pearlee at the door. The grocer called after them: "It's about five
miles not counting the kinks in the road."

When they were in the truck, Pearlee said, "That was not much of a
recommendation for Cross Creek." Tom laughed and replied, "Everybody in Alabama said the same thing about the people over in Georgia."
He patted his wife's knee. "Now, ain't you glad I didn't listen?" He didn't
get a response and continued, "I always figure a man's got to see for
hisself and then make up his own mind."

A quarter of a mile west of the railroad the village ended. Thin
yellow pines shaded thick patches of scrub palmettos. Titis and gall
berries provided the rest of the ground cover. Cat faces, cuts made in
the pines to extract turpentine, extended two feet above the dense
ground foliage. Pearlee thought they looked like Oriental masks peeking above the palmettos.

Around a turn in the narrow road a young man stood waving a blue
handkerchief, indicating he wanted the truck to stop. Tom brought
Moses to a halt parallel to the young Cracker. They all said howdy.
The man, who was barely grown, removed his tired sweat-stained

straw hat when he saw Pearlee. "I'm Pete Johnson, I live to Cow Hammock."

Tom introduced himself and his family, adding, "We're from Georgia."

Pete grinned. "Just about everybody is." They all laughed. "How far you folks goin'?"

"To a place called Cross Creek—if we can find it."

The young Floridian looked at the overloaded truck. "If it won't be puttin' you folks out any, I would be obliged if you could give me a ride. I could show you the way."

"The only space we got left is the running board," Tom replied. "You're welcome to stand on it and I'll try to keep the bushes from wipin' you off."

Pete climbed onto the side of the truck and immediately assumed the role of local guide. He shouted above the engine, perilously releasing one hand to point out landmarks. "That's Right Arm Prairie over yonder to the north and Pee Gee Marsh on this side. This ain't nothing along in here but piney woods. All the good hammock land is at the Creek."

A small herd of half-breed cows scurried from where they had been feeding on wild grass, acting as if they had never seen an automobile. The cows leaped the narrow ditch and crashed through palmettos, behaving more like a herd of wild deer than cows. Pearlee asked, "Are they wild?"

Pete responded, "No, ma'am. Them's Hoyt Haymans' cows. He's my boss and owns Cow Hammock. The reason I was over here this mornin' was to run 'em back this-a-way. They was gettin' too close to the railroad."

Tom asked, "Does your boss own all this land?"

Pete looked around. It was obvious he had never thought of who owned the flat woods. "Could be nobody owns it, or maybe the turpentine company." They had driven more than a half-mile before he stuck his head into the cab and said, "I hear most folks that owns land like this gets it if they pay the taxes. It's all open range. A feller don't have to own land to own cows. Cows is as free as panthers or bears, they got a right to go any place that ain't fenced. 'Cept I'm suppose to keep them off the railroad."

As they approached a massive hammock and a fork in the road, Pete yelled, "We got to keep to the right 'cause that road to the left goes back in there to Big Hammock and Cane Hammock. They is close to a thousand acres of orange grove back there owned by the Fairbanks family and different folks." Tom was amazed that anything like that could exist in a place so wild.

The road skirted the massive hammock composed primarily of live oak, hickory, and sweetgum with an occasional giant pine protruding above the forest. The vegetation in the flat woods became more dense, then unexpectedly opened on a place that looked like the pictures of western ranches Pearlee had seen through her family's stereoscope. Except this place had lush green-leaved orange trees and hammocks in the background. Tom pushed in the clutch, and the truck rolled to a stop.

A new gray one-story house sided with milled novelty pine siding sat only a few feet back from the road. A man was slapping blue-gray paint onto the moldings that decorated a small screened porch. A tenant house, a large corral, a low barn, and another tenant house all faced a cleared right-of-way leading to the largest lake they had ever seen. Pearlee was astonished. "Tom, it looks like the ocean!"

Exuding pride, Pete said, "This here is Cow Hammock where I work, and that's Orange Lake, yonder. It ain't the ocean but it's five to six miles wide and seventeen miles long, and there's more fish in it than the whole New-nited States could ever eat."

"How do I get to Cross Creek from here?" Tom wanted to know.

"Well, you been in it since we left Big Hammock," Pete said, "but most everybody lives nearer to the Bridge."

"How far is that?" Tom asked.

A big smile spread across Pete's face, "It's a mile and a half—and I've decided I'm goin' with you. I can't think of a better way to spend the day than showin' outsiders how purty Cross Creek is."

Tom started the engine and moved off, following Pete's directions.

The narrow road turned north, jogged west, then back north, and led directly into a massive hammock.

They entered through a small passage leading directly into the dense woods. The subtropical sunlight vanished, leaving them sightless for a moment, but gradually their eyes became accustomed to the soft amber light of the interior. Tom allowed the T-model to coast to a stop. They climbed from the truck mesmerized. High overhead, live oak limbs curled and twisted in concentric patterns that supported a roof of foliage. Intermittent shafts of sunlight penetrated through small openings, sustaining ferns and air plants that lined the limbs meandering out from the trunks of ancient trees. Dwarf palmettos grew near the roots of the oaks and occasionally in the forks of the giant trees. Violets were sprinkled in profusion over the floor of fallen leaves. Tom and Pearlee breathed in the oxygen-rich air scented with natural humus and yellow jasmine that announced the beginning of spring at Cross Creek.

Without looking at Pete, Pearlee asked, "Why didn't you tell us it was so beautiful?"

"Some would say it's purty, lots would say it's ugly. It depends on who's lookin'." Pete grinned. "You folks is gonna like Cross Creek." They drove on through the hammock, frequently looking back, not sure the magic would be there when they returned.

The Glissons emerged abruptly into blinding sunlight with a young orange grove on their left and the snags left from the Big Freeze on their right. The citrus branches, burdened with golden fruit, thrashed against the sides of the truck as they squeezed by. A hundred yards from the hammock a drive led off into the grove past a primitive barn to an unpainted, unadorned two-story house. The old dwelling sat comfortably in the shade of a magnolia whose leaves were the same color as the citrus trees. Both threatened to envelop the house.

Past the driveway and parallel to the barn on both sides of the road, pecan trees formed an arch over the passing vehicle and led into larger groves. Pete pointed to a home that adjoined the house they had passed, hidden except for a small area of hand-hewn cypress shingles. "That's the Armstrong place," he shouted. Neither Tom nor Pearlee mentioned that it was Mr. Armstrong they had come to Cross Creek to see. They both preferred to see more of "the Creek," as Pete called it, before deciding if it was the place they were looking for.

The orange trees were set in perfect rows with scarcely enough room for vehicles to pass. Tom asked, "Pete, how far back from this road do the groves go?"

"They go back to the hammock that's left along the edge of the lake or marshes. Anybody what knows citrus always leaves a strip of hammock around the grove. It's fer cold protection." He pointed to the cabbage palmettos standing twenty to fifty feet over the grove. "They's left there fer the same reason. Cold is the most likely bad thing can happen to oranges, 'specially this far north."

Pearlee said, "I would leave them even if they didn't help. They make the groves look like an ornamental garden."

On their right they passed the most formidable barn they had seen in Florida, adjacent to a prim two-story house set snugly in a grove. Pete stooped to get his head inside the cab so Pearlee could hear. "That's the Axline place. Mr. Axline moved away like practically everybody else that was here before the freezes. It's one of them houses where most of the fancy parts was made somewheres else and they shipped 'em here to be built. Mr. Brice, that runs one of the stores in Island Grove, lives there now. Most of the groves at the Creek is his now." Pete laughed heartily. "Course, he's from Georgia too."

Past the Axline place grapefruit trees grew on the left, and vermilion-red tangerines hung like oversized grapes across the road on the right. "To think I spent all year waiting for Christmas to get two or three tangerines in my stocking," Pearlee exclaimed. Directly behind the row of grapefruit trees carpenters were busy building a frame house. A worker was troweling the finish cement on a sidewalk that curved around a grapefruit tree. Young orange trees were set within a few feet of the half-finished house.

Anticipating their question, Pete said, "The reason they set trees so close to the house is because most citrus only grows good on hammock ground, and it costs a lot more to clear the land than to buy it."

"I wouldn't mind how close the trees were. They are pretty as flowers," Pearlee said. She thought a moment. "Tom, while I'm wishing, that's the house I want someday, or one exactly like it."

The road continued north, passing a hammock on the left and a field that was being cleared on the right before it intersected another sand-rut road going east and west. Pete said, "Let's turn to the left, it'll take us straight to the Bridge. They's only two families what lives back the other way."

Going west they passed a two-story house that had aged into a soft silver-gray nestled in the edge of the hammock that ran along the north side of the road. A hundred and fifty yards farther on the same side, an abandoned but well-constructed church complete with a steeple and tall, narrow windows stood in the center of a one-acre clearing. No weeds or grass grew in the snow-white sand surrounding the lonely monument to humanity's erratic belief in God. A single row of water oaks partially shaded the front, leaving the remaining yard bare to the sun. A matched pair of outdoor toilets sat along the back edge of the clearing. "The church ain't never been used. The folks who built it all got froze out," the young Cracker elaborated. "The ninety-eight freeze hit the week they finished it. They put the pews they ordered from Jacksonville in it and canceled the openin'." He then divulged an observation to which he had apparently given a great deal of thought. "They figgered God let 'em down. It wan't God. Was ol' nature, sometimes that Ol' Gal'll get in cahoots with the devil hisself jest to have her way." Beyond the church was continuous hammock. Across the road on the south side a field set with little citrus trees led to a single cottage nestled in a swamp that bordered Cross Creek.

Pete motioned Tom to stop. He stepped from the running board and removed his hat. "I'll be gettin' on back to Cow Hammock. You people don't need no help to see the creek itself. There is about five families scattered in the woods over there 'cross the Bridge. I am glad to of met you folks, and I hope you decide to settle here at the Creek." He turned and walked down the center of the road in the direction they had come.

The Cross Creek Bridge was as imposing as the steel bridges they had crossed on the way from Georgia. The creek below joined Lake

Lochloosa, three-quarters of a mile to the north, and Orange Lake, a quarter-mile south. Tom stopped the truck near the center. They got out and looked down at the gentle stream. The water was not the red clay color they were accustomed to; it was the clear amber of good Kentucky bourbon. Giant cypresses along the banks mirrored the blue overhead. A hundred yards upstream to the north, where the open channel ended, two homemade cypress boats floated beneath a huge live oak leaning out over half the width of the creek. The boats were the only sign of human existence in the area other than the Bridge itself. Wildlife was everywhere: egrets, cranes, and curlews waded along the edges, feeding on minnows and frogs, and soft-shell and alligator turtles poked their heads up for air, then disappeared beneath the surface.

Pearlee and Tom stood without speaking. They had come a long way. Tom looked at his wife holding their baby daughter in her arms, their son tugging at her skirt.

"What do you think?" he asked.

"You brought me all the way down here, but now that I am here I would be willing to bet you, you're not man enough to drag me away from this place." Tom had come to recognize his wife's characteristic habit of separating each word when she was positive of her decision, as she was doing now. "Let's go back and see what kind of deal you can make with that Armstrong fellow."

They backtracked the half-mile to the Armstrong place. It was midafternoon when they turned in past the barn and parked in front of the old two-story house, and Tom had climbed out of the truck before he realized the house was vacant. He walked to the one-story house next door. When he knocked and called "Hello" a man came to the door, and they talked briefly through the screen.

Back at the truck Tom reported, "He says he definitely wants to hire me to take care of the grove. Says he has to go to Hawthorne tonight and we can work out the details in the morning. He wants us to move in this place, but I think we should only unload the things we need till we've closed the deal."

Pearlee, with Marjorie in her arms, followed her husband and son to the house. The steps were dangerously rotten, and the porch would have to be repaired before Carlton could play there. Inside, the unpainted walls were grimy from years of absorbing smoke and collecting dirt. The ceiling was black, with the exception of a half-dozen varieties of spiderwebs hung from everything on which they could anchor. Dirt-dauber nests, some probably dating back before the house was finished and others in the process of being built, gave the ceiling and upper walls a knobby texture. The floor was covered with dirt and debris accumulated from fallen nests. A single window with one of the original eight panes missing admitted a muted light that was almost absorbed by the gloom. Pearlee forced the door open to an adjoining room that had been used as a kitchen. A small, antiquated cast-iron stove stood in one corner, teetering on three legs and a stack of bricks. The only furnishing was a table with a top made of two rough-sawed pine boards and a bench nailed to the wall. The asphalt-impregnated backing of what had been a linoleum rug covered the floor beneath the table.

A nine-inch skink raced across the floor and scurried up onto the windowsill, where it stared at the intruders defiantly through its tiny serpent eyes. Pearlee and Tom were appalled by the snakelike creature's yellow-and-blue-striped body and legs. Had it been in a cage, they might have thought it fascinating or even beautiful, but right there in the house the combination of shiny skin, brilliant blood-red throat, and forked tongue was too much. Pearlee picked up a discarded shoe and hurled it at the lizard. "One of us has got to go—whatever you are! And better you than me!"

Tom laughed, "Go git 'em, Pearlee. It's your house now."

Tired and disappointed with the condition of the house, she snapped, "Instead of standing around laughing, get my mop and broom and scrub bucket off the truck. I'm not putting any of my things in this place until I clean it."

Tom bowed and went back out the front door whistling. The baby slept on the truck seat while Pearlee scrubbed the front room and the makeshift kitchen. Tom and Carlton gathered wood for the stove and set up two beds in the front room. When Pearlee finished scrubbing, she went out to the truck and retrieved a side of bacon, some flour, a bottle of cane syrup, and two jars of vegetables preserved back in Georgia.

The shadows were long before they sat down to their supper in their first Florida home. They ate mostly in silence. Only once Pearlee spoke, talking partly to her husband and partly to herself. "We'll have to get a cow to milk. I can get by without most things as long as there is plenty of milk."

After they finished eating they continued to sit contemplating their luck and the future. The house wasn't much, but Florida was better than they had expected.

In the distance beyond the grove and lake hammock, the sun set, and the short, dramatic Cross Creek twilight began. Flights of ibis and egrets, anticipating the oncoming night, passed over the grove returning to their roosts. Millions of frogs representing dozens of varieties, impatient for the coming darkness, all began to croak as if directed by a single wave of a conductor's baton. Two wood ducks flew low over the grove toward their nest in the hammock.

The Glisson family stood looking out the window, fascinated with their new world. Tom finally spoke. "It's different and kinda wild, but I never seen a place I liked so much. Why I—" He was interrupted by a high-pitched hum that started in the same manner as the frogs'. It immediately grew in volume until they were in the center of a constant roar. A long second passed, and there was no doubting its source— mosquitoes! Billions of Cross Creek mosquitoes, all with ravenous appetites, came whining from every shadow, all searching for blood. Pearlee attempted to brush them away from the baby while they bored into the fair skin on her arms and legs. Carlton flailed and slapped in a futile effort to defend himself. He then tried to hide in the folds of his mother's skirt.

"Tom, do something!" Pearlee shouted.

Tom did the only thing he knew. It at least worked on honey bees. He pulled a fat splinter from the firebox of the wood stove and smothered out the flames with a dish towel. Then he herded his family into the front room. The smoke from the acrid pine combined with the burning cotton dish towel filled the room while Pearlee attempted to hang a quilt over the window with the missing pane. The kitchen door, jammed by the house's sagging foundation, promptly separated from its hinges when Tom tried to close it forcibly.

He remembered Spanish moss hanging on a crape myrtle growing near the barn. "I'll be back in a minute," he said into the smoke. He came back and threw a large pile of what he later came to call Florida cotton on the floor and lit a candle retrieved from the truck. He then proceeded to stuff the moss in the cracks around the door. In the faint candlelight Pearlee discovered several mosquitoes filled with blood attached to the baby's face. Carlton was coughing uncontrollably from the smoke and frantically scratching the bites on his fingers and toes. Welts covered his face.

With the window partially sealed and moss stuffed into the cracks around the doors, the smoke was unbearable. It was also ineffective, so Pearlee pulled the quilt back from the window and Tom tossed their smoker out into the yard.

A cloud of despair and fatigue settled over everyone huddled in the room. Even though they tried to chink moss into every crack, the hellish mosquitoes continued to find their way in. The hot, stale air made the bites sting even more. Pearlee suggested that Tom try to sleep so he would be fit to deal with problems the following day. She wrapped a quilt over her feet and legs and sat all night fanning mosquitoes away from the children. Her husband slept intermittently with the covers pulled over his head, waking regularly to choose between suffocation and mosquitoes. Eventually the candle burned out, leaving Pearlee fanning in the darkness.

The Armstrong rooster announced the coming of daylight after the longest night Pearlee could remember. Slivers of light seeped in through cracks in the walls and ceiling, and the mosquitoes withdrew as suddenly as they had appeared. Pearlee slipped into the kitchen.

Tom awoke to the smell of coffee. He and Carlton shuffled into the kitchen with the skin around their eyes puffed and smudged from smoke and loss of sleep. Pearlee did not look in their direction or acknowledge their existence. They quietly settled on the bench by the table. Pearlee was preparing breakfast, her anger reflected in her movements, which exhibited the deliberate efficiency of a short-order cook.

Tom winked at the boy and spoke to his wife. "Now, Pearlee—I hope you're not going to let a few Florida mosquitoes lower your opinion of Cross Creek." He didn't have to wait for a response.

She didn't turn in their direction. "Don't joke with me. I had the whole night to think, and it is important that this morning we make good sound decisions." She spoke as if she had spent the night rehearsing what she had to say. "Yesterday when it was daylight, Cross Creek seemed to be as close to a heaven on this earth as any place could possibly be. Then last night it changed into a hell the devil wouldn't put up with." She continued, choosing each word carefully. "It will probably never be easy living here, and God only knows what other surprises the Creek has waiting for us. But come what may, I am game to stay and tackle it if you are."

Tom started to speak.

"Let me finish," she said. "I want to start by all of us washing this smoke off. Then let's put all our things back on the truck, and we will leave them there until we find a decent place to live."

An hour later, after making it clear to Armstrong that his lack of concern for their well-being had eliminated him as a potential employer, they were off. The truck was entering the road when they were forced to stop for a splendid blue Buick roadster with sand boiling up behind the red clincher-rim tires. It skidded to a stop directly in front of the truck. A young man wearing an infectious smile and a three-piece suit tipped his stylish touring cap and climbed out of the automobile as if he had encountered a long-lost friend. Ignoring the noise of the two clanking engines, he tipped his cap to Pearlee and stuck out his hand to Tom. "I'm Hoyt Haymans from Gainesville. Me and my family are going to live out here as soon as we finish the house there." He pointed to the house being built next door to the Armstrong place. "Pete said you folks are looking for a full-time job and a place to live. At Cow Hammock I've got seven hundred acres of cattle land plus over a thousand five hundred acres in open range." He paused to calculate his additional holdings. "There is twelve acres of oranges and thirty acres cleared for truck farming. Florida is booming and I need a good man to run it. He looked past Tom and nodded to Pearlee, "Mrs. Glisson, I have a brand new house waitin' for you to move in. If you haven't made a deal with Armstrong, then I would like to make you a offer."

"We didn't," said Tom.

"Hell! Then you folks follow me. I'll show you the place and you can meet my wife, Sally, and we'll make us a deal."

When night fell across Orange Lake, Tom Glisson and his family slept in their new home at Cow Hammock, with screened windows and a water pump on the back porch.

🌿 One man's paradise is another man's hell. (Old Joe McKay, the Creek's oldest resident, habitually scratched the back of his hands. Bernie Bass once asked him why he didn't doctor them. Old Joe answered, "If I didn't have a place that itched, I wouldn't enjoy scratchin' it.") Tom and Pearlee had indeed found their place in the sun: warm winters, open space, and new opportunities. Like Old Joe's itching, Cross Creek's long hot summers, bugs, snakes, and irritating plants made surviving there a satisfying experience.

It was a place where they had an opportunity to accumulate land and security. They knew the second half of their goal—earning and saving the necessary money to buy land—would be like their trip from Georgia, for they could not predict what barrier lay around the next corner. The trick would be to take only the necessary detours and continue moving ahead.

The Glissons continued their rural Georgia custom of rising early and beginning their working day at dawn. They knew their survival depended on learning and adapting. Tom loved the wild untamed environment. He planted twenty acres of Irish potatoes and ford hook beans and laid out a family garden. He told Pearlee everything he planted grew faster than he believed possible. She pointed out that the weeds also grew faster and bigger. But Tom did not care. "I can't stand anything that drags around," he said. "It don't matter to me if it's potatoes, weeds, or people."

Pearlee laughed. "I'll try to remember that."

Tom's original deal with Hoyt was for salary and a percentage of profit. After a few weeks they changed their arrangement to a straight percentage.

The cows foraged in the woods and marshes for their food. They required only 10 percent of Tom's time and were more profitable than anything else. Most of the time they only required someone to check where they were grazing to keep them from straying onto the railroad. It was necessary to round them up twice a year and run them through a dipping vat to protect them from a new strain of ticks that was Florida's latest plague. In the late spring roundup they were dipped, castrated, and branded. Those that were ready for market were butchered and shipped to packers in Jacksonville or Tampa. With luck and a little help the whole operation usually could be done in twenty days.

The orange trees were special from the start. There was security in working a crop that with reasonable care could provide a bountiful harvest annually for more than a hundred years.

Some of the things Tom learned were discouraging. Gradually he came to realize that the land at Cow Hammock was marginal for citrus and truck farming. The groves closer to the creek where the Haymanses lived were not a part of his responsibility and received sporadic care, yet they were healthier than the Cow Hammock grove. He also learned that without constant rain, moisture filtered down through the sandy soil, leaving the crops thirsty and shriveled. Following the normal spring drought thunderstorms came with regularity. The often violent rain beat the beans and other plants into the ground. With prolonged rain the crops became blighted with mold and fungus.

In the evenings after their supper was finished and Carlton and Marjorie were in bed, Tom and Pearlee rarely lit a lamp, preferring to sit together in the darkness of the screened porch resting and sharing their thoughts. On one occasion Tom remarked he had learned to like the drone of mosquitoes buzzing outside the screens. His wife jokingly asked if he had come down with a fever. Tom thrived on the work, enjoying the sweltering heat and the challenge of voracious weeds and insects. He told his wife, "Them men that got rich in the goldfields out in California didn't find it just layin' around on top of the ground, they got a shovel and started digging, and when they found some, they hired some more men to help dig." He summed up his philosophy: "It seems to me the trick is to get somebody digging for you while you look for new places to dig."

At the Creek, Nature (referred to by the Crackers as the Ol' Gal), was not simply an all-encompassing deity but a loving mother and a bitchy mistress. Her contrary side became abundantly clear as the Glissons' first year progressed. Pearlee had a bout with malaria and spent endless hours doctoring stings, bites, and funguses on herself and the children.

During the first three years they lived in Cow Hammock, the Florida boom was a major factor in the national economy. Men at the cattle market told Tom he should have gone farther south, where everyone was getting rich. He told Pearlee, "Cross Creek won't ever have a boom, but it'll be here for people who want to work for a living after all the others is gone."

The end of the boom and Florida's ongoing plagues had a serious effect on the Haymanses. The State became obsessed with the real or imagined citrus fruit fly and imposed an embargo on all fruit. National Guard checkpoints were established along the major highways to search every vehicle for citrus and flies, until the courts finally ordered them to stop. The private citrus industry was devastated. The oranges at Cow Hammock could not be sold and consequently dried up over-ripe on the trees. In addition the Haymans investments and holdings elsewhere were threatened by the collapse of the economy. The family would have to move back to Gainesville where they could protect their more important interests, and they decided to terminate their farming operations including the range cows.

Tom and Hoyt dissolved their partnership in the spring of 1926, but the Haymanses remained respected friends through the rest of Tom and Pearlee's lives. They asked the Glissons to continue to live in the Cow Hammock house and look after their property at the Creek.

Although for Tom the change meant more freedom to pursue his personal interests, it also meant reassessing the family's future in Florida.

Tom and Pearlee sat late into the nights talking and planning. Their savings were near two thousand dollars; in addition, Tom had taken stock cattle as part of his share in the close-out of the partnership and now had a small herd of his own on the open range.

In April of that year Pete Johnson came by and insisted Tom go bream fishing with him. "You been here at the Creek without wettin' a line longer than anybody ever has been, and I told my ol' lady it was time we changed that." He laughed. "We got a rule here, don't nobody charge a feller for a mess of fish, and I don't mind giving you a mess, but they taste better when you catch 'em yourself."

Pearlee insisted that Tom go. He left with Pete at daylight the next morning and returned in time for lunch with a string of fish and a transformed view of Cross Creek. In the evening the family feasted on corn bread, potato salad, grits, watermelon rind pickles, and the fresh-caught fish. Tom was exuberant. By lunch they had caught eighty bream weighing a total of sixty-one pounds. Pete had explained that panfish were bringing four cents a pound, and Tom calculated the bream they caught with a pole and line at two dollars and forty-four cents. In addition Pete fished five old rusting fish traps and caught another eighty-one pounds. His fish for the day were worth five dollars and sixty-four cents. "No wonder he won't work for a dollar a day," Tom said.

Several of the Crackers had been fishing at the bream beds, including wives and children. Tom said it was more like a neighborhood get-together than folks working for a living.

Pearlee contained her misgivings until Tom questioned her. "I heard people talking about a whole Sunday school on an outing," she said. "They were from across the lake and they were caught in a sudden storm on Orange Lake. Six of them poor souls drowned."

Tom brushed the thought aside. "That was a long time ago, and besides, nobody from the Creek has ever drowned on either lake." He continued to talk of the beauty of the lake and promised to take Pearlee and the young'uns fishing.

After they were in bed and she thought he was asleep, he laughed out loud.

"What now?" Pearlee asked.

"That has got to be the best fishing lake in the world. Hell, you don't even have to dig for bait, you just split open the stem of a lily pad and get a big juicy worm out of it and then catch three or four fish on the same worm." The fishing trip on Orange Lake was the beginning of a love affair that would last the rest of Tom Glisson's life.

❦ One morning in that same spring Tom announced he was going to Gainesville to buy some supplies and intended to stop and visit the Haymanses while he was there. Pearlee worked in her garden early, ironed and mended clothes through the heat of the day, and in the afternoon returned to her garden and did the evening chores. After supper with the children she retired to her rocker on the porch. An hour later Tom returned, parked the T-model in the tool shed, and joined her. The last light along the west hammock had faded and darkness covered the Creek. He sat for several minutes before he spoke. "Hoyt and Sally are moving back to Gainesville, and I asked if they would rent us the house they've been living in."

Pearlee stopped rocking. "And what did they say?" she asked.

Tom had not forgotten the day they arrived at the Creek when she had said she wanted that house. He could not resist the temptation to tease her. "Well, Hoyt said he will do it if I look after his things here at Cow Hammock in exchange for rent. They think they may farm here later on so he wants to keep the mules and horses in good shape." Tom sat for a minute without continuing.

Pearlee was anxious to learn about the house. "You are awful quick to talk unless it's something you know I want to hear. Then you make me drag it out of you. What did you tell him?"

Tom, enjoying the moment, said, "Well, I know I should have asked you first, but because it would save a trip all the way back to town, I told him we would move tomorrow."

Pearlee clapped her hands. "If it was not so late we would move tonight!"

Tom's casual tone was exaggerated. "They also said they would give me the first option to buy the place." He got up from the rocker. "I think I am going to bed," he said, and left her sitting in the dark.

When they moved into the Haymans house the next day it was the last time they would ever move. The identity of rural property changes slowly, as if the words of the legal title must be earned rather than traded or bought by those who might merely stay on the property without becoming a part of it or the community. But the Haymans place became the Glisson place almost immediately. There was no doubt that the Glissons were at Cross Creek to stay.

In the excitement of telling Pearlee about the house Tom neglected to tell her he had purchased a roll of poultry wire to make fish traps. When he remembered, she told him he might fall overboard and drown with no one to save him. He laughed at her fear, pointing out that if he was going to start running scared he would be more afraid of getting kicked in the head by a mule or struck by a rattlesnake than falling in the lake. She then said trap fishing was against the law, and he should not go into anything that would hurt his reputation. He had obviously given that argument some consideration. "If everybody that fishes traps at Cross Creek leaves, we would be the only family between Micanopy and Island Grove," he said, adding, "The law is to protect the local fishermen from outsiders." He had made up his mind, and she knew that nothing, including her, would change it.

In the weeks that followed Tom mended the fences around their new home and pruned and hoed the half-grown orange trees. Pearlee laid out her garden in the rich soil along the back side of the ten acres near the creek and then had the mules brought from Cow Hammock to break the ground. When Tom saw the area she had reserved, he said it was the equivalent of a one-horse Georgia farm with the capacity to feed everybody at the Creek. Her comeback was, it was inexcusable for any family not to raise all their food. He conceded, "O.K., Miss Pearlee Josey, I'll fish and you farm."

I came into the Glisson family simultaneously with the Ides of March in 1927. My entry was probably more of an itch than a scratch. My birth would not have altered my family's life any more than any other young'un's at the Creek except that I had clubfeet complicated by multiple deformities. Without a series of events in the mid-twenties, I would have never walked.

For my parents the deformities were unacceptable. They swore to have them corrected regardless of any personal hardships they might suffer. During my first three months of life they exhausted their savings rushing from one medical facility to another. Orthopedic surgery was in its infancy, and many deformities were considered impossible to correct. Help came from a source they didn't know existed.

I would almost certainly have spent my life confined to a wheelchair but for the Shriners of North America. At their 1921 convention in St. Louis they committed their vast organization to building and operating hospitals for crippled children. Fortunately for me, Talmage Dupree, a citrus grower from nearby Citra, attended that convention and returned home enthusiastic about the program. Seven years later when the first hospitals were coming on line, he overheard a local physician talking about a severely crippled child he had recently delivered to a family in the backwoods. Mr. Dupree contacted my parents for permission to apply for treatment.

The country doctor who had delivered me said it was impossible to take a baby off to a place two states away to attempt to correct a deformity that God had chosen to give him. My parents remained determined, so with great apprehension, Pearlee, my mamma, boarded the train in Ocala with me in her arms for the journey of two days and nights to Greenville, South Carolina. It was the first time she had traveled alone, and the longest trip she had ever made. When she arrived, she found herself in the midst of the hospital's grand opening celebration. I was admitted at the opening ceremonies as the first patient in the Greenville Shriners Hospital for Crippled Children, on September 1, 1927. At that time I was five months old, and until I was nine, I alternated between six months at the hospital and six months at home in Cross Creek.

Mamma told me years later that leaving me there was the most difficult decision she had ever made. Torn between fear and the possibility that her child would walk like other children, she handed her baby to the staff and made a tearful departure. Many more trips were ahead; some said that I would never walk and that it was cruel to send a little baby off to be experimented on. My parents put their faith in the Shriners hospital.

When I was three, Mamma came to Greenville for one of my regular trips home. When she walked into the station she was astounded to see me running across the waiting room to greet her. It was a great moment in her life—her child could not only walk but could run. My parents' faith was well-founded.

Because of my clubfeet they were forced to postpone buying the Haymans house and its adjoining ten acres for six years while they used their income to pay for braces and travel.

❦ Meanwhile Cross Creek was changing little by little. The road across Pee Gee Marsh connecting Island Grove with Citra was built shortly after my folks came to the Creek, making it easier to go to

Ocala than to Gainesville. In 1928, the year after I was born, the State paved the road from Island Grove to the Cross Creek Bridge. In November of that year a new family, the Rawlingses, moved into the Armstrong house next door to us. No one could have known that Charles Rawlings's shy, pretty wife would ultimately bring about more change in Cross Creek than all of the roads and Crackers combined.

That same year Tom asked for a family fishing territory on Orange Lake. The Cracker families met on the Bridge and agreed on an appropriate area of the lake for the Glisson territory. It extended from Samson Point to Little Hammock, then north along the east shore to a hurricane root (a fallen live oak), three hundred yards south of the mouth of Cross Creek and back to Samson Point. The territory was joined by the McKay family's on the north, and what later became the Bass family territory on the south side.

Although the fish traps were basically the same, all the local fishermen insisted their own personal variations were necessary to catch fish. Tom had more advice than he needed. His neighbors' sincerity and concern was proof of his welcome into the closed society of the Creek.

From the beginning Dad fished his traps in the late evenings and at night. The air was cooler then, and the wind was usually calm; he also loved the peacefulness of Orange Lake at night. He felt a bond between his inner being and the lake in the same way he had known it with the soil. The territory became his farm. He weeded out the shad, suckers, and garfish to provide a better habitat for the eatable varieties. Several years would pass before he would confront the Creek's need for a dependable market for his and his neighbors' catches.

Three. The Ol' Gal

$\mathcal{B}$EFORE I stopped believing in Santa Claus I was convinced Mother Nature presided over Cross Creek with a firm hand. Everyone made constant references to her. We accused her of being fickle, contrary, stingy, and downright mean. Sometimes we praised her, but more often we blamed the Ol' Gal for her ornery creations and inconsiderate control of the weather. Even though I knew she was part myth and part joke, she seemed more real than fantasy.

Because the preachers in Island Grove never mentioned the Ol' Gal when I was growing up, I assumed she was like a wild and unpredictable relative, one of those disreputable characters whose conduct a family would sometimes like to forget. Some of my best friends were like that, and they were exciting too. My friend Bernie Bass and I developed the theory that the Ol' Gal had conceded most of Florida to governments and outsiders, reserving the garden spot for herself.

Everyone knew that those who chose to live at the Creek would be tried and tested by nature's diabolical balancing scheme; the losers would be forced to move out into the tame, civilized world. Minor variations of nature affected every facet of our lives. High and low water, freezes, wind, increases and decreases of any creature could mean feast or famine. Optimist or pessimist, we viewed the continuous changes from our individual perspectives. To some, nature was like a spoiled child; to others, the Ol' Gal was a sweet, loving grandmother.

Whether she was cruel or forgiving, miserly or generous, treacherous or compassionate, the Ol' Gal was family, and she had to be dealt with.

Which of the Ol' Gal's progeny had the highest nuisance value depended on which one we had last encountered. A Cracker who had recently stepped near a rattler would definitely say snakes. The poor soul who inadvertently disturbed a red wasp nest would unequivocally say bugs. And anyone hoeing orange trees in the midsummer sun would find it hard to choose between weeds and weather.

Promoters called Florida the Sunshine State, for good reason. Outsiders unanimously describe our summers as long, hot, humid, and oppressive. (I am convinced that we owe 90 percent of the population increase in Florida since World War II to the man who invented the air conditioner.) A soldier who visited the Creek wrote his friends back home: "There are only two degrees difference in the annual temperature at Cross Creek, miserable and worse." Summertime and malaria were synonymous, and no one can get closer to hell on this earth than to have come down with a high fever in our midsummer heat. Winters at the Creek are mild by the standards of anyplace to the north. No one prepared for the humid cold spells that consistently came in January and February or the occasional early or late frost that slipped in when least expected. Without heat and warm clothing, winter at the Creek could be downright miserable, and sometimes several layers of our light garments were necessary. My friend Bernie Bass once joked that he was looking forward to spring, when he could find out "what all clothes he had on."

We did not use the word *insects,* feeling that term implied more dignity than the tormenting little bastards deserved. We referred to them as bugs, damn bugs, or worse. Of those capable of mounting an aerial attack we had a dozen varieties: mosquitoes, deerflies, horseflies, green flies, black flies, houseflies, sand flies, and jillions of gnats. We also had guinea wasps, black wasps, and red wasps, plus yellow jackets and hornets. Honeybees and butterflies seemed to be the Ol' Gal's way of apologizing for her other bugs. The current population explosion is in lovebugs, proof she has joined the sexual revolution.

Leaders among the crawling bugs were ants in various forms. They were black, red, bull, sugar, piss, and one particular variety we called a cow ant. The cow ant is an inch long with an elegant red and black velvetlike coat. Fortunately they don't attack humans; however, I picked one up when I was a child and it bit me with the ferocity of a wet hornet. Our current scourge is fire ants; they, like our worst weather, came from Texas. Other little crawling devils included red bugs, chiggers, ticks of various shapes and sizes, and a little gray worm about one-half inch long that inflicted more excruciating pain wherever it touched the skin than even the Ol' Gal's centipede.

I never thought of leeches as worms but have recently been informed that they are. Our parents discouraged swimming in the creek, but we occasionally fell in and swam around until we were caught. Leeches attached themselves to our skin, but they dissolved when doused with table salt and didn't infect. I think all the insects at Cross Creek were capable of infecting anyone that had not developed an immunity to their individual bites and stings.

Spiders were not considered a menace, since they did not attack unless provoked. However, black widows insisted on taking up residence in outdoor toilets and could not be totally ignored; I have a strong aversion to this spider, which is frequently more than three inches in diameter and builds a strong web coated with a sticky substance. We walked with an arm extended in front of our faces in the hammock at night to avoid having a sticky web over our faces and an unhappy spider on the loose.

Everyone agreed. Dealing with the insects was relatively simple: Learn to live with them. We often laughed at outsiders' attempts to defend themselves from mosquitoes. They slapped and flailed at one with such a vengeance that they exhausted and bruised themselves, while a million more waited to take its place. In time they learned to calmly brush them away or blow them off. The most important thing was to take sulfur pills and to keep moving when it was possible. In the evenings, when darkness descended over the Creek, the mosquitoes took flight with a hum like airplanes droning in the distance. During the summer tens of thousands would cover the window screens, making it difficult to see a lamp burning in a house from the outside.

The Ol' Gal's plants, too, often had special sadistic capabilities. A sample of her collection included bamboo vine, about the thickness of a pencil, which had camouflaged thorns several inches apart and grew in the hammocks, slashing unsuspecting victims who rubbed against it. Briars grew ten feet high along the edges of the marshes and ponds. They may have offered a haven for Br'er Rabbit but they could be pure hell when we were chasing cows or running from the game wardens. Scrub palmettos covered the flat woods with their sawtooth stems, making it impractical to use horses there. Stinging nettles loved cultivated ground and had only one redeeming feature: Once children experienced the horrible itch they were careful to look where they walked. There was also wild cherry, which is highly toxic in the spring. Deadly nightshade adorned with white flowers and shiny black berries grew along fences to tempt the unsuspecting. We lost several cows to nightshade and wild cherry but only one to alligators.

I have no problem identifying with the poor souls of biblical times who agonized over and endured the plagues that descended upon them. Plagues were a way of life at the Creek. They came in all types and from all directions. Southeast Asian water lettuce clogged the lakes and marshes during the 1930s, making it difficult to fish and for a few years impossible to frog hunt. Water hyacinths from South America followed the water lettuce, and now hydrilla is the Ol' Gal's scourge in aquatic plants. On cultivated land maiden cane grass spread like wildfire through our groves and fields. The south side of Mrs. Rawlings's east grove was finally abandoned because maiden cane was so prolific and impossible to fight on the lower ground. Once introduced, Bermuda grass became a menace, as tenacious as our native sandspurs. The two thrive in the same places, obviously a pact the Ol' Gal made with the devil.

I was convinced as a child that the Creek had more prolific stubborn grasses and weeds than any other place on this planet. A few of them were smut grass, Bermuda grass, redtop grass, Bahia grass, wire grass, maiden cane grass, saw grass, crabgrass, and six varieties of sandspurs. Charley Fields, the Creek's resident poet, and I once talked about what we didn't like about some of the plants on Burnt Island, where he lived. After we had finished with them, he looked around his camp. "She didn't make a plant that was not beautiful: roses without thorns are not roses." I didn't know if he was quoting, but I understood that everything had a right to defend itself.

But the Ol' Gal's specialty was snakes. Since way back when she loaned one to the devil, they have terrorized or mesmerized those who came in contact with them regularly. We assumed snakes could be anyplace at any time, and we were right. A lady I knew sat on her chamber pot in the middle of the night once and discovered a snake in it. Little children were taught before they learned to walk never to put their hands or feet anyplace they could not see.

"Snake!" Whispered or shouted, the word produced a knee-jerk reaction born of our respect for the reptiles as the greatest single threat to life at Cross Creek. I cannot explain why drowning or communicable diseases did not win this honor, but I am sure the reason no Cracker at the Creek ever died of snakebite was our instinctive wariness toward snakes.

Even though nonpoisonous snakes often ate our eggs and baby chickens, they represented a minor nuisance compared to the poisonous varieties. Poisonous snakes were in the hammocks, the flat woods, the swamps, the marshes, and the lakes. Occasionally they moved into our houses and utility buildings searching for food or shelter. The coral snakes were the most deadly of the four poisonous snakes at the Creek but the least feared. They are small, normally twelve to fourteen inches, and do not coil and strike as diamondback rattlers and cottonmouths do. Ground rattlers or pygmy rattlesnakes, though common, seldom grew to a length of more than twelve inches at the Creek. They have short fangs and are considered to have insufficient venom to be lethal.

The diamondback rattlesnake grows to a length of six feet and to almost four inches in diameter. I have seen them seven feet long downstate but never as thick-bodied as the rattlers in our area. Rattlesnakes have a wide range of habitats and are common in the flat woods and the hammocks and along the lakes. I once saw one swimming across the creek with his nose and rattles above the water, dispelling the myth that rattlers cannot swim. They appear to have less fear of humans than is commonly thought. Rattlesnakes will attempt to escape under normal conditions, but this is not a behavior to count on when it could mean life or death. I have seen them strike and sing their rattles afterward, which dispels another common myth, that they give a "gentleman's warning."

We considered the cottonmouth the most dangerous of the poisonous snakes. They did not grow as long as rattlers—it was rare for one to be more than four feet—but they had a bulky girth, often more than four-and-a-half inches. I once saw a big cottonmouth at a distance of more than fifty feet when it was not aware of my presence. I scuffed my foot in the leaves, careful to conceal any upper-body movement that would alert the snake to my closeness. The cottonmouth immediately coiled, ready to attack anything that passed within striking distance.

No one at the Creek liked rules and laws, so mostly we had obligations. One of those was an obligation to pursue and kill poisonous snakes. We understood the delicate food chain and the role it played in the balance of nature, and anyone killing just for the pleasure of it would have been called into account on the Bridge. If they repeated the behavior they would surely have been driven from the community. The love of wildlife and respect for all of the Ol' Gal's creatures extended to everything except snakes. The consensus was that the snake was the equivalent of a maniac with a pistol and would strike a little child as quickly as it would a rabbit.

Superstition held that hanging a dead snake on a fence would make it rain. I, of course, did not believe that, but I always hung any snakes I killed on a fence, just in case. Rattlesnakes and cottonmouths were so common during the summer that it was rare not to see three or four hanging on the fence along the road to Island Grove. Some were killed when they were spotted by the children on the school bus. The bus always stopped for something that important.

There were as many snake stories at the Creek as there was time to tell them. Everyone had their private collection of rattles, usually kept in a cigar box along with the flint arrowheads collected over the years, and every specimen had a story. The young'uns believed if they got the dust from a rattle in their eyes it would blind them, a story probably started by a mother who didn't want her children playing with anything that had been connected to a snake. Some families kept bantam chickens because of the distinct clucking sound they made when they spotted a snake. A dog that would not kill or hold at bay a poisonous snake was not considered worth his grub.

When I was about seven my mother sent me to her garden to get a hoe. Once I was out of her sight, the errand turned into play. I ran down through the orange grove playing with my dog, siccing him on imaginary creatures and throwing sticks for him to retrieve. This old bulldog had been my protector and companion since I was an infant. We came to the fence that enclosed the garden, and while I climbed over, the dog slipped under the wire and ran ahead to drink at the water hole. Grass had grown knee high along the sides of the depression. I saw the dog run up to the hole and rear back on his hind legs, letting out a single yelp. He was dead when I got to him. A cottonmouth had struck him in the throat, probably in an artery. I killed the relatively small snake with the hoe.

I asked my dad how my dog, who was capable of killing any snake, could allow himself to get bitten so easily. He said the dog had made a little mistake, running into a place he couldn't see. He thought a moment and added, "Little mistakes can get you the same as big ones." He paused again. "You ought to remember that." In my grief his philosophy was lost on me, but years later, when it was as important as life itself, he would repeat it.

Not all snake stories have bad endings. One Sunday evening my mother stayed home while my dad, Marjorie, and I went to church in Island Grove. Mamma sat on the back porch until it was dark and decided to go to bed without bothering to light a kerosene lamp. She passed through the kitchen and into the dining room, turned to go into the bedroom, and felt something scratch her leg. She thought it was a piece of wire I had carelessly left there. Kicking her foot to get clear of it, she stepped on something alive. She grabbed the flashlight from the mantel, shined it on the floor, and saw a dark snake slithering around on the polished surface. Blood trickled across her foot. Terrified, she yelled, "Lord—I am bit—by a moccasin!" She grabbed a pistol and shot two holes in the dining room floor, then killed the snake with a mop.

Mamma couldn't think of anyone to go to for help. Our neighbors the Brices were at church, and Mrs. Rawlings, the next closest, was away on a trip. She grabbed the keys to the pickup, intending to drive herself to the nearest doctor, in McIntosh. Then she reconsidered. McIntosh was twenty miles around the south end of Orange Lake. If the poison reached her heart before she got there, she could die on the way. She decided there was nothing to do but accept her fate. She lay down on the window seat across the room from the dead snake, waiting for its poison to take effect. Five or ten minutes passed, and nothing happened. She remembered people saying that the venom felt like a hot branding iron. There was no burning sensation. She had seen blood on her leg but didn't remember seeing any fang marks. She didn't even feel bad. She got up and lit a lamp and inspected the dead snake. It was a little nonpoisonous chicken snake. I do not remember ever seeing my mamma as jubilant as she was when we got home that night. Over her protests, Dad took her to Dr. Strange, who said it was not serious but she might feel bad for a day or so.

The next morning before daylight Mamma had us up looking for the place where the snake had gotten into the house. Dad found it: a three-quarter-inch hole in the floor in the corner of the kitchen. My parents had bought a new icebox but placed it in a different spot than our old one, which had drained water from the melted ice through a pipe that extended through a hole in the floor and under the house. That hole had been plugged with a cork stopper until a day or so before, when I had removed the cork to use on a fishing line. I considered that my mamma was in a happy mood, but not good enough for me to confess.

That night, just as my mother blew out the light, I heard my dad say to her, "Pearlee, you suppose there was more than one snake came through that hole?"

My mamma said in her no-nonsense voice, "If I thought there was a snake in this house I would get up and burn it to the ground right now."

The snake population did not decrease at the Creek until the nineteen-fifties. Of course, the possibility still exists that the Ol' Gal is holding them for release when another unsuspecting generation moves into her garden.

Four. Young'uns

AGIC is a woodpile that glows green in the night. The only time I have ever seen fox fire was in our woodpile. I was a little young'un, and it was one of the biggest events of my life up to that time. We came home after visiting a sick neighbor about an hour after dark and discovered the woodpile glowing a brilliant green. I didn't know that this was a rare, unpredictable phenomenon that occurs only on cold nights. My sister, Marjorie, and I were enchanted; we ran to see where the light was coming from. All of the recently split wood and chips were covered with a green fluorescence that illuminated the yard.

Awed by the beauty, we picked up wood pieces and tossed them into the air. Marjorie ran around the yard swinging her arms, creating luminous trails through the darkness. We laughed at my dog, who thought we had gone mad and barked at the back door trying to report our insanity.

I was disappointed when my folks remained in the house. They had seen fox fire back in Georgia, they said. It seemed to me necessary to draw them into the excitement, so I carried some glowing chips into the dark kitchen. My dad was sitting in a straight chair just inside the dining room next to the swinging door that separated it from the kitchen. I pulled the door open and called from the darkness, "Dad! See the green light!" He poked his head in the door opening at the very moment I accidentally released the eighty-pound door, which hit him full in the face, knocking him out of his chair flat on his back. He sat up and said, "Pearlee, you ought to see that stuff J.T.'s got in there. Damn if it ain't got real stars in it."

Being a young'un at the Creek was like that night: gloriously happy one minute, then in trouble, then happy again. The Creek had a special place in its heart for young'uns. Even the Ol' Gal showed a tenderness to them. Some families always had a new baby like others had kinfolks or dogs. The men at the Creek seemed to hold and talk to little babies more than men did in other places, making the little ones feel welcome and wanted.

When a child had learned to walk and had demonstrated a minimal degree of responsibility, he or she was called a "yard young'un," with new freedom in a limited area around the house where the yard had been swept and the shrubs trimmed to make it possible to see any snakes that might crawl there. Days spent exploring that little world were Creek children's first lessons in surviving and understanding nature and the Creek. Bushes and shrubs exaggerated the subtle seasons in the confines of a young'un's yard. Each child watched domestic and wild plants flower and seed in that small space, providing food and shelter for the various small creatures that crawled, hopped, or flew about the yard. Colorful butterflies and birds competed with the seasonal brilliance of flowers creating a kaleidoscope that kids in another place might have missed.

When I was seven I was no longer a yard young'un, and my world expanded to the outside perimeters of the surrounding lakes and marshes. Unlike the other young'uns at the Creek, I had routinely known two completely different worlds since birth. When I was at the hospital, Cross Creek was like a distant planet, and back at the Creek the hospital seemed eons away. The contrast was so great I am today unable to associate one with the other.

Because of the cost of traveling to and from Greenville I was allowed to travel alone after I was five. I liked the trips and could not understand why anyone found the idea so traumatic. I went back and

forth on the train until I was nine. The conductors put a tag on me and always seated me next to some kind, violet-scented grandmother. The Travelers' Aid Society met the train in Jacksonville and Atlanta and took me to the station restaurant and let me order anything I wanted. Then they handed me over to the conductor of the connecting train to Greenville.

On one of the trips I brought along a baby snapping turtle. During the long trip, the shoe box I kept it in came apart, and the turtle got loose in the train. I made a lot of new friends, as the passengers in the car all helped find it several times. One of them was a lady whose son was with the Hershey chocolate company. She asked me about the hospital and then did the most extraordinary thing I could imagine anyone doing. She opened her briefcase filled with Hershey bars and said, "Take all you want." The next day I arrived at the hospital with melted chocolate oozing from all my pockets and a sticky brown turtle.

The hospital was my second home, the treatments and cast necessary nuisances. I am eternally grateful to the Shriners and my parents for the gift of normal feet and all the freedom it entailed. By the time I was four I could run and play with only minor noticeable impediments. The only clue to my condition was the leg braces I wore until I was ten.

❦ The first contact most Creek young'uns had with government and the outside world was the Island Grove public school. In a place where school attendance had invariably depended on how well fish were biting, that meeting was at best a clash of cultures and priorities. The county, my dad, and the mothers all joined in an uncomfortable alliance dedicated to the proposition that young'uns at the Creek needed as much education as could be forced on them.

Each morning the county school bus came collecting all the young'uns that could be found. Mothers of families living away from the road stood at each stop, herding their little ones onto the bus with the same determination they demonstrated at bath time. Children old enough to go to school were capable of roaming through the hammocks and swamps without an escort, and the temptation to miss the bus was more than most could handle. I do not remember any occasion when a mother stood by the road waiting to help her brood off the bus.

The Island Grove Elementary School was two rooms joined by a wide, roofed breezeway on two acres of prime sandspur land in the center of the village, surrounded by modest houses and a hog-breeding pen. The two identical wood-framed structures sat on piers high enough to provide space for all of the Island Grove young'uns' dogs to spend their days scratching and fighting beneath the classroom floors.

In one room Mrs. Howard, a middle-aged woman with a full figure and a sincere belief in a child's need for education taught the first, second, third, and fourth grades. In the other the principal, Mrs. Ida Pring, who wore small gold-rimmed glasses, taught the fifth, sixth, seventh, and eighth grades. Mrs. Ida Pring's room had a stage across the front raised eight inches above the floor, used for presentations, disciplinary proceedings, and the principal's desk. Outside, two well-worn paths led across the school yard to a pair of sturdy four-hole toilets located on two corners of the property.

Folks said, "You can lead a horse to water, but you can't make him drink," and even though Island Grove's educational facility was con-sidered adequate, some who were forcibly led to that trough of en-lightenment refused to drink. Skink Strop's collision with the Island Grove Elementary School set a record that was never equaled.

The first time I saw Skink he was standing across the road from our house at the edge of the tangerine grove. The only thing he had on was a pair of overalls two sizes too small. His sandy hair and green eyes looked lighter than they were because of his pale white skin. I thought, "Hot dog. A new neighbor."

I had never been happier to see anyone and went out the gate and said "Hey." He acted as if he didn't hear. He didn't move. I ventured closer and tried smiling. He still didn't move. I took one more step. Suddenly all my instincts told me to get back in the yard, and I turned to run, but not soon enough. He caught me as I desperately tried to unlatch the gate. When he bit me on the leg, I let out a yelp and kicked. Even though I was wearing leg braces, he managed to bite me a second time. Marjorie and my dog both came to the rescue, screaming and barking. Skink turned loose and ran back toward the creek, keeping close to the fence that would give him an avenue of escape if pursued.

After being bitten twice, I had no desire to know or understand this strange boy. I was scared to death of Skink Strop. My dad said if I bit him back we would probably become friends; I nevertheless avoided him through the rest of the summer. The last thing I expected to do that summer, or ever, was to end up respecting Skink.

I felt my dad had betrayed all the young'uns at the Creek when I heard him tell Mamma he had talked to Mr. Strop about the need for Skink to go to school. Skink was eleven, four years older than he looked standing in the tangerine grove, and still in the second grade.

I never liked goldenrod because when it bloomed, only a few more days of freedom remained before the school year began. That year I disliked it more than ever, as once again, all of the Creek young'uns that could be rounded up were forced to leave blue skies and freedom to sit in dismal gray classrooms for the next seven months.

The first day Skink's dad, with a stick in one hand and Skink in the other, put him on the bus. Apparently all the young'uns had met Skink, because when he selected a place in the front of the bus everyone else sat in the back; going home after school, he chose to sit in the back and we all crowded up front. The driver, who normally didn't put up with any violation of the rules, ignored Skink's tobacco chewing and allowed him to spit out of any window he chose.

Each morning the Island Grove Elementary School opened with two teacher's pets raising Old Glory up a twenty-foot cypress pole while we all stood with our hands over our hearts in the yard and recited the Pledge of Allegiance. Mrs. Pring then lowered the cactus-thorn needle onto her morning glory phonograph, and John Philip Sousa's *Stars and Stripes Forever* inspired us as we marched into class.

The first morning Skink attended school he broke out of line and charged into the room, thinking he would select his seat the way he had on the bus. With great patience Mrs. Howard coaxed him into the second-grade row long enough to call the roll, then let him sit by the window in a bigger seat. Skink was two heads taller than the other children in his class and sat sulking and staring at the blue sky out the window. In the afternoon he bit off a piece of his chewing tobacco. He would probably have gotten away with chewing it if he had spit in the stove's wood box rather than on the floor. Skink got the first whipping of the school year for that, and one or two nearly every day thereafter. In fact, he became such a disrupting element that eventually he was allowed to sleep or wander around the room at will as long as he didn't disturb the other children.

By far the most popular spot at the school was the outdoor toilets. We all took turns going there to escape the monotony of the classroom. The older boys smoked and chewed in the outhouse, and the rest thought of it as a student lounge. A few minutes after school began, the first young'un asked permission and headed for the sanctuary at the corner of the yard. As soon as that student returned, hands shot up, seeking permission to be the next. It was impossible for the teacher to keep track of who had been excused when and still teach four grades in the same room, especially with boys and girls going at the same time. We all competed for a turn, and obtaining permission was like winning a lottery.

The affair that broke the fragile relationship between Skink and the Island Grove public school was directly related to the outhouses. One morning Skink and another boy raised their hands simultaneously. Skink protested that he had raised his hand before the other child but was overruled. When the boy returned, Skink assumed he had permission to go and sailed out the door. Mrs. Howard was busy with the third grade's reading lesson and did not notice the time passing. When she finished, she faced a roomful of hands waving, some attached to apparently desperate children. Skink had not returned.

Mrs. Howard told her students to stay in their seats and study their reading. She selected one of the paddles from her desk and left the room. All of the young'uns immediately jumped to the window to watch the show. Someone said, "She's going to whip him all the way back to the room." Ten feet from the toilet she called, "Skink, you come out of there!" Whereupon Skink threw his overalls and shirt out the outhouse door. It was clear that he had begun Island Groves School's first sit-in.

Mrs. Pring, teaching in the next room, looked out her window just in time to see Skink's clothes go flying. She told her charges to stay in their seats and hurried out to support her colleague. When all threats had failed, Mrs. Pring returned to the school to reestablish order while Mrs. Howard scurried down the road to the school trustee, Mr. Austin, for some masculine help in handling the rather delicate predicament.

Mr. Austin was plainly angry at being called from his farm work. As Mrs. Howard discreetly turned her back, he picked up Skink's clothes and jerked the door open. A white cloud of toilet paper billowed out into the yard. The muscular farmer-trustee probed into the mass of paper, grabbed Skink, and stuffed his naked frame back into his overalls. That done, he tucked Skink under his arm and, trailing streamers of toilet paper, headed back to the classroom looking like a bald-headed bride carrying her skinny groom to the altar. The teachers, both carrying all the toilet paper they could manage, made up the procession back to the school rooms. The flag raisers were dispatched to bring the rest of the unrolled paper to the stage in the principal's room. Skink had unrolled every bit of it. Classes were suspended so everyone could witness him being soundly spanked in the center of the stage.

Following the public spanking Skink was ordered to restore the toilet paper to its original condition. He sat all day on the stage, five days a week, rerolling the three rolls of paper he had unrolled. Principal Pring was unyielding in the perfection she demanded of Skink's efforts. When his deft fingers strayed from the flawlessness of the original manufacture, she made him unroll the paper down to the flaw, then roll it up again.

After the first few days Skink settled into his task with intense interest. Legs crossed, he sat in the corner of the stage facing the wall and rerolling paper. From the time he got off the bus in the morning until he reboarded it in the afternoon he stopped only to eat his lunch. It was almost possible to feel sympathy for the lonely figure humbly concentrating on his work.

The teachers exuded pride in the obvious success of their disciplinary program when, after two weeks, a second roll of perfectly rolled paper was displayed on Mrs. Pring's desk. Almost everyone agreed that all Skink needed was to find something he was good at to transform him into a good boy. Marjorie and I were more skeptical: I had scars that proved his bite was worse than his bark.

By the end of the third week all the students watched as Skink came to the end of the last roll. Everyone in the village seemed proud of Skink's rehabilitation. He finished in time to catch the bus on Friday afternoon. The following Monday he didn't come to school. In fact, Skink never returned to Island Grove School. It was apparent he knew his folks would be moving, and he had worked diligently to right a wrong and make peace before leaving.

The Creek young'uns were all a little disappointed at Skink's submission to the will of the school and county government, until some of the older girls came running out of the privy, some screaming and the others snickering. One of the flag raisers ran to Mrs. Pring waving a roll of paper, one of the very rolls of paper Skink had rerolled. A quick inspection revealed a collection of four-letter words that would shame a buzzard, crudely printed a few feet apart with purple crayon. A quick investigation located the second and third rolls, also with personalized inscriptions. Skink had struck his final blow!

❦ The first thing I learned about work was that you can't do it and fun things at the same time. My sister Marjorie had five more years' experience in avoiding work than I and kindly shared her wisdom with me. She had developed some basic rules: Always play out of sight of your parents; when you could be seen, look as if you were on the way to do a job that needed immediate attention; never announce you had finished the work you were supposed to be doing; create the illusion with your mother that you were doing some important tasks for your father; and let your father believe you were doing jobs for your mother.

The best times were summers and Sundays. The quality of my summer was dependent on the amount of work I could avoid. On Sundays, or more accurately on Sunday afternoons, I did not have to hide in order to play. I was free to do anything I had planned during the week.

Like everything else at the Creek, Sunday afternoons had a price: church on Sunday morning, where you were not supposed to sleep, look back, talk, or—a rule established specifically for me—yawn. This rule came about one Sunday when my dad saw me yawn every time the preacher looked in my direction. I had been doing the phony yawns for three Sundays in a row. The yawning was born out of a desire to persuade the preacher to shorten his sermon. I thought if he saw how tired I was he would cut it short. It appeared to have worked the first two Sundays, although the time may have seemed shorter because I had something to do. On the Sunday I was caught I had yawned twenty-six times after Dad started counting.

When we finally got home my mind was centered on Mamma's Sunday dinner and the total freedom I would have all afternoon. As I went past Dad into the house, he caught me by my collar and guided me into my bedroom. "Son," he said, "I was noticing you in church, and it became obvious that you are not getting enough sleep." Uh-oh. He continued softly, "You get your Sunday clothes off and get in that bed. Your sister can bring you some nourishment when it is ready." Before he closed the door he said, "I want you to sleep until breakfast tomorrow. Then you won't have to yawn every minute and might even feel like helping the family with some work."

To this day I make it a practice never to yawn in church.

Most Sunday afternoons presented a greater choice of activities than a toy store. I could fish in the creek, paddle a boat out on the lake, hunt a bee tree or a gator nest—the list was endless. One of my favorites was going visiting and eating, which I considered one activity. Everyone in the Creek welcomed me as if I were family, lavishing food and hospitality on me. I drank coffee with the Basses, had onion-and-biscuit sandwiches at the Slaters, ate gopher with the Mickenses, and tasted my first sweet potatoes and gator tail with Mr. Story. Mrs. Brice had dainty little cookies, and Mrs. Rawlings always had something new and different. The only food I ever refused was the gator tail my sister Marjorie and I cooked in the yard over an open fire (Mamma wouldn't let us bring it in her house). It didn't smell right, so we gave it to the cat. She lived, but all her kittens died.

There was no one I liked to visit more than my friend W.C. Calton. He was only a few months younger than I and lived around the curve close to the Bridge. Since my brother, Carlton, was ten years older than me, he had left for college by the time I was seven, and I was glad to have a boy my age to play with. W.C. had his mother's pleasant, gentle nature, and like most of the young'uns at the Creek, he had a nickname: Monk. I truly envied Monk. His stepfather owned a farm but preferred trap fishing over tilling soil. Monk consequently had time to roam free. In addition, he had his brother C.J., only a few years older, for a companion. When we got together, Monk and I usually made things like minnow traps to put in the creek or sling shots from forked sticks and strips of automobile inner tubes.

One Sunday afternoon (when I hadn't yawned in church) we examined our options and decided to search the hammocks for the world's best grapevine swing. Monk's mamma told him to be careful and for both of us to look out for snakes, which was the same thing all mammas said at the Creek.

We headed into the woods, zigzagging back and forth through the hammock and testing vines to determine if they were securely attached to the tops of the trees and if there was enough open space to swing. We found several that were pretty good but none that were perfect. Monk showed me a bee tree his uncle had found, and we discovered a wood duck nest in the hollow of a dead cabbage palmetto. After an hour of searching we explored the richer soil nearer to the creek.

Finally we found a wild grapevine hanging unencumbered from a series of limbs in the top of a live oak, sixty feet above the ground. The area beneath the oak was clear except for a few beauty berry bushes. We trimmed the bushes and cut the vine with our pocketknives at a point where it would swing clear, about a foot off the ground. Next we tested it by pulling ourselves up together and bouncing our weight up and down. We assumed that if our combined weight could not break or pull the vine loose from the limbs it had attached itself to, it would certainly hold us individually.

I don't know if Monk was wiser or just more polite, but he usually let me be the first to try out such contraptions. I ran as far as I could in one direction holding the vine, then lifted myself up on it, pulled my knees under my chin, and swung back across the clearing. It was a perfect swing. We took turns running and swinging until we became bored with the game. We were ready to abandon it when Monk had a great idea. A young sweet gum stood at the edge of the clearing. If we climbed up into the sweet gum and jumped out holding onto the vine, we would get a fantastic ride. Again, he let me try it first. After I climbed ten feet up the tree, he lifted the end of the vine up to me by attaching it to the end of a long stick.

I got a good grip and jumped. The momentum was incredible; it carried me more than forty feet across the clearing and then back to where I could catch onto the tree I had jumped from. We had found the ultimate grapevine swing. I swung out and back several times before offering him a turn. I was surprised when he told me, "You go ahead and I'll swing later."

One of the hardest things for a young'un to learn is when he has pushed his luck too far. I thought that if swinging this way was exhilarating, swinging through open flames would have to be better. I gathered dry palmetto fans and set them on fire at the point the swing came closest to the ground. By the time I climbed back up the sweet gum and Monk passed up the vine the flames were five or six feet high. I jumped out, closed my eyes, and held my breath. I swooshed down, pushing the air in front of my body, sailed through the flames, and dropped off on the other side—fantastic! "Now it's your turn," I told Monk, who had been watching skeptically. He said maybe he would do it another time. I pointed out that a grapevine swing was only good for one-time use. In two or three days the vine would start to rot and would break if we tried to use it.

"I'll do it one time and that's all," he said. While he shinnied up the tree I gathered more palmetto fans for the dying fire. When Monk was ready the fire was burning higher than before. I yelled, "Come on!" He hesitated, and then with a look of absolute determination he jumped and came flying down toward the fire. In the split second before he reached the flames, the vine's hold on the tree slipped and lowered Monk just enough that his butt struck the ground, sending him crash-

ing and rolling through the burning fans, throwing flames and charred palmetto in every direction. The momentum carried him past the fire and into the brush beyond the clearing.

Monk was surprised to be alive. He rolled to his feet and stood staring in my direction, his face blank. By some miracle his clothes had not caught fire, but the flames had singed the hair on his arms as well as his eyebrows and lashes. When he tried to wipe the smut and dirt from his face, he wiped his eyebrows and lashes off. His hair, too, was singed and smelled awful.

Neither Monk nor I had time to be concerned with the near-tragedy he had escaped: we were already more terrified of the consequences when our folks found out. We tried to be calm, but Monk panicked at my reaction to his bald face and his hair kinked down on his scalp, smelling up the hammock. I had an idea that I desperately hoped was inspired by divine providence: We should go to the creek and wash the stink out of his hair, and maybe I could paint him some new eyebrows that would last until the originals grew back. Monk didn't think much of my suggestion, but for lack of alternatives he agreed.

Something about burnt hair makes it oily, and without soap his normally blond hair turned a rusty orange. We scrubbed until his scalp was sore but couldn't get the tint or the smell out. He thought it might be more natural when it dried. I agreed, then began what turned out to be my first and last makeup job. We burned the ends of some sticks to make charcoal eyebrow pencils. When I attempted to duplicate the brows he had lost they looked more like Groucho Marx's than Monk's. I tried to wipe some off and only succeeded in giving the skin on his brow a deep blue cast that looked like a five o'clock shadow.

There is a phenomenon that I have observed many times as an artist: The longer you work on a project, the more you will think it looks the way you intended it. Someone else, though, will see it as it is, and that is why one should never show one's creative work until one can see it objectively. After more than an hour and a lot of smut, I decided Monk looked natural and convinced him and myself that no one would notice any change.

We stopped worrying and relaxed. We decided, just in case his mother might notice some little difference, that it would be best if we stayed in the woods until sundown. Then we strolled nonchalantly up the road to Monk's house.

Overconfidence combined with deceit is a treacherous thing. When we were fifty yards from his house, Monk's mother ran out, letting the door slam behind her, yelling, "W.C., what in the world happened to your face?"

I did the cowardly thing and ran across the ditch on the opposite side of the road, slithered under the fence, and cut through the grove home. I spent the next month waiting for Monk's mamma to tell my folks about the stupid, dangerous escapade I had enticed her son into. Bless her heart, she never did. I have always loved her for it.

Monk's mother died while we were still kids, and he had to leave the Creek and live with an uncle in Gainesville. Everyone missed him, and especially me.

Five. The Poet of Burnt Island

CHARLEY held more titles than anyone at Cross Creek with the exception of Mrs. Rawlings. Charley was the "tallest," "most generous," "gentlest," "quietest," and even though he destroyed all his poems, he was the poet of Burnt Island. After all was said and done, we wished we had called him Mister Charley back when we had the chance.

A title Charley never had was "the drunk." When we referred to "Charley's drunk," we were talking about an annual happening at the Creek. At Cross Creek we didn't discuss a man's drinking lightly and especially not with anyone that wasn't raised on creek water and naturally immunized from red bugs and mosquitoes. I am still a little reluctant to talk about it, but in that so much time has passed and Charley is dead, I'm sure he won't mind.

Charley only drank on one occasion each year. Educated folks would give a dozen different reasons why a man would go on an annual drunk, but at the Creek we didn't analyze much; we dealt with what we saw and assumed everybody was the way they were because that was the way they were. If it didn't make sense, it didn't matter. As long as the sun rose in the east every morning and Mrs. Rawlings continued to wreck her Oldsmobile, we knew Charley would go on his drunk every summer.

To appreciate Charley's drunk one has to understand that we are not talking about an ordinary drunk. These were world-class drunks. No one I ever knew before or since could drink that much cheap booze under those circumstances and survive.

Mrs. Rawlings achieved national celebrity status, and she should have become the most celebrated person at Cross Creek, but she had to share that distinction with Charley, a self-described nobody from nowhere. Charley appeared to be about forty when he came to the Creek, and he never seemed to age. He never said where he was from and, in keeping with custom at the Creek, no one asked. Charley was exceptionally tall and slumped. He had clear, light-blue eyes, and wore long sleeves and a striped denim cap to protect his milk-white skin from blistering in the searing Florida sun. In total he looked and walked like an oversized great blue heron, stalking minnows along the shore.

Charley derived his living by fishing with a cane pole for brim and speckled perch when they were biting. When that failed he put out a trotline for catfish, baiting it at night and running it in the morning. He stored the fish in a wire pen set in the water and tied to a cypress tree in front of his camp at Lochloosa Lake. When a fisherman from the Creek fished on Lochloosa, he would pick up Charley's fish and sell them to my dad.

The payment was sent by the next person going to Lochloosa and deposited in Charley's bank, a Prince Albert tobacco can nailed on a tree out in the lake. Occasionally the bank contained a polite note from Charley with a request for whoever came by: "Would you please purchase two pounds of cornmeal? I will be most grateful. Thanks." There was no signature and none was needed. Other items necessary for his secluded existence might be coffee, tobacco, salt, sulfur for mosquitoes, and Crisco during the early spring when catfish didn't have enough fat in them for grease. There was never a hint of urgency. He assumed that someone would drop the item off when it was convenient. More than enough money to cover the cost of the purchase was always folded in the note.

For twenty years Charley was the sole resident on Burnt Island in Lochloosa Lake. He lived in a hut made of palmetto fans with no furnishings but a thick layer of Spanish moss for a bed. The structure was only half as tall as Charley's six-foot-six height. His camp occupied an area half the size of a tennis court on a sandy knoll with the lake in front and a swamp in back. I visited there often. I have always thought it was one of the most tranquil, beautiful places on earth. Lake cypress draped with gray folds of Spanish moss formed a curtain obscuring the campsite from the lake. In the afternoon the reflections of sun and shadow created by undulations of the water moved lazily to and fro on the huge limbs and foliage of an ancient live oak that formed a roof over the camp. When I was a kid I wished everyone could see Charley's camp but I knew if they did it would not be special anymore.

Once I was guiding a friend of my father on the lake, and we passed within a few yards of the camp. I wanted to share that special place but knew that Dad's friend would not appreciate its beauty. It would be, I knew, like meddling in someone's home without their knowledge.

With one exception that I know of, Charley left the lakes only twice each year—once to buy clothes and once to get drunk. Charley was a man who had time to think. His decision to get drunk every summer was clearly deliberate. In Florida, when a man set out to paddle twenty miles to a liquor store in a heavy cypress boat in July or August, his was a premeditated, calculated drunk.

Normally Charley passed through the Creek and into Orange Lake before sunup, thus avoiding greetings and conversations that would detain him in his quest for the spirits that could only be obtained at the south end of the seventeen-mile lake. Of course no one moved about the Creek without detection, and inevitably the word went around: "Charley's going on his drunk."

If the wind didn't get up he could reach the little village of Orange Lake by eleven, park his boat, and walk to the liquor store in half an hour. There he purchased four gallons of wine and two quarts of gin. He tied two jugs together with catline, one to hang in front of him and one in back over his left shoulder. He hung the other two the same

way over the right shoulder, which left his hands free to carry the two bottles of gin. (Bernie Bass always said the only thing harder for a man to carry was two watermelons and a fishing pole.) With luck Charley was back in his boat by noon, while the temperature was still in the low nineties. If he had been an alcoholic he might not have resisted taking a nip before shoving off, but Charley didn't drink just anywhere. He paddled four more hours back to our end of the lake. There he would pick out one of the hundreds of floating mud tussocks, pull the boat up on it, conceal it with foliage, lie down on the bottom of the boat in the hundred-degree direct sun, and pop the cork.

When the word went out that Charley was going on his annual sabbatical, the ritual was always the same, with only a few variations in the script. No one would have dared try to stop Charley from buying the liquor or drinking it. That was his business. And rushing into a premature search would have been useless because he always hid completely out of sight on one of those mud tussocks, which were unique to Orange Lake. But once he was underway, for some reason everyone talked about him in the past tense. They told stories of his drunks over the years, and of the annual search to find him.

The tussocks were the result of layers of muck that periodically broke loose from the bottom of the lake and floated to the surface, creating thousands of floating islands. Exotic plants thrived in the rich muck and subtropical sun, causing the roots to solidify the muck enough that in some instances it would support a man's weight. For centuries the tussocks had grounded in shallow water between the open lake and its shallower marshes, forming an inner barrier that encircled the entire lake. We called that barrier "the shore tussocks." The remaining floating islands drifted back and forth across the lake, shifting before the wind, or temporarily lodged in deep-water grasses or lily pads.

Once Charley hid his boat it was impossible to find him until the vegetation he damaged by dragging his boat onto the tussocks had time to start decaying. That took three days. This was the tell-tale sign that would lead them to his hiding place. Charley could not survive more than four days lying in the direct sun without food or water and under attack by black ants by day and millions of mosquitoes by night. So there was only one day to find him, and no extensions. The search required every skill Creek people had, including tenacious optimism. It sounds cruel to describe these hunts as fun or enjoyable, but in their way they were. The deadly serious event would have been less effective if it had been approached without a spirit of sportsmanlike competition.

My most vivid memory of the searches is of the first one in which I was allowed to participate, when I was about ten. On that day every able-bodied man and some of the women from the Creek were on Orange Lake when the sun came up. Their cypress boats moved with the deliberate ease of big alligators in open water, circling the perimeters of the shore tussocks. The simple, efficient design of the homemade boats evolved by trial and error from the time of the first settlers up to the mid-1940s. Their low profile made them easy to paddle in the lake winds and difficult for game wardens to see.

On the search day the only objective was to find Charley. I went with Bernie Bass. Even though his oldest boy, Alfred, was only a few years younger than I, I thought of Bernie as a special buddy, and he was the perfect one for me to go with. Brimming with excitement, I met him at his boat just before daybreak. "You think we can be the ones to find Charley?" I asked before even saying hello. I normally tried to hide my enthusiasm around grown people, but it wasn't necessary with Bernie.

"Darned if you ain't settin' on go fer so early in the morning. You kick the snakes out of the back of the boat and let's go see," he joked.

We moved down the trail to the creek and into the lake by the first light of day. "We're going to start at Seventeen Sisters," Bernie said. The Seventeen Sisters were seventeen cabbage palmettos standing in a clump out in the edge of the open lake. Our search area had been selected as part of the plan agreed on at the meeting of the participants on the Bridge the night before. I remember being glad Charley went on the drunk in the summer, or I would have been in school and missed it. While we covered our area, we swapped stories on some favorite Creek subjects: fishing, snakes, and running from the game warden. Bernie also liked hard-times stories. "They ought to give me one of them Ph.D.'s for hard times," he said, " 'cause I got so much experience with 'em." One of the many things I learned from him was that you can't put a man down who has learned to look poverty in the face and make a joke of it.

The sun glared down hard. It *would* be one of the hottest days of the summer. We all widened our individual search areas with a growing feeling of urgency. When Bernie and I came near to one of the other boats, they yelled joking remarks. "Y'all fishin' or huntin'?" My dad said, "It looks like that kid in the back ain't doin' much of the paddlin'."

Bernie answered, "He ain't no kid, he's my kicker"—meaning his outboard motor. "He runs on biscuits and he's about to run out."

There would be no need to ask if someone had found Charley. Whoever found him would announce it by bumping the side of their boat with a paddle.

The search extended from Little Hammock to Twenty Brothers. At noon we moved out into the open water to eat our lunch away from the bugs, hoping for a little breeze. I swapped with Bernie, since it always seemed more like a picnic if I was eating somebody else's dinner. We drank lake water and speculated on how good a cold drink would be. Neither of us spoke the thought constantly on our minds— that Charley's time was running out. After we ate we swapped search areas with one of the Townsends, a way to jog our memories so we wouldn't overlook anything.

When we started out I'd had visions of Bernie and me finding Charley. I pictured us bringing him in, while everyone envied us. We would be remembered as the men who found Charley. But with the passing of each hour I wasn't so sure I even wanted to be present when or if he was found. For the first time since he went on his drunk I suspected some of the reality of what we were about. He could really be dead. I imagined his body in his boat covered with the ferocious black ants and flies that immediately gathered to anything dead. I erased the thought from my mind to avoid being sick. Panicked, I paddled harder.

Bernie said, "J.T., don't push yourself in this sun. You'll give out and be of no use."

My frustration turned to anger. "Why do you suppose Charley goes and does a thing like this?"

Bernie said he had been studying on it every year when it happened. He said, "Know why?" Which was not a question but the beginning of his answer.

"Why?"

"Charley ain't like the rest of us. He carries a big load. It could of been he had bad trouble. And again it could be in his mind. He's so smart he sees and understands things that's deeper than this lake. He don't have no family except us here at the Creek. You want to know what I think?"

"What?"

"I think he wants to prove to hisself we want him. Every year he goes on his drunk, and we come and hunt him up. It's simple. If we decide we don't want him, all we got to do is not try our dead level best to find him. If we didn't, he wouldn't ever wake up. The gators would get him and we wouldn't even have to bury him. The thing is, Charley don't want to be any trouble to nobody, but, J.T., there ain't nobody that don't want to be wanted." Bernie turned and looked over his shoulder. "J.T., my idea is between us, and all I know is, I'll always be glad to hunt Charley. The same as everybody that really knows him."

We circled a big tussock lodged in a patch of bonnets in a silence that Bernie was the first to break. "If me and you ever go on a drunk, he's probably the only one who'd come looking for us." We both laughed half-heartedly. We moved past Grassy Point, stopping every twenty feet to stand on the boat seat and look out over the foliage for any sign of Charley's boat.

The lake had been like glass all day, and the glare made boats and tussocks in the distance appear suspended several feet above the surface. About three o'clock the calm began to change; ripples appeared and were transformed into waves. A thunderstorm rising halfway between the lake and the Gulf of Mexico soon became a serious threat.

The storm was a bad one, an old cackler, as we called them. It billowed up into the stratosphere, an anvil head protruding forward. A black and purple curtain rolled across the sky. On the underside the light green that identifies a severe thunderstorm boiled like an angry cauldron. In twenty minutes the clouds had covered the entire west side of the lake. In a normal situation we would all be on our way to shore and home, but this was not a normal situation. The increasing wind made it impossible to handle our boat alongside the tussocks. We were forced to move out farther, making it more difficult to see over the foliage. Bernie was frustrated. "Orange Lake is like a mean old woman. She's always seeing how far she can push a feller." The temperature of the first gust was twenty degrees lower than the air it pushed from its path.

Bernie motioned for me to come forward. "J.T., we can make it to the Creek before it hits full force, if you want to go." But I knew we could ride out a bad lake storm providing we didn't do anything foolish. The most important thing would be staying low in the boat to avoid lightning. If we went to shore and the storm continued to move east and pass over, there would not be time enough to come back and resume the search before night. There was no choice. We couldn't desert Charley.

We pulled the boat up on a grounded shore tussock and huddled in the bottom. Lightning split the atmosphere around us like evil, probing fingers searching for prey. Within seconds the rain came down like a wall. The smell of ozone filled the air after each bolt of lightning and then was washed away in the deluge of water. It is hard to believe that a person sweltering in Florida's oppressive heat can within a few seconds be freezing. I am sure the gusts of wind reached seventy miles an hour. It came in waves, whistling and then roaring across where we lay, jostling the boat in spite of our weight. I could taste lake water picked up by the wind and mixed with the rain. Bernie shielded me from the stinging pellets, hovering over me like an old setting hen. The storm seemed interminable. I thought of Charley on a similar tussock, possibly only a few yards away. I choked on the thought of him dead and his peaceful camp deserted. My mind drifted to a more pleasant time, the one and only time he had left the lakes apart from his annual drunk and his annual trip to Gainesville to buy his clothes. That was his fateful trip to Island Grove.

❧ The Methodists and Baptists in Island Grove had been forced into an ecumenical existence because neither could afford a full-time preacher. For the survival of both churches they had settled on a service every other Sunday. The Baptists had to attend the Methodist services on one Sunday and the Methodists listened to a Baptist preacher the next. It was the only way to have a congregation large enough to sing and pay the preachers. Naturally, both insisted on holding their own week-long revivals in the summer. The revivals were held at night, since everyone worked during the day.

I am sure that the longest sermons in history were at the Island Grove summer revivals. If it had not been a sin, I would have sworn that they lasted eight hours. In truth they were only about an hour not counting the praying and singing, but their length was amplified by the sadistic design of the pews, possibly created by some demented Catholic as retribution for the Reformation. Even at five years old I knew God didn't create any anatomy capable of fitting that ridiculous shape. As I grew older and taller I became even more positive. It seemed appropriate to me that if Bernie got a Ph.D. for hard times, I should get one for sitting in those hard Methodist pews during summer revivals. To add to my burden, I was forced to sit between my father and mother because I had once been involved in a ruckus in the back of the Baptist church. The combination of severe restriction, hard pews, and endless sermons was seriously threatening my spirituality when a single event made it all worthwhile.

We were nearing the end of a revival. The preacher was giving his all to a congregation that was physically tired, hot, and sleepy. The windows were closed because of the mosquitoes and bugs. The lack of fresh air was compounded by the hundred-fifty-watt naked light bulbs (the power companies did not charge churches for electricity back then) that hung on cords low over the congregation and created a stifling and unholy heat and glare. Everyone was perspiring and fanning themselves with the fans furnished by an Ocala funeral home. The preacher, who looked as if he had fallen into the creek, was bent on making his point. He paused and reached toward the ceiling with both hands.

Before he could speak, the loudest "Amen" I have ever heard came from the back of the church. I tried to turn to see who had shouted but my parents' reflexes were faster than mine. Mamma leaned on me, and Dad gave me a firm pinch on my leg. It was not polite to look back in church. The preacher, apparently encouraged, continued but was drowned out again "Amen! Amen!"

We had one or two old brothers at the Baptist church who occasionally sanctioned the preacher's statements with weak amens. This was considered unfashionable in the Methodist church. But I had never heard anything in any church like this. Out of the corner of my eye I could see others looking back. I tried to turn my head, but Mamma leaned harder and my dad pinched harder.

The amens were coming up the aisle and drowning out the preacher. He stopped. His expression was one of disbelief at what he had wrought. The amens were coming faster than a cattle auctioneer's chant. Dad's and Mamma's restraint broke. They both looked back at the same time, releasing me. I stood up and looked back. It was Charley. His denim shirt was unbuttoned to his belt, he was barefoot, and he didn't have his cap. He had either been seized by the Holy Ghost and delivered there from Burnt Island or he was—God forbid *plain drunk.*

Everyone was on their feet giving him plenty of room. He looked scary. The bright lights obliterated the blue of his eyes, causing them to look like two fresh-peeled boiled eggs. He continued to shout, "Amen! Amen! Amen! Amen!" and he waved his arms, gesturing for the congregation to join him. Two of the deacons recovered and rushed forward to seize him, while mothers herded their children away. Other men joined in and hauled him out of church into the darkness. Charley was still shouting "Amen!"

The congregation stood with their mouths open, staring at the door. Thankfully, no one knew who he was except my folks and me. The preacher recovered and directed us to bow our heads for benediction. I don't think anyone did, but when he finished, everyone said, "Amen" and broke for the door.

My dad didn't stop to talk to anyone. He headed straight for our car with Mamma trying to keep up and pull me along at the same time. We jumped in the car as if we were stealing it and drove out as if by association we were responsible for Charley's dastardly act. The darkness of the Creek road was a welcome relief. I have always felt guilt in the presence of catastrophes and disasters. That night I was afraid I could be blamed for just knowing Charley. I didn't know what would happen to a person who came in a Methodist church barefoot, drunk, and shouting "Amen."

In situations where I didn't know how to feel I watched my dad for leads. He always breathed hard through his nose when he was mad. I was leaning toward him to see how he was breathing when suddenly he exploded into uncontrollable laughter. With the revelation that it was all right, I broke up too. Mamma's feeble effort to protest in the name of decency and religion was lost on my dad and me. Still laughing, he said, "Island Grove has always thought we are uncivilized at Cross Creek. Now they've got something to talk about." He wiped his eyes. "Talk about a revival. They should give the collection to Charley. Nobody'll miss a meeting from now on because they'll be afraid Charley'll come back. Damned if he ain't revived us again." I fell asleep that night proud of Charley, and proud of my dad and his loyalty to Cross Creek.

The next day two of the Island Grove elders came out to see my dad. The spokesman said, "We decided that in the light of the unforgivable conduct of that scoundrel you got out here, we think it best for everyone that he moves some place outside the county."

His companion mumbled, "White trash." My dad looked at them and said nothing.

The spokesman said, "What do you think, Tom?"

My dad answered, "You asked me, so I'm going to tell you. I have been thinkin' about him since last night. That scoundrel's name is Charley. He don't lie, cuss, or steal. He would give the last mouthful of food he had to a total stranger. You fellers ain't got many in Island

Grove you could say that much about. The answer is no." He paused
and laughed. "If you fellers would calm down and think about it, that
was probably the best preachin' you ever had in that church."

❦ The lightning subsided, and the deluge began to taper off. I rose up
and looked around. The lake was completely different; I had never
seen anything like it. The wind had shifted all the floating tussocks and
blown them against the shore tussocks. Their tender foliage lay flat,
blown down by the high winds. Nothing on them protruded more than
twelve inches from the surface. A thin yellow line over Evinston, a
village west of the lake, was spreading south over Boardman and
down to Sampson Point. The wind calmed as the dying storm moved
off to the east. Within a few seconds the thin yellow line in the west
became an orange glow over the lake and the trees along the shore.
The angry waves were dissolved into soft swells of molten gold. I felt
the mysterious euphoria and peace that permeate the air after a violent
storm.

Bernie broke the spell. "Old Ma Nature shore creates a ruckus to
then turn around and make things so purty when it's all over. Ain't this
sumpin'?"

The bumping of a boat paddle signaled the end of the search. In the
distance three boats moved along the shore tussocks toward the mouth
of the creek. Without speaking we both dug in with our paddles to
intersect with them. "Mr. Story found him, and he's gonna make it,"
Marcel Ferguson yelled. We drew parallel to the procession as Mr.
Story's boat glided past with Charley lying in the back, his head
propped up against the live well. Charley's unbuttoned shirt was hanging off one shoulder. He looked exactly like a picture I had seen on a
calendar of Jesus as they took him down from the cross. He was blue-
gray, cold, and gaunt, a fragile human being hovering between life and
death.

Bernie was aware of my distress at the grotesque figure and said
reassuringly, "J.T., Aunt Martha'll kill a fat old hen and spoon-feed
him chicken soup. He'll be on his feet and back at his camp in a couple
a weeks."

Trying to be grown up had its disadvantages. I would have to wait until the men met on the Bridge and went through the ritual of spitting and beating around the bush before they would tell their individual experiences of the search for Charley. Whatever the experiences at the Creek were like while they were happening, they were all great adventures when they got to the telling.

When we finally sat down for supper my impatience was partly relieved by my mamma's insisting to know what had happened. I started to tell everything I knew but got a look from Dad that clearly meant he would do the telling; Mamma would not approve of my being exposed to the entire reality of the search. "It wasn't much," Dad said. "We weren't having any luck till a thundershower come up. The wind blowed the flags and weeds flat on all the tussocks. When it was over and the rain let up, the first thing Mr. Story seen was a empty gin bottle floatin'. He followed in the direction that had been upwind. Then he found a wine jug, and then there was Charley's ol' boat like Noah's ark settin' in the middle of a tussock. We had searched that same tussock twice before and couldn't see nothin' of him."

I thought Dad sure told a poor story, at least when he was telling it to Mamma. What about the wind and all that lightning? My dad buttered another biscuit. "If that shower hadn't come up we wouldn't of found him. And if the sun earlier hadn't of shrunk and opened up the bottom boards on his boat lettin' all the rainwater out, it would of filled up and drowned him for sure." He thought a minute and added, "He sure had the Lord out there with him today. He must of made him a friend at the Methodist revival."

I said, "I sure wish I could be the one to find him next time." I got a despairing look from my mamma.

❦ It was the simple act of purchasing his annual wardrobe that brought Charley to his final destiny. Every year he went to town and bought exactly the same items: a blue denim shirt with long sleeves, a pair of denim bell-bottom trousers, a pair of tennis shoes (the old high-tops with round rubber reinforcement over the toes and ankle), and a striped denim railroad cap. He always put the new clothes on in the store and threw his old ones in the trash.

In March of 1947, Charley caught a ride to Gainesville with one of the fishermen. They parked three blocks from the courthouse to avoid the parking meters and to conform to the Creek habit of being as inconspicuous as possible. Charley walked to the clothing store on Southwest First Street and made his purchase. He had no reason to hurry, since it would be an hour or more before his friends finished buying their groceries. He walked along the west side of Rice Hardware, probably a little uncomfortable in his new clothes and eager to be back in his camp on Lochloosa.

We only have the account of the eyewitnesses as to exactly what happened next. A convertible going east on Garden Street struck a car on Masonic Street and careened across the street toward the brick building directly behind the old Commercial Hotel. The witnesses said they heard car tires screeching and saw the car speeding out of control. They saw a man of no particular distinction walking directly into its path. And they saw a tall, lanky man move with unbelievable speed and push the pedestrian to safety. In less than a second Charley was faced with a decision: his life, or the life of a stranger whose face he would never see.

The newspaper said Mr. Charles Fields was crushed between the car and a brick wall. His death was instantaneous. The people from Cross Creek went to Gainesville to claim the body. At the morgue an official asked, "What is your relation to Mr. Fields?"

There was an embarrassed silence. Then someone said, "We're kin."

Six. That Woman
Next Door

WHEN Charles Rawlings and his wife Marjorie came to Florida for a two-week vacation in the spring of 1928, neither could have suspected how their lives would become unalterably entangled with Cross Creek and the Crackers who lived there.

They arrived in Jacksonville on a steamship from New York and were met by a petite, vivacious lady named Zelma Cason, who guided them about the city. From there they journeyed southwest down the peninsula to the village of Island Grove, where Charles's two brothers ran a service station. Together they explored the countryside, the lakes, and the rivers and even ventured into the Big Scrub (later Ocala National Forest). By the time they left they had fallen in love with this untamed place in the sun.

Mrs. Rawlings asked her brothers-in-law to find a farm that could support Charles and her while they tried to write. Three months later they had found one: seventy-four acres with over thirty acres of orange groves, a rambling farmhouse, barn, and tenant house in a tiny hamlet off the beaten path called Cross Creek. Mrs. Rawlings bought it, using part of the money she had inherited from her father's estate. In November 1928 the Rawlingses moved into the solid but rundown farmhouse on what had previously been the Armstrong place, 200 yards south of our house. They were as enthusiastic about Cross Creek as my parents had been five years earlier.

In a letter she wrote to the editor of *Scribner's Magazine,* Marjorie Rawlings summed up her first impression of her neighbors:

> I had met only two or three of the neighboring Crackers when I realized that isolation had done something to these people. Rather, perhaps civilization had remained too remote, physically and spiritually, to take something from them, something vital. They have a primal quality against their background of jungle hammock, moss-hung against the tremendous silence of the scrub country. The only ingredients of their lives are the elemental things. They are a people of dignity, speaking often in Chaucerian phrases, aloof: but friendly and neighborly once even a Yankee has proved himself not too hopelessly alien.*

My dad and Charles Rawlings liked each other from the time of their first meeting. Charles, as he introduced himself, was a personable man with a quick wit and a love of satire. He clearly enjoyed feeling akin to the other Creek men and found great satisfaction in physical labor. Charles told my dad he was a writer and had written for newspapers and magazines; he said his wife was also a writer who was interested in poetry and planned to write fiction. He was from upper New York State and his wife was from the Rock Creek area just outside the District of Columbia.

The Rawlings grove and ours needed extensive pruning to put them in productive condition, so Dad and his new neighbor decided to share the work, setting additional trees and clearing back the encroaching hammocks. The Cow Hammock mules were ideal for hauling the pruned brush as well as muck shoveled from the marsh that would enrich the soil beneath the new trees. By the end of the second sum-

---

*Marjorie Kinnan Rawlings to Alfred S. Dashiell, March 1930, Rawlings Collection, Department of Rare Books and Manuscripts, University of Florida Library, Gainesville.

mer the twenty acres across the road from the Rawlings house had
been set and the bare spaces filled in around the house. On our place
most of the trees were pruned and the open spaces set with the popular
Parson Brown and pineapple varieties of oranges.

Charles talked of his plans for writing but did not set aside time for
it. He seemed intent on finishing the job at hand before tackling
another. Occasionally Mrs. Rawlings, a pretty woman who examined
everything with an unquenchable thirst for the smallest details, came
to the grove with lemonade or water. My dad told Mamma she was
high-strung and likable. Mamma gave them her highest compliment:
"We are lucky to have honest neighbors."

One afternoon when a thunderstorm drove the two men from the
field, they found sanctuary from the lightning and stinging cold rain in
the Rawlings barn. Charles showed my dad a Pflueger rod and Shake-
speare reel he had brought from the North. They discussed whether
the old silk line was rotten or if it could be depended on to hold one of
the largemouth bass in Orange Lake. My dad said, "Why don't we try
it? The lightning has passed, and bass hit better in the rain than the
sunshine."

Charles's reply was, "Why not?" So they left their shoes and shirts in the barn, raced out into the downpour, vaulted over the fence, and crossed the Brice grove to the landing, where my dad docked his homemade cypress boat. One bailed the rain water from the boat while the other paddled. Near the mouth of the creek they spotted a school of bass. On his first cast into the school Charles caught a two pounder. On the next six casts he caught six bass, all about the same size. "Tom," he wanted to know, "how could you dare criticize a fine silk line like this?"

Before my dad could answer the water rolled in front of the artificial plug and then exploded. The white mouth and red gills of a monstrous bass shot out of the water, whipping back and forth to dislodge the hooks. Dad yelled, "You've done made their daddy mad. Now we'll see how long that New York line holds out."

Charles told him to relax and watch a master handle a fish. He played the bass beautifully. When it tailwalked, he pushed the rod beneath the surface and forced the fish back into the water. When the bass headed toward a tussock, he slowed it gradually and turned it without straining the line. Finally he brought the exhausted fish alongside the boat. The bass lay on its side until it was in reach, then gave another powerful lurch, banging into the side of the boat, and fell back belly up. Charles eased his hand in over the lower jaw and lifted the fish into the boat. Dad told him to look at his line. It hung limp from the end of the rod, not connected to anything, severed when the fish struck the boat.

The thunderstorm that had passed began backing up, bringing new clashes of lightning and heavy rain that forced the men to rush back to shore. In only thirty minutes from the time they left the barn they were back with seven fish. It was an amazing number in so short a time, but Charles was cheated out of his glory. When he showed his prize fish to his wife, she said she had seen him run to the barn when the storm began and it was ridiculous to expect anyone to believe he had slipped out for a few minutes in the rain and caught the fish. Behind his back she confided to my dad that she had seen them both return from fishing but wanted to tease Charles. Dad joined the conspiracy, refusing to corroborate Charles's story, saying he would not be in the middle of a man's dispute with his wife. Charles said it was bad enough that his friend and his wife would not give him credit for such a great feat, but when he gave the big bass to Aunt Martha Mickens and told her he had caught it, she said, "Sho' you did," and laughed.

🌿 In the early spring of 1933, five years after their first visit to the Creek, Charles and Marjorie Rawlings came to our house on a weekday morning. Because it was not customary to visit anyone during the middle of the day, when they would be working or taking a rest, a visit at that time indicated something extremely important. They came onto the screened porch but declined my dad's invitation to sit in one of the rockers, saying they only had a minute.

Charles extended his hand to Mamma and then to Dad. "I am going to be leaving the Creek today and I wanted to say good-bye to you and Pearlee—"

Dad interrupted him. "Where are you going?"

"Marjorie and I are too high-strung to live together," Charles said, "so I am leaving. I never had a better friend than you, Tom, and I wanted to tell you." He looked at his wife standing at his side. "I also wanted to ask you, please don't let my leaving affect the wonderful relationship you and your family have with Marjorie."

Dad asked, "Will you come back to the Creek, ever' now and then?"

"No," Charles said, "we think it is best in situations like this to go our separate ways without infringing on one another." He shook my dad's hand again and turned to the door. Everyone exchanged good-byes, and they walked back down the road toward their house together. None of us at the Creek ever saw Charles Rawlings again. The depot agent in Island Grove said the couple went there together and kissed good-bye, and Mr. Rawlings boarded the south-bound train.

After that Charles Rawlings's stories appeared infrequently in popular magazines, both fiction and accounts of his adventures in places a world away from the Creek. Shortly after he left, Mrs. Rawlings gave his old fishing rod and reel to my brother, Carlton, and told him that Charles wanted him to have it. The rod became a proud family memento of a good friend we had lost.

❦ Cross Creek will always be known as the home of Pulitzer Prize–winning novelist Marjorie Kinnan Rawlings, and it should be. But with the exception of the four families that lived east of the Bridge, Mrs. Rawlings had little contact with most of the Crackers, having set herself apart from them by displaying an air of intellectual and social superiority. Whether or not this was deliberate, she was perceived as wanting to keep herself distant from the local inhabitants. When she needed to have close contact with the local culture she chose the Leonard Fiddia family, who lived east of the Oklawaha River twenty miles from the Creek.

The Creek folks were comfortable with their status and fiercely independent. They believed that as long as the lakes existed they would be financially secure. Although they might have appeared poverty-stricken to a stranger, they were not like small farmers who lived under the constant threat of crop and financial failure. Their simple needs allowed them to remain unaffected by changes in the national economy and by the deepening depression. Bernie Bass once told me, "Compared to Gilchrist County, there ain't no hard times at the Creek." To emphasize his point he added, "Only convicts and rich folks is as secure as us fishermen." His outlook generally reflected the attitude of everyone at the Creek. The Crackers were not humbled by or envious of social or academic status. They viewed Mrs. Rawlings's stature as a burden that isolated her from the camaraderie and excitement of their world.

I am sure Mrs. Rawlings was unaware of the responsibility back-woods culture demanded of Crackers toward their neighbors, especially toward those who lived alone. Wealth and academic credentials were useless in the wake of fires, natural disasters, sudden sickness and unexpected death. Wives regularly stopped by to visit, using one pretense or another, to see if Mrs. Rawlings was all right. On two occasions, well-meaning families attempted to draw her into their community of friends, only to have her misinterpret their overtures as attempts to obtain charity. She would later write of those sincere offers of friendship from the bias of her own misunderstanding.

She was of little or no real consequence in the daily lives of most of the Crackers at the Creek, although they felt a neighborly responsibility to her and continued to extend offers of neighborly friendship. Their survival centered around fishing and hunting. They were naturally secretive, and the quasi-illegal status of their fishing activities caused them to be more so. They excluded her from their comings and goings not because she wasn't trusted, but because they saw no reason why she should know how they conducted their lives.

Not that the folks at the Creek were unaware of Mrs. Rawlings's presence. She exuded an aura of energy and controversy. She was charismatic and antisocial and unyielding, a force that could not be ignored. She smoked in public at a time when most women smoked in secret and publicized her taste for good liquor when most of the country buried their empty bottles. Her fast driving, reckless accusations, and occasional profanity all created an image not always admired but never ignored.

My family and the Brices were Mrs. Rawlings's closest neighbors. Our properties all adjoined orange groves. The Townsends occupied the Cow Hammock house for several years after my folks moved in the Haymans house, then they moved across the creek. The Creek's only black family, the Mickenses, worked for the first three families, providing an indirect link.

During Mrs. Rawlings's first years at the Creek, Mrs. Slater, a widow lady, and her four children did odd jobs for her. But the needs of her children eventually forced Mrs. Slater to move back to her birthplace in South Carolina. Only her eldest son, Snow, remained at the Creek to fish and tend Mrs. Rawlings's grove.

Mrs. Rawlings was looked upon as a temperamental character who vacillated from warm and friendly to snobbish. She clearly valued her independence and privacy. But to be fair to her, that same description fit most everybody at the Creek.

Creek folks didn't visit much except on the Bridge or out on the lake when bream were bedding and the boats gathered close together over the beds. So on those rare occasions when a neighbor knocked at the door, it usually meant something important had happened or was about to. That was never more certain than when Mrs. Rawlings came to our door. During the twenty-five years she was our neighbor, she came to our house to introduce her friends, fight with my dad, bring something she had cooked, apologize to my dad, invite me on a junket, fight with my dad, deliver her latest book, apologize to my dad, bring her holiday gifts, and fight with my dad.

When I visited her, it was a casual rather than a prescribed event. She made me welcome to open the little ornamental gate, walk up her pine-straw walkway, and call, "Miz Rawlings, it's J.T." She always called, "Hello. Do come in," over the friendly barking of her bird dog. Looking back, I am impressed by her tolerance of my interruptions, and especially of some of the ridiculous favors I asked of her. When I was six or seven, my dad would say to her, "Don't let that boy bother you. When he does just tell him to git." She would answer him in a feminine tone that made him uncomfortable, "Now Tom, J.T. and I have lots of things that are just between us." I wasn't sure what all they were, but I felt ten feet tall because she said so.

The first favor I asked of her was permission to trap small animals on her land. I was nine or ten and had heard George Fairbanks, a bachelor hermit who lived west of the Creek, talk about trapping and selling raccoons and wildcats. He had sold the pelts to Sears, Roebuck for what sounded like a fortune to me. I had immediately decided to become an animal trapper, starting with eleven rusty steel traps I found in our toolshed and plenty of coons at the Creek. I also needed my folks' permission.

My mamma objected. "The hides are not worth killing the little animals."

Dad said, "You might as well find out what it is really all about," and overrode her veto with two provisions: I could only set a trapline when there was no school the next day, and I was not to put traps where other people were trapping for a living. The hammock on Mrs. Rawlings's land was just the place. I asked her if it would be all right and she said, "Well . . . yes."

As I put the traps in the trails along the fence and in the edge of the water where the hammock joined the swamp, I envisioned genuine manly recognition and big money. The following morning in the gray light of dawn I ran past her house and turned into the hammock. The first trap was just as I had left it. The second had a large male coon working desperately to free his paw from the steel jaws of the trap. It looked directly at me, whimpering, and I was consumed with pity for the terrorized creature with its pleading eyes. I would have liked to set it free, but there was no way to remove it from the trap without killing it. I was heartbroken and ashamed when I shot it. It was a relief to find the rest of the traps empty, with the exception of a single fat possum.

Once I was out of the hammock and back on the road I put the horror of the steel traps and the killing behind me and fancied myself a great hunter coming home with the kill. I felt secure that no one would ever know I had cried when I killed the coon and even when I shot the lowly possum. I hoped in vain that Mrs. Rawlings would notice me passing and give me an opportunity to brag on my trapping ability. She was nowhere to be seen.

My friend Henry Fountain skinned the coon and possum for the meat and restored my diminished ego when he thanked me for providing more meat than a big family could eat in a week. I spent the morning stretching the coon hide on the side of our outdoor toilet. The Creek fishermen congratulated me, telling me my daddy was a lucky man to have a son that was willing to help him make a living. I acted as if killing coons was an everyday occurrence. I became committed to the trapping by accepting praise for the killing while remaining silent about the unpleasantness. I simply did not have the courage to tell anyone I hated it.

The following Friday I reset my traps, feeling like a coward for hesitating and disgusted with myself for doing it anyway. The next morning there was a coon in three of the traps. One had nearly chewed its foot off trying to escape and rolled into a ball when I came near. Suddenly I didn't care who thought it was manly to trap with steel traps. I was finished.

Most of the experiences that bring us face to face with the hard realities of life harden our sensitivity. That was not the case for me. The memory of the coon and possum only made my second experience more traumatic. I shot and removed the three animals from the traps. Then I sprung the remaining traps and threw all of them into the swamp. I considered throwing the dead animals away but didn't want to compound my shame by wasting the wildlife. When I lugged the heavy carcasses past Mrs. Rawlings's house, she was in the yard near her pump house. I was thankful that she acted busy and pretended not to see me.

Several weeks later I was in her backyard playing with her half-grown pet coon, Racket, who was trying to climb on my head and pick a fight with her dog at the same time. She heard the commotion and came outside just as the coon managed to get inside my shirt. I tried to pull him out by his furry tail but he insisted on going around my back, causing me to dance up and down when his cold paws tickled my skin. Mrs. Rawlings laughed while I extricated him by pulling my shirttail out and shaking him to the ground. I told her I had once tried to tame a coon but he was too old, and I'd had no choice but to turn him loose.

She asked, "Do you still trap animals?" I told her, "No, I didn't like it." She gave me a knowing smile and said, "I did not think you would."

I unknowingly had forced her to make a painful decision by asking permission to trap on her land. She was in the first stages of writing *The Yearling,* a story about a boy growing up in the forest that reflected her passionate love of animals. When she gave me permission to trap on her land her wisdom superseded her emotional inclination.

❦ In spite of Mrs. Rawlings's continuing kindness, her relationship with my parents shifted like the winds on the lakes. She would be warm and friendly, then for no apparent reason not speak to them for weeks. When my mamma would inquire of Aunt Martha Mickens if Mrs. Rawlings was ill, the Creek's informant and prognosticator would say, "She's havin' one of her black spells, bless her heart." I am sure that acclimating herself to living alone in a strange environment contributed to her radical changes in temperament. But my dad had little or no patience with her moods. If she was mad about something, Mrs. Rawlings would race up to our house, then skid to a stop and refuse to come in. She would state her grievance from the top step. Most of the time the crisis was about something my folks had never heard of. If it became evident that she was mistaken or had been misled she would step inside and apologize for the misunderstanding, then leave as suddenly as she had come.

As volatile as my friend next door could be, she was in many ways more a creature of habit than were her neighbors. I was sure to see her every day when Mr. Baker, the mailman, came at eleven o'clock. Frequently his was the only car to come through the Creek all day long, so his passing was important for our communication with the rest of the world. At the sound of his car I ran to the front yard in case he stopped to deliver a letter from Georgia or a package from Sears,

Roebuck. Looking down the road, I could be certain, if Mrs. Rawlings was home, that she would come from her yard and cross the road to collect her mail. I thought she showed real class by not rushing out when the carrier stopped at her box. She waited until he drove away, then rushed out. Ordinarily she sorted through her mail right then, placing part of it on the weathered mailbox that sat precariously on a tilted cypress post. She usually opened and read a letter or a card. It was as if the moments spent lingering near the box were her only connecting thread to the outside world and fulfilled her need for it.

From the time she came to the Creek she walked daily along the road south of her home, a routine that became a ritual. Regardless of the season, when the sun hovered an hour above the western horizon, she came out her front gate walking as if she had a thunderstorm at her back. Her appearance would lead any observer to believe she was totally without vanity. She wore the clothes she had worn throughout the day—always dresses, never slacks. The only time she wore pants was when she wore riding britches and boots for hunting. Her bird dog, Mandy or later Pat, was invariably a part of the afternoon walk. The dog frolicked a few yards ahead sniffing the air for coveys of quail that had left their scent along the right-of-way. She maintained a breakneck pace for the two miles to Big Hammock, and then she strolled casually back, timing her return before the mosquitoes descended on the Creek.

During the 1930s, when the rest of the country was struggling through the depression and the convenience of automobiles was less than two decades old, it was assumed any pedestrian would prefer to ride than to walk. Occasionally a stranger would come upon the slightly overweight woman who appeared to be either fleeing or pursuing something and would stop to offer assistance. Mrs. Rawlings usually rewarded the samaritan with a curt refusal and would be flat-out insulted if asked why she was walking.

Those walks home were the only times Marjorie Rawlings ever appeared to be relaxed. On the occasions when I encountered her walking *toward* the hammock, I did not speak, nor did she. On her return she was warm and congenial, waving long before we reached

speaking distance. Our chance meetings along the road back from the hammock and the resulting conversations are some of my fondest memories of my literary neighbor.

One afternoon she noticed a flutter mill (a tiny toy waterwheel made with palm fronds) that I had put in a ditch that drained from the road into Right Arm Prairie. She asked who had shown me how to make it and why I had placed it there. I told her Mr. Story, a fisherman who lived on Lochloosa, showed me how, and I explained that the ditch was the only place except the creek itself where there was flowing water. She helped me clear the pine straw that had clogged the device until it was turning freely. We watched it in silence for a few minutes and left it flipping, neither of us admitting it would be clogged again in a short time. I like to think that my flutter mill inspired Jody's down in the Big Scrub in her book *The Yearling*.

In spite of her daily walks, excess weight plagued Mrs. Rawlings from her early thirties until her death, and the size of her derriere attested to the quality and quantity of the rich food and drink she enjoyed. Her overweight was compounded by the many hours she spent sitting at her typewriter. She was not a beautiful woman, but she was certainly not ugly. She was what the Crackers would describe as "a handsome woman," with beautiful eyes.

With that same combination of handsome and plain, her home was a rambling frame structure painted white with dark green trim, sitting comfortably in a sea of overgrown orange and tangerine trees grown from root stock after the Big Freeze in the 1890s. Hibiscus and turk's cap bloomed in profusion around the foundation in the few spots where the sun shone through the canopy of citrus. Some summers a row of petunias struggled against the heat on both sides of the entrance to the front screened porch, giving the house its only non-native touch.

A round table that held a typewriter and a vase of flowers dominated the north end of the porch. A glider (a swinging couch, popular at that time) and matching steel-spring chair were the only furniture on the south end, which joined the carport. The living room was small and dark until Mrs. Rawlings tore out part of the wall and installed French doors. The house was not elaborately furnished, but everything was in good taste. Matching colorful slipcovers and drapes ironed with crisp pleats and snow-white bleached curtains gave the house a comfortable, well-kept look. I do not remember a time when there were not fresh-cut flowers or greenery throughout the house, which gave it a feeling of native hospitality.

Owning real property was a new experience for Mrs. Rawlings. Savoring her good fortune with the selfish pride typical of the first-time landowner, she rejected the concept of open range, a policy which allowed livestock to roam freely over the countryside. Individuals who did not want cattle or hogs to graze in their yards or groves fenced them. When cows or hogs intruded on someone's land, it was the property owner's responsibility to drive them out and fix the fence to keep them out. That was the custom and the law. The open range was not an extraordinary practice if one considers that only a minute percentage of Florida was cultivated at that time. In addition to range cattle, the open woods at the Creek still had a large number of wild hogs that could do tremendous damage to unfenced crops and gardens.

The fences around Mrs. Rawlings's property were old and in need of rebuilding when she purchased the place, a factor that was reflected in the purchase price. She could not afford new fences and tried to repair the old ones, which resulted in livestock coming and going at will on her property, an intrusion she frequently chose to blame on her neighbors. Sometimes she would accuse a neighbor of tearing down her fences when they had fallen because of rotten posts. On several occasions she threatened to shoot invading livestock, and she did shoot Mr. Martin's pig when it rooted in her petunia bed.

Shooting, or threatening to shoot, someone's cows was a serious business at a time when the Crackers at the Creek frowned upon anyone asking the law to intervene in their affairs. Just how serious is reflected in the court records of Florida during that period, showing the large number of people who were shot for killing someone else's livestock. But neither custom nor law were equipped to deal with the threat when it was made by Mrs. Rawlings. The other families at the

Creek had little sympathy for her dislike of open range. Even I had a brood sow that roamed freely, raising several pigs every year. (I've always been thankful the sow preferred a diet of scrap fish over petunias and ranged near the creek.)

My mamma typically defended Mrs. Rawlings, saying one had to admire her for being forthright in expressing her grievances. Dad always said, "She was acting the fool. When she gets her tail up above her head her brain don't work."

I remember the time we heard gunshots at two in the morning that sounded like the FBI's shoot-out with Ma Barker. They were followed by hysterical screaming. I asked my dad, who had been awakened by the commotion, what was going on. He said, "Sounds like that woman is having another understanding with her help." Mrs. Rawlings had just returned from a trip. A few minutes passed, and we heard the sound of bare feet running through the grove, then the creaking of the fence as the fleeing blacks hurled themselves over and into our yard. They stopped outside my parents' bedroom window.

"Mr. Tom!" they yelled. "That womern is done gone crazy. She tryin' to kill all us!"

Dad answered them through the screen. "Maybe I ought to get up and help her. Y'all been partyin' and raisin' hell down there ever since she left and my first guess is, it's been while you've been drinking her good liquor." He paused. "Y'all ain't scared of that little woman, are you?"

Adrenna, one of Aunt Martha's daughters, answered in her high-pitched voice, "Don't fun us. I is scared of her tongue and that thirty-eight special."

"Do somethin'!" they insisted. "Please do somethin' afore she get here!"

Dad said, "Y'all go stay in the garage. There's a cot in there, you can take turns sleeping on it. I'll talk to her tomorrow."

The next day Mrs. Rawlings ran up to our house and skidded to a stop. Dad joked with her that he was afraid she would shoot him. She laughed and said she wasn't going to shoot anyone, she just wanted to get her help back. Her tantrums receded as fast as they rose.

Still, she often was too quick to brandish about accusations or threats in her bursts of temper. No man at the Creek had ever had a dispute with a woman other than his wife and they were all totally unprepared to deal with the situation Mrs. Rawlings presented. Dad decided to keep as much distance from her as possible.

The word went out through the Creek one day that Mrs. Rawlings was claiming her dog, Mandy, had been poisoned. Poisoning was an offense that was simply unacceptable at the Creek. Everyone believed the dog had gotten into some poison by accident or that Mrs. Rawlings had incorrectly diagnosed the reason for her death. In a community of people who never locked anything and dealt with their problems face to face, no one wanted to believe her accusation.

It was a common folk belief that when something died of poison the buzzards would refuse to eat the carcass, so the first question everyone asked was, "Did the buzzards eat the dog?" Unfortunately, Mrs. Rawlings had buried the animal and eliminated the only test that proved poisoning. The Creek folks talked about her allegation on the Bridge and within their families. At our house Dad said, "Poisoning someone's dog is the equivalent of shooting your neighbor in the back." Mamma agreed: "Only a sneak would do such a thing." Everyone felt sure that none of their neighbors would poison a dog.

A week passed before Aunt Martha Mickens told my folks, "That womern is saying, Mr. Tom, you done poisoned her dog. She say she knows it on good authority."

Dad laughed. "Ever since Charles Rawlings left the Creek she's been trying to find somebody to fight with."

"What do you plan to do about it?" Mamma asked.

"Pearlee," he said, "people who know me, know me. She can't hurt me with them." He thought for a moment, then concluded, "It takes two fools to have a row and I don't plan to be one."

The summer passed without further incident. Mrs. Rawlings always spoke to me when I passed, and I to her. Dad said, "There ain't nobody you can't speak to and look straight in the eye, but you can pick the ones you have anything to do with." Gradually, we all came to believe her suspicions had passed. Then one of the women who worked for Mrs. Rawlings came up late one afternoon with a note and said she was supposed to give it to Dad personally. He came to the door smiling, saying he didn't get much mail hand-delivered.

He read it and reached for his hat. I ran out the door behind him, followed him to the garage, and hopped in the truck when he didn't say I couldn't go. We drove to Mrs. Rawlings's house. He told me to stay in the truck and went through her gate, leaving it open. I could see her through the screened porch standing by the living room door. Dad didn't stop and knock, he just opened the screen door and went in the porch. A twelve-gauge shotgun leaned against the door casing. Dad picked it up, breached it, and stood it back where it had been. They stood toe to toe. I could not hear well enough to understand what was being said, which meant they didn't cuss because cussing was always louder. After about five or maybe ten minutes they began to talk calmly. She followed him out the door, and they talked for another minute before Dad got in the truck and made a U-turn back toward our house. "J.T.," he said, "what do you suppose Mamma's got for supper?"

Over supper he explained he had gotten mad about the note, which said, "Tom Glisson, I wish to see you. Be quick about it." When he went in, he asked her who the hell she thought she was. "I don't owe you anything and never did," he told her. "I never had any business with you, and you sure as hell don't have anything I want." She flared up when he suggested she run for queen in the next election, and then she said something about her poisoned dog. He answered, "O.K., lay your cards on the table and let's see what kind of hand you've got." She mumbled something about someone who had sworn her to secrecy and told her Dad had poisoned her dog. She admitted that the sneaky accuser had no proof and that she was wrong to have entered into a pact of secrecy. They talked out the whole thing, including Dad's aversion to being sent demanding notes.

The next day we were resting after midday dinner. Dad was lying on the windowseat when Mrs. Rawlings slid to a stop in front of our gate. Mamma motioned for me to stay where I was and went to the door. As Mrs. Rawlings came up the walk, Mamma latched the door. Mrs. Rawlings said, "May I come in? I want to speak to you and Tom."

Mamma answered, "No, Miz Rawlings. Now, why don't you go and let us alone?"

Mrs. Rawlings stepped back. "I deserve that," she said. "I did not come to cause trouble. Yesterday I admitted I was wrong but I did not apologize. I wanted to tell you how ashamed I am."

Dad interrupted her from inside the house: "Miz Rawlings, come on in. It's too hot to forgive or forget out there in the sun." Mamma opened the door. The three of them sat in the big rockers on the porch while my sister Marjorie and I eavesdropped from the living room. Much to our delight, Mrs. Rawlings stayed until it was nearing sundown and kept us from having to go back to work. When she left, Dad said, "It makes a feller tired even when he's getting forgiven by that woman; let's go over to Orange Springs to cool off."

It was not the last time Mrs. Rawlings disagreed with Dad, but that afternoon the relations between her and my family changed. A bond began to grow that ultimately became a true friendship.

❧ When I encountered anything uncommon at the Creek that was outside the realm of nature, I assumed it had something to do with Mrs. Rawlings, and I was usually right. So it was only natural, when I came upon a heavyset man wearing gold-rimmed glasses and the first pair of knickers I'd ever seen, to assume he was her company. He was engrossed in a sketch he was making that included a tall palmetto standing at the edge of the hammock.

I advanced to what I considered a respectable distance and shuffled around, waiting for recognition. He motioned me to come closer and introduced himself, and I told him I was J.T. He said Mrs. Rawlings said he might run into me. As we talked he continued to sketch. The drawing that materialized while I watched was more wonderful than anything I could imagine. At the hospital in Greenville they had encouraged us to draw and I enjoyed trying, but he did it so easily and the result was better than drawings in Mrs. Rawlings's magazines. It was the Creek, and better than the real thing. The stranger cordially told me that it was a matter of seeing and practice.

Having been taught that it was bad manners to visit someone when they had company, I waited for Mrs. Rawlings's guest to leave. When I was sure he was gone, I rushed to ask her about him. She said her publisher had sent him from up north to illustrate her new book. I was impressed to learn they had paid his expenses *and* given him *additional* money for his pictures. Mrs. Rawlings seemed surprised that I was interested in his art. She apologized, saying she had intended to have me show him around the Creek but had been so busy arranging their schedule she did not have the opportunity. From her library she showed me two books with pictures he had drawn. I think that was the moment the idea of being a professional artist first occurred to me. Mrs. Rawlings said I should remember his name: Mr. N.C. Wyeth.

I was proud to have a friend who had such impressive company and even prouder a few months later when her next book was published. I came home from school, and there it was, *The Yearling,* by Marjorie Kinnan Rawlings. She had placed it in the seat of one of the porch rockers in front of our living room door. A boy, kind of pale, nuzzling a half-grown deer, adorned the book jacket. I was as excited as if I had written it myself. The inside cover and first page displayed a panorama: a boy and a fawn running across a Florida sand bed with scrub pines and a live oak in the background. On the title page it said "*The Yearling,* by Marjorie Kinnan Rawlings, with pictures by N.C. Wyeth," with a drawing of a bear standing in the edge of the water, and then "Charles Scribner's Sons, New York."

Hot dog! This was big stuff. A book by Mrs. Rawlings and Mr. Wyeth. I riffled the pages, inhaling the printer's ink. Then it got even better. A full-page picture in color of a boy lying on his belly watching a flutter mill in the little stream flowing from the sand boils at the head of Silver Glen Springs. It was the best picture of a hammock I had ever seen. In fact, it was *the* best picture I had ever seen. I rushed through the pages. Every picture was equally exhilarating. *The Fight with Old*

Slewfoot was real. Dogs barking, the bear raising hell, the man yelling and grabbing the bear to save the dog. I could smell the gunpowder, saw grass, sweat, and springwater.

I wished someone was around to show the pictures to. Then I remembered I was lucky my folks were not home. I could waste a little time looking at the book and then go into the kitchen and read the note Mamma always left pinned on the icebox door, "Change your school clothes and hoe the green beans" or "Go pick five boxes of oranges" or—the note could wait. I fluttered the pages again, making sure I hadn't missed any pictures when I first skimmed through.

Then I thought I would read enough to see what it was about. "A column of smoke rose thin and straight from the cabin chimney. The smoke was blue . . . ." It was about real people and real things. In a few minutes I was hooked on the story, and although I didn't know it then, I was hooked for life on good literature. This book was not about something that happened in Boston or a castle in France, it was Florida—my Florida, the piney woods and hammocks, the Big Scrub. While I moved my finger beneath each word I became the boy, Jody, romping through the pages. The time passed like Jody's did when he was playing off at the sand boils.

I was jolted out of my trance by the sound of my parents stopping in front of the garage. It was getting dark, and I had not only skipped the chores Mamma had assigned, I had neglected to milk the cow, feed the chickens, and pump water into the water tank.

Believing that the best defense was a good offense, I charged out to meet them, waving the book. I showed them the illustrations painted by Mr. Wyeth and tried to tell them about Jody and Slewfoot. Dad interrupted, "Did you pick the tangerines?"

I said, "No, sir," and tried to get back to the story.

"What *have* you done?" he asked. I was in trouble.

"Well, I came home, and the book was on the porch where Miz Rawlings left it, and, well, I got to reading it and forgot everything."

I never learned to predict my mamma's reactions. She came to my defense. "Tom, at least he was reading, and that's what they have been trying to get him to do at school." She started toward the house, saying, "We can move about quick and have all the things attended to before it gets too dark."

The Yearling was the first full-length novel I ever read, and I couldn't have made a better choice. The north central Florida–based book became a part of my life. Although at that time no one knew it, the book would ultimately affect all our lives by attracting attention to the Creek. For me the characters were so real that it was like a new family had moved permanently to the Creek.

The reviews of the book were rhapsodic, and the Book-of-the-Month Club chose the novel as a main selection. On top of that, Mrs. Rawlings told me Hollywood was going to make *The Yearling* into a movie, and she was going to be a consultant. MGM bought the movie rights for $30,000. Accolades poured in.

We didn't have any phones at the Creek, but Mrs. Rawlings had an arrangement with the railroad freight and telegraph agent in Island Grove to deliver any important telegrams to her for fifty cents. When wires came that were obviously unimportant he was to mail them and let them go to Hawthorne and then out on the RFD to the Creek, which usually took two or three days unless it was near the weekend.

One May afternoon in 1939 she received a wire in her regular mail (because the agent didn't think it was important) notifying her she had won the Pulitzer Prize and inviting her to the award dinner in New York that very evening. Later, talking to my mamma, she said she was happy about the award and had tried to forget the disappointment of missing the dinner. She sat down at her typewriter and attempted to calm herself by continuing to write but could not concentrate. She just had to tell someone, but there was no one around but Aunt Martha. She called her out to the porch and said, "Martha, you know how I have written day and night for all these years? You see, this telegram I received in today's mail, it says I have been awarded the Pulitzer Prize for literature." Aunt Martha patted her on the shoulder and said, "Sho' nuff? Sugar, I bet you is the only one at the Creek what's got one."

Mrs. Rawlings began receiving invitations to speak at celebrated affairs across the nation. Most of her neighbors were happy for her financial success but not really interested in the content of the book that had secured it. I was particularly impressed when she told me she had been a guest of Mrs. Roosevelt and stayed in the White House when she was in Washington. I was disappointed that my friends at the Creek took this honor for granted. Their attitude was, if she was in Washington, why *wouldn't* she stay there?

When she was home Mrs. Rawlings told me that they weren't making much progress on the movie, and that Spencer Tracy was going to play Jody's father, Penny Baxter. Finally she went out to Hollywood. When she returned she said the only thing positive she saw was a man who was growing corn in buckets, in a range of sizes. The studio people would bury some of the buckets in a field and film it, enabling them to show the passage of time by filming the "corn field" in whatever stage of "growth" was required by the story. I thought this was fantastic. MGM eventually came to Ocala to shoot in the Big Scrub. Then in June 1941 they stopped all production, packed up, and returned to Hollywood. Even though it was rumored that the postponement of the film was Spencer Tracy's fault, Mrs. Rawlings said they were all a bunch of nuts.

❦ In the late summer of 1941 Dad and I were building a skinning bench for the catfishermen in the shade of the big water oaks behind our garage. Dad saw Mrs. Rawlings walking up the road toward our house. "Here comes that woman again," he laughed. "I still don't know whether to get ready to fight or cry when I see her comin'."

My mamma, who had brought out a pitcher of ice tea, spoke persuasively: "Tom, she don't mean any harm, she's just high-strung." He replied, lowering his voice as Mrs. Rawlings approached, "She's like a Cadillac without a throttle. It'll run over you before you can get out of the way." He looked at Mamma. "I think she's got a little of the Josey family in her." Mamma did not have time to respond before Mrs. Rawlings was there. We exchanged the usual greetings, followed by talk about citrus and Mrs. Rawlings's aging cow, Dora.

Then Mrs. Rawlings came to the point of her visit: "Tom, I have something I wish to ask you." He stopped what he was doing in order to pay close attention. She began, "During the years I have lived at the

Creek I have made notes of our life here, a chronicle. I did not intend to publish any of the material during our lifetimes; however, my last book has done exceptionally well, and my publisher is impatient to publish another book as soon as possible. I will not do something that is of lesser quality than I am capable, and that leaves me only the book about Cross Creek." She paused for him to absorb what she was saying. "Now, I have used the actual names and incidents that have occurred here at the Creek, and it was of course necessary to change the chronology in some instances and color some events. And I have portrayed everyone at a common level, like in a family, or else Cross Creek would be like any small community." She hesitated. "I have used your name and referred to your lovely family—what do you think?"

A long silence followed. I had no idea how he would respond. He looked directly at her and said, "People who know me, know me. As far as the ones that don't, I don't give a damn."

She seemed relieved. "That is how I thought you would feel."

"You are sure runnin' short on something to write about if you're down to Cross Creek," he smiled. "But times is hard. If you can sell it, you better do it while you can."

She laughed heartily. "Tom, that is good advice for any writer." She turned and asked Mamma something about recipes while we continued our work.

Meanwhile, the casual friendship between Mrs. Rawlings and me continued to develop. At each stage of my growth she seemed perfectly conscious of my exact level of maturity and always gave me the impression she liked me the way I was. Her own life was changing too. She had found a new maid who brought a calmness to her house that did not exist before. And on October 27, 1941, totally unexpected by anyone at the Creek, she married Norton Baskin, a hotel man from Ocala. We heard that the newspapers said they were going to live in St. Augustine. I was upset.

I do not know what I expected, but I believed Mrs. Rawlings would be changed by her marriage. Although she had spoken to me of her friend Norton, I had never met him and was greatly relieved when she returned to the Creek a few weeks after her marriage and immediately came up to our house for a visit. She said she would never give up her place at Cross Creek and would be spending part of her time in St. Augustine and part at the Creek. "Norton," she explained, "will be busy running his newly acquired hotel." Mamma counseled, "You better not neglect him. Husbands trickle away when they are left alone."

The following year I entered ninth grade, making it necessary to ride the school bus twenty miles to the nearest high school, in Hawthorne. In the spring I came home from school and found a new book waiting for me. It had been placed on the same chair as *The Yearling* had been, nearly four years before. "*Cross Creek,* by Marjorie Kinnan Rawlings," the cover read. Hallelujah! There were people who lived less than ten miles from us who had never heard of Cross Creek, and there it was on the cover of a book. To my untrained eye the jacket was a gaudy yellow and the cover art was loose, almost cartoonlike, but I dove into it.

The picture on the endleaves was instantly recognizable, a green-and-white drawing of the Brice grove on the east side of the road between Mrs. Rawlings's house and the Brices. On page one, a black-and-white drawing decorated the chapter head, depicting the Creek in the foreground and the Brice place up the road. I loved the drawing and studied its details. I was in the process of turning the page when my eye caught the word "Glissons." The sentence read, "We are five white families: 'Old Boss' Brice, the Glissons, the McKays and the Bernie Basses; and two colored families, Henry Woodward and the Mickens." This was heady stuff!

I flipped through the pages, ignoring the beautiful illustrations, scanning for the word "Glisson." On page fourteen I hit pay dirt.

Tom Glisson lives on the same side of the road as I do, and opposite Old Boss. Tom has prospered. He and his wife are Georgia folk, too, and as hard workers as I have ever known. I am not at all sure that Tom can read or write, but he talks well, with a flair for the picturesque and the dramatic. He was put to the plow when he was so small he could scarcely reach the plow handles, he told me. He was given no education.

It was a shock to see my family reduced to ink on a printed page. The encounter was similar to unexpectedly seeing oneself in a mirror. It was irritating to read that she didn't know whether my Dad could read or write. If she didn't know whether he could read or write, why did she send him notes?

"It has been good to see the three children grow tall and bright and handsome." I thought, *Now she's stretching it the other way.*

Then, there it was:

The youngest, "J.T.," was a tragic little cripple when I first knew him. I would see him hobbling down the road on his crooked legs, with the luminous expression on his face that seems peculiar to those we call the "afflicted." Tom and his wife were not the breed to accept an evil that could be changed, and they worked day and night to save money to send the boy away for braces and treatment. Now he too is tall and strong, and I saw him ride by yesterday on his own dwarf-mule, talking to himself and lifting his hand to an invisible audience. He was, I knew, the Lone Ranger or perhaps Buck Rogers, but he took time out courteously from his duties to call "Hey!" to me, then returned to his important and secret activities.

I didn't care for the "luminous expression" nor the word "afflicted" but liked the "tall and strong" part.

There was more:

The Glisson house is small and brown, well kept, and the yard has been slowly given shrubs and a bit of grass. Tom raises hogs and some cattle, has built up a little grove, and he and his wife do anything profitable they can turn their hands to. They have fought ill health as well as poverty, and it is sometimes hard to feel sympathy for what seem offhand less fortunate people, knowing what can be done with courage and hard work and thrift. Tom and I began with a strange mistrust of each other, and had some harsh encounters. I was in the wrong, and that is a story, too, and now I know him for a friend and would turn to him in any trouble.*

I thought, *I am going to enjoy kidding my folks about the "doing anything profitable" part.* It was good that she didn't write the book during the times she was mad at my dad.

I skimmed to see what she had written about my neighbors. Some things were flattering and others were humbling—there was a difference in the telling. I turned back to the first chapter and began to read. Everything was familiar yet also strange: the Creek I knew and a Creek I had never seen. There were blatant omissions and skillful enhancements of the people and the place. It was like the impressionist art I had only recently begun to admire and understand. Mrs. Rawlings's version of the Creek was in some ways more vibrant, yet more simplified, than the real-life Creek. Even the truth laid bare was as savory as it was offensive. The book was a gift of a place and a time that was passing, though I was too young to know it.

Again I neglected my work and the chores. When my folks came home I was still standing by the door reading. I made the same excuse I had made before. My dad said, "I'm glad that woman don't write a book every day, or I'd have to hire somebody to do your work."

Cross Creek received instant recognition. It was highly acclaimed by national reviewers and received a lot of notice even while the shock of Pearl Harbor permeated the national consciousness. The war commanded the immediate attention of everyone at the Creek, although I was surprised none of the teachers in Hawthorne mentioned the book, especially after a condensed version appeared in *Reader's Digest.* It was as if anything written locally could not be important. When I asked the families that had been given autographed copies of the book by Mrs. Rawlings, most said they had not read it, and those who had either reckoned it was okay or seemed defensive about the stories and descriptions of their neighbors: "She ought not to of wrote some of the things she did about some, even if it was true." But no one said they

*All *Cross Creek* quotations are from the 1942 Scribner's edition, pp. 1, 14, 15.

were angry about the book, nor did anyone appear angry with Mrs. Rawlings.

🌿 The Japanese attack on Pearl Harbor and America's involvement in World War II caused a sudden change in my priorities. When I was small and wore leg braces, strangers would say, "Well, he won't ever have to go in the army." They were, of course, trying to be kind but I resented the statement. I had been taught at the hospital that I could do anything if I really tried; in addition my dad considered the word *can't* obscene. When the war escalated and a storm of patriotism swept the country, I decided I would get into service in spite of my feet. I was quite serious about it, although I was only fifteen. My first move was to enlist the support of my friend the writer.

The perfect opportunity came when she asked me if I would like to go with her on a jaunt to the Big Scrub to visit a friend. We crossed the Oklawaha on the Orange Springs ferry and talked about the war and the effect it would have on the Creek. She was not optimistic about an early victory and believed Norton would not go into the military. On the other side of the river she turned the Oldsmobile south paralleling the east bank. The car plowed through the deep sand rut for several miles and finally became mired in dry, ball-bearing sand. I said, "It is a pity the CCC's ain't graded the road," and struck an unexpected nerve. She snapped, "I would junk the car and walk rather than have them spoil this beautiful country." We lined the ruts in three different places before reaching her friend's cabin. She visited with the old man for an hour before we started back to the Creek.

We agreed that it would be easier to return through Eureka. As we drove along she counseled me: "You should not become distracted by the war and neglect your education." I confessed that I was not at the top in my class in school. She told me there had to be a branch that would accept me, and when I was eighteen I could enlist, and if I was turned down I should keep trying.

🌿 In August of 1942 Mrs. Rawlings placed *Cross Creek Cookery* in the seat of the rocking chair by our living room door, inscribed "To Mrs.

Glisson and family." The book was difficult for me to read since I considered cooking women's work. My only expertise in that area was in the eating. So when I next saw Mrs. Rawlings I avoided expressing my personal opinion of the cookbook. When she brought up the subject, I told her my mamma thought it was a fine book. Mamma had also said that if the war brides used it to learn to cook, their husbands would be willing to stay home when the war was over.

In truth I was far more interested in the N.C. Wyeth painting Mrs. Rawlings had recently acquired and hung over the fireplace in her living room. Entitled *The Dance of the Whooping Cranes,* it was even more exciting than the reproduction that illustrated *The Yearling*. I stopped to study its every detail any time I had the opportunity.

Cross Creek Cookery had been published only a few weeks when Mrs. Rawlings brought her car to a stop in front of our house in the usual cloud of dust and blew the horn, which indicated she wanted to see me. If she had stopped to visit with my folks, she would have come to the door and called. I dropped what I was doing and ran to the gate. "J.T., I want you to take me frog hunting." Before I could tell her it was a poor time to frog hunt, she continued, "I have some people from the *Saturday Evening Post* who would like to take pictures of me gigging frogs for an article that will promote my cookbook. We will need a second boat for the photographer. You get someone who can handle that boat." She cranked the engine and raced away, tires spinning, before I could explain that the new moon would not set until ten o'clock, and no self-respecting frog would rise before then. Our neighbor Bernie Bass said he would come, but pointed out we'd be hard put to find frogs in any place that we could reach in rowboats.

Two photographers from the magazine, Norton, Mrs. Rawlings, Bernie, and I set out for Lochloosa that night about nine o'clock. I had hoped we would pick up several frogs along the edges of the creek. That was not to be, since we made such a racket we sounded more like fishermen and game wardens having a chase than frog hunters. When we reached the lake we had not seen a single frog big enough to gig. Desperate, I tried to find some in the aquatic coontail or among the lily pads. Mrs. Rawlings said I should slow down and relax: "It's too beautiful to rush around and miss a beautiful night like this." I thought, *These men have come all the way to Cross Creek from New York City, and for the first time I can remember you ain't in a hurry.*

We were making so much noise bumping the boat that when I finally did spot a big old bullfrog he sank out of sight. Without warning, Mrs. Rawlings began to sing "I Don't Want to Set the World on Fire." Norton joined her, followed by the photographer, all sounding more like the frogs we were after than the singers that had recorded the song. I finally found the dumbest frog at Cross Creek. He sat while I moved the boat into gigging position to the accompaniment of the first singalong ever held in the middle of Lochloosa. The flashbulbs went off, and even after Mrs. Rawlings missed him, he sat there and let her get him on the second try.

There has never before or since been so much cheering at the Creek over the capture of a single frog. I gave up and joined the merriment. Bernie told me that if the game wardens were hiding on the lake, they would think we were a decoy for someone pulling a seine.

I found the *Post* magazine propped in the chair by the living room door a few weeks later. The title of the article was "She Hunts For Her Supper," and I was in the photo with Mrs. Rawlings and the frog.

❧ Because of the war, a severe teacher shortage—especially in rural schools—forced school boards to hire anybody they could find. One of the teachers who had come in to my high school in Hawthorne was a former college instructor, desperate to find material that would stimulate interest in social science among her small-town and backwoods students, consisting of fifteen girls from Hawthorne and one other boy from Lochloosa Station and me. One day she referred to Florida's Pulitzer Prize–winning novelist Marjorie Kinnan Rawlings, triggering the first surge of interest she had received from the class. It was obvious she did not know that Mrs. Rawlings lived only fifteen miles away or that I was from Cross Creek. I signaled to the other students to keep quiet about the proximity of the Creek. For several days thereafter all the students encouraged the unsuspecting teacher to tell us more about that unique place. She was delighted to have found something to which the students would respond.

I reported what she said each day to Mrs. Rawlings, who enjoyed a good laugh and then reminded me of what a mean joke I was playing.

With the class's encouragement our teacher soon began to improvise beyond her source material. A student asked, "How can a child raised in such a remote environment ever hope to be a part of the modern world?" It was the kind of question the teacher loved. She said motivation was the first step. Someone else looked at me and asked, "How could children in such a backwoods area become motivated?" while the entire class snickered.

She thought for a moment, searching for the right hypothesis. "There might possibly be a surveyor or maybe an explorer who would come to the area, and he might drop, let us say, a pineapple, into that stream, and it might float down, and one of the children would see it and know it was different from anything he had seen before. Curiosity would cause him to pick it up. The smell would be pleasant, so he might investigate further, cut it open, and discover the wonderful flavor that had been unknown to him before. That kind of chance happening could ignite a spark of curiosity lying dormant in a child's mind, causing him to wonder what was out there beyond the isolation of his remote community."

When all the students laughed, she was not suspicious. We urged her on: "Is that kind of thing likely?" She said, "There was one child there, a cripple, who for some reason became so motivated that he would hobble more than four miles on his crooked legs to school because the desire to learn was burning inside him." The entire class fell out of our seats laughing. The teacher said it was not funny to laugh at those less fortunate than ourselves. On the spur of the moment a student proposed a class trip to visit that unique anthropological model. The teacher hesitated to go on such a long trip but promised to think about it.

Mrs. Rawlings said it would be restitution for the terrible joke to bring my teacher out to the Creek and have a little picnic for her and the class. The next morning I rushed into social science class and found the teacher waiting for me. It is a frightening experience to find your-self face to face with someone who has a clear desire to kill you with their bare hands. Someone had told. The teacher now knew where Cross Creek was.

She lunged at me and began to shake me furiously. I pulled her hand loose from one part of my person only to have her grab me in another, while all my classmates fled the building. Only when she was ex-hausted could I finally dislodge her and run too. The following morn-ing the school principal assembled my class in his office. He said it was a terrible thing we had done; however, the teacher had agreed to stay on, providing the boy from Lochloosa and I, the culprit from Cross Creek, sit in the back corners of the classroom and speak only when spoken to.

The year I reached my seventeenth birthday I became totally preoc-cupied with being accepted into the military as soon as I turned eigh-teen. In fact, I compounded my problems by making failing grades. A solution presented itself unexpectedly when the social science teacher referred to Mrs. Rawlings as a literary genius. I raised my hand, even though I was still not supposed to speak first. She nodded at me, and I said, "If I got Miz Rawlings to come and give us a lecture, would I pass the subjects you teach?"

She was enthralled with the idea and agreed: "It would be worth the entire year for all of us if she would do that."

When the bus passed Mrs. Rawlings's house on the way home, I could see her car in the carport; my luck was holding. I dashed into the house, ignored my mamma's work assignment note, grabbed some food from the icebox, and ran next door. Halfway there I began think-ing of the prestigious universities that had awarded her honorary doctorates. She had told me about refusing invitations to speak from cities all across the country. Scribner's had suggested an author tour, and she had refused. I decelerated my pace to a slow walk. Even before *Cross Creek* was published, I remembered, she had spent the weekend at the White House as a guest of Mrs. Roosevelt.

I walked through the gate and up the pine straw walk. For the first time I could remember, I was afraid to talk to her. Normally I would have stepped inside the screen door, onto the porch and called. This time I decided to call from outside on the steps.

She answered from the living room, "Come in, J.T."

"No thank you, I only wanted to see you a minute."

She came out on the porch. "Is something wrong?"

"No ma'am."

She was becoming impatient. "Then why are you so formal?"

"Miz Rawlings," I blurted, "I am flunking some of my schoolwork at Hawthorne and we got a new teacher and she said if I could get you to come give us a speech, I would pass."

She put her hands over her mouth in what I interpreted as shock and disbelief that I would make such a stupid request. I had turned to leave when she laughed loud enough to be heard out on Orange Lake. I looked back to see her coming out the screen door.

"That has to be the damnedest invitation I have ever received." Still laughing, she asked, "When would you like me to come?"

I thought, *Hot dang.* Without any consideration for the school's scheduling problems, I said, "Tomorrow at one o'clock."

The next morning when I told the teacher Mrs. Rawlings was coming, she went into raptures and rushed out to inform the principal. She returned ecstatic. It was settled. Mrs. Rawlings would speak to all the students from the third grade through the twelfth. I was to wait outside the building and escort her in to meet the principal.

When she arrived I told her I had to introduce her to the principal, but that he was all right. I explained she didn't have to say much, what was important was that she came. In the principal's office I made the introductions: "Miz Rawlings, this is Mr. Benson, he's the principal, and this is my social science teacher." Mrs. Rawlings said she was glad to meet any friends of mine and she wanted to confirm the principal's agreement to our deal.

A look of astonishment came over his face. "What deal?"

Mrs. Rawlings put her hand on my shoulder and said, "It is my understanding that J.T. will pass whatever study he is having trouble with if I speak to your students." His face reddened. He said he had never heard of such a deal and glared at me. The social science teacher came to my rescue. She confirmed what she had promised and said she was certain the lecture would benefit the entire school.

Mr. Benson thought for a moment, then put out his hand for Mrs. Rawlings to shake. "It is certainly not my idea of education," he said, then laughed, "But since I have over two hundred students waiting in the auditorium, Mrs. Rawlings, we have a deal."

In the auditorium several chairs had been placed across the stage just behind the podium. When they led Mrs. Rawlings to the steps, she stopped and said, "If you don't mind, I came to talk to the children and would prefer to stay down here with them."

The principal told me to introduce my guest. I said, "This is Miz Rawlings, and she's all right," and then I sat down. The principal then elaborated on my introduction.

I was surprised that the young'uns loved her. She walked up and down the aisles, making contact with them all. At one point she stopped, pulled out her cigarettes, glanced at the principal, said, "You don't mind if I smoke?" and lit one. Although it was against the rules for anyone to smoke anywhere near the building, Mr. Benson shrugged with a look that said, "Why not? You're doing everything else your way."

She told us about the man who was still raising corn in buckets out in California for the movie *The Yearling*. And she answered questions. One child asked, "Why did you write about a boy instead of a girl?"

Her answer was straightforward: "When I was growing up I thought boys were the lucky ones. They could run and play with such freedom and dirty their clothes and do all kinds of adventuresome things." She smiled at the girls in the audience. "I like boys. They're special."

She spoke through the entire afternoon session, holding every kid spellbound with her stories and explanations. I began to see her from a new perspective. She was professional, yet still understandable. I was downright proud of her and Cross Creek.

After she said good-bye and we were out in her car, she roared with laughter. "We did it, J.T. We did it!"

Seven. The Hutchenson Buick

I BELIEVE the first time I heard the story about the Hutchensons and the Buick, it was told by my friend W.C. Calton. It caught my imagination then and still does. During the years I was growing up I am sure I asked every man and most of the women at the Creek what they knew about the Buick and whether they believed the story. More than once when I tramped through the hammocks with one of the old-timers, he would stop and stomp the ground where there was a large depression and then shrug his shoulders and walk on. When I was old enough to ask specific questions, I discovered there was no single version of what had happened, and everyone had a different interpretation. Today the Buick remains Cross Creek's greatest unsolved mystery. I have pieced fact and fiction together and settled on my own version.

The Hutchenson family consisted of Mr. Hutchenson, a widower stooped from hard work and other burdens; the older son, Wilbur, twenty-two, who was taller than his daddy, and the younger son, Clyde, the only Hutchenson with light hair. Clyde was only two years younger than Wilbur and appeared to have retained his baby fat. He kept an unfriendly distance from everyone except his brother, usually standing back cleaning his fingernails with a simulated pearl–handled switchblade. His eyes were expressionless spots set deep behind squinting lids.

Wilbur looked like a young version of his dad. Both had black unruly hair and skin so thoroughly tanned that it was impossible to guess the color of their behinds beneath their britches. All similarities ended there. Wilbur, the young buck, gestured wildly when he spoke and strutted about cocksure and arrogant. He was a ladies' man. In fact, women were the only thing he talked about. The word from down in the Big Scrub was that Wilbur was Bull Gator in the jukes on Saturday night. "It's that mop of hair sticking out above his undershirt" (the only shirt he wore), they said. "It's the clean one he wears when he is dressed up, along with them rust-colored britches and brown-and-white shoes. That's what gets the gals."

His brother Clyde's skin was the color of milk from a range cow, white with a bluish tint that would have been the envy of most women except for several blemishes that refused to clear up.

One day on the Bridge, Dad asked Pete Johnson, who was about the only one willing to listen to Wilbur's version of his escapades on Saturday night, what Clyde did at the jukes while Wilbur was charming all the gals. "He jest waits around hoping they is a fight," Pete said. "Clyde's a fighter, he ain't no lover."

Everyone on the Bridge laughed except Mr. Story, who commented to no one in particular, "He better get his insurance paid up, or build him a six-foot box, 'cause somebody down in that Scrub'll cut him down to size." Everyone nodded in agreement.

Occasionally Mr. Hutchenson walked down to the Bridge to be with whoever was there. He was a pleasant man who seldom spoke, old and tired before his time—a man of integrity. When he had first arrived at the Creek, the fishermen suggested he be given a territory on one of the lakes. He had declined the offer, saying he was not sure he would be staying at the Creek. He planned to fish with a pole and line, and Old Joe had given him permission to put six traps in his territory. Mr. Hutchenson ventured that if his boys showed any interest in fishing, he would possibly ask for a territory later.

From time to time the two young Hutchensons came down to the

Bridge, always walking several yards in front of or behind their father. They had no apparent interest in knowing the fishermen there and stood off to themselves leaning on the rail with their backs turned. Wilbur looked bored, and Clyde cleaned his nails and picked his teeth with his knife. Mr. Hutchenson and the boys never alluded to what had happened to Mrs. Hutchenson or where they came from, and no one asked.

Even though nature provided for those at the Creek who were willing to work, the only sweating of the brow the Hutchenson boys did was jukin' on Saturday night. It was obvious that the few fish the old man caught could not support the three of them. Wilbur had mentioned to Pete he might make 'shine for a living, and Pete told him that there was only one family that ever made liquor at the Creek, and that theirs was a small operation. Pete made it clear the local Crackers didn't want the Creek to become a haven for moonshiners, and they wouldn't tolerate Wilbur running moonshine.

Late one afternoon it suddenly became clear that Wilbur and Clyde had decided on an occupation when seventy-five shots fired in close succession from twelve-gauge pump shotguns rumbled over the Creek from the direction of the Hutchenson place. Their shack was directly in the flyway between Orange Lake and Right Arm Prairie, where thousands of ducks flew daily to and from their feeding areas and the roosts. Wilbur and Clyde were killing ducks to sell to restaurants.

Duck hunters from outside slaughtered ducks in excess of bag limits in the name of sport without much fear of the law, but although killing ducks had never been a part of the unwritten agreements that existed between the Creek fishermen and the game wardens, the Crackers disapproved of any commercial killing of migratory birds.

A cloud of anger spread over the Creek. Two lazy hooligans were jeopardizing the principles of the entire place. The boys were confident no one would break the backwoods code and report them to the law for anything less than a capital crime, and they were right. They also knew they would not be invited to meet with the men of the community on the Bridge until the men had agreed on a solution. Really, the only thing the locals could do was run them off, and the boys believed the Creek's respect for their old man would prevent that.

Everyone liked the old man and wanted to avoid putting him in direct conflict with his sons. The responsibility in situations like this was with the head of the family, but there was no doubt the two culprits would ignore their dad if he tried to stop them. The Creek fishermen nevertheless refused to be bullied by Wilbur and Clyde, nor would they allow the continued slaughtering of ducks.

Cool heads prevailed. They would allow a week to pass before scheduling a meeting on the Bridge. This was the Creek's way of giving Wilbur and Clyde enough rope to hang themselves or an opportunity to back off. A confrontation would be far more serious than the boys thought.

The young Hutchensons blasted away every evening and roared past our house in their Model-A at ten o'clock every morning on their way to Ocala. They had made the rumble seat, or at least the place where there had been a rumble seat, a compartment for transporting ducks, all killed out of season without a license. On Saturday morning they passed an hour later than usual. The Model-A had undergone a major alteration. Its natural rust-brown and black finish had disappeared beneath a brush-painted, brilliant blue, McCrory's Five-and-Dime coat of enamel. The ragged cloth top thrashed in the wind like so many gray pennants and did nothing to improve the overall appearance. My dad said, "For two men bootleggin' illegal ducks they sure know how to keep from attractin' attention." No one expected them back that afternoon. Saturday night was jukin' time.

My family was at church on Sunday morning and missed seeing them return. Tom Morrison (the Creek's only Spanish American War veteran) said Clyde slowed down to pass him on the narrow sand road leading to the Hutchenson place. He tried to describe the encounter: "Apparently the enamel paint dried slow and got sprinkled with duck feathers blown on it before they left on Saturday." Then during the weekend a collection of sand and dirt had mixed with the tacky paint. Clyde was driving, and all Tom saw of Wilbur was his feet in those brown-and-white shoes, without socks, sticking up out of the rear compartment. Tom assumed Wilbur had had a hard night and was resting.

The Bridge meeting was scheduled for Wednesday of that week, and it looked as if a confrontation was inevitable.

On Monday morning a strange sedan came through the Creek, crossed the Bridge, and continued toward Micanopy. There was no way the wardens could know about the duck shooting, and no one was pulling a seine at that time, so the passing car was of little concern.

When the first flight of ducks flew over, the shotguns opened up but immediately stopped. An hour passed. Then our dog announced that someone was at the front gate. It was old Mr. Hutchenson, barefoot and breathing hard. A game warden and a skinny little man wearing a badge stood in the road behind him. My dad invited them in.

The warden said, "This ain't no social call, Tom. Out of respect for you and the other people here at the Creek I agreed to see if you would stand good for this feller and us not take him in. We tagged him for shootin' ducks out of season with no license." The warden's lack of enthusiasm was obvious.

Mr. Hutchenson said, "Tom, that little feller, he's a constable, he tagged me sittin' on the steps there at the house—I ain't even shot a blue pete since I come to the Creek, and they arrested me 'cause the boys wuz shootin' ducks out back of the house and when these pimps with badges stepped out of the palmettos my boys run, so they arrested me and said they are gonna swear out a warrant for them when they get to town."

The little constable said, "They was all in it. The whole place is ass-deep in duck feathers."

My dad walked out of the gate past Mr. Hutchenson and spoke directly to the warden. "If he says he was not shootin', mister, he wasn't shootin'."

The warden said, more calmly, "I don't want no big thing. I seen them two young men shoot and kill a duck apiece and the ol' man was sittin' right there."

The little constable interrupted, "And if you had waited like I told you to do, we'd of got 'em with over the bag limit."

The warden's patience with his companion apparently had run out.

He told him he had no jurisdiction in this county and that he, the warden, would decide what should and would be done.

Dad said, "You know everybody at the Creek knows everything that goes on, and like I said, Mr. Hutchenson ain't shot no ducks. Now, if you want to be reasonable about this, if it is all right with Mr. Hutchenson, he can call the boys up here and you can tag them and save yourself a lot of trouble." The warden shrugged, indicating approval.

Dad turned to Mr. Hutchenson. "I think this man" (indicating the warden) "will drop anything against you. And I'm sure he will swear out a warrant against Wilbur and Clyde, and they will have to give theirself up. So I think the whole thing will go easier if we get it all straight now."

The old man thought for a second and said, "Yeah, I know you're right." He walked down the road only a few feet and called, "Wilbur, come up here and bring Clyde!" He paused and shouted again, "Do it now!"

In the growing darkness the two came out of the hammock and ambled up the road. Dad was glad to see they had discarded their shotguns. When they were thirty feet away the constable said in his squeaky voice, "Mister Wilbur, you are both under arrest!"

Wilbur started toward him, and Dad and the warden both stepped in the way. Wilbur said, "You little pimpy son of a bitch, 'cause I took your gal you turned us up."

The little man looked pleased with himself. "You didn't know I was a constable, now, did you, when you was braggin' about gettin' rich killing ducks?"

Clyde was circling like a shadow toward the constable. Dad spoke in a positive voice: "Clyde, you stand back over here with your brother, and don't try to clean your damn fingernails." Clyde walked back behind his brother.

The warden said in a soft voice, looking directly at Wilbur and Clyde, "You fellers are charged with illegal shootin' of wild ducks."

Dad held up his hand before either one could speak. "You boys are in enough trouble now. Keep your mouth shut before you end up six foot under or on the chain gang." He approached the warden, "It looks like these boys and that little constable feller already know one another, so if you can see your way clear, how about you askin' your partner to walk on down the road to wherever you got your car hid."

The constable waved both arms. "What the hell y'all tryin' to do? I'm a part of this arrest and I ain't goin' nowhere before we take them two and their old man to jail." He put his hand on his little pistol and holster.

The warden lost all his patience. "God dammit! I shouldn't of let you come in the first place. Now get back to the car or so help me, I will kick you back to it." The constable turned and walked down the road in the direction of the Bridge, mumbling to himself.

Dad took out his tobacco and started rolling a cigarette. "If Mr. Hutchenson gives you his word he'll have his boys at the courthouse on whatever day and time you say, I'll give you my word they will plead guilty, and I'll forfeit whatever bond the judge wants if they don't show up." While the warden considered the proposition, Dad laughed, and added, "It'll beat hell out of having to ride around all night with your little buddy."

The warden looked at all three Hutchensons, and they nodded approval. "I ain't got no case against you, Mr. Hutchenson, but I am also taking your word that you'll have them there Wednesday at eleven o'clock waitin' on the east side of the courthouse." The old man agreed.

The Hutchensons climbed the fence, taking a shortcut through the tangerine grove back to their place. Dad asked the warden in for supper, but he declined, saying, "You were right, I want to take the little bastard straight home. I wouldn't of been here except that Wilbur fellow apparently told everybody he was gettin' rich sellin' ducks so it was only a matter of time before somebody would turn him up—and I didn't know he was wanting to use me to get even for a row over some hussy they had in a juke."

Dad shook his hand. "Well, you did us a favor. 'Cause all of us at the Creek had already decided the duck shootin' was gonna stop this week."

On Wednesday the Hutchenson Model-A came out of the hammock road with the Hutchenson boys in it, on their way to Gainesville to appear before the judge. Mr. Hutchenson sat in the front with Wilbur driving, and Clyde sat with his head sticking up in the back. They pleaded guilty—it was a first offense. The judge's sentence was ten dollars each, total twenty dollars, and an emphatic "Don't come back on another duck charge." They paid fourteen dollars on the spot with six dollars due in ten days.

Dad loaned Mr. Hutchenson six dollars based on the promise that his sons would apply for jobs as laborers with the road construction company that was rebuilding the fill across the marsh between Island Grove and Citra. The following Saturday Wilbur stopped at our house wearing his jukin' clothes and paid Dad the six dollars they owed. He said they had quit the job because it didn't pay enough. "Me and Clyde is going to gather moss and sell it," Wilbur added.

The Spanish moss business was probably the least profitable occupation at the Creek. Black folks used long bamboo poles with nails in the tips to snare moss and pull it from the trees. The moss factory in Gainesville (which prepared the moss to be used as padding in automobile seats) paid only 20 percent as much for green moss as they did for moss with the outer surface rotted off. As hard as times were, no one sold their moss green. Moss gatherers soaked it for ninety days in lye water and sold it when it was black. The Hutchenson boys pulled moss Monday through Thursday and hauled it to the factory on Friday. Aunt Martha observed that if a ten-year-old of hers couldn't pull more moss than the two Hutchensons hauled to the market, she would remind his rear what his hands weren't doing.

Mr. Hutchenson continued to fish with his few traps and with a pole and line, selling the market fish and carrying the mud fish (bowfins) and jacks (pickerel) home to eat.

Two or three weeks passed and the two young Hutchensons began staying overnight in Gainesville when they delivered their moss, often returning late Saturday afternoon. They bought a new canvas top for the roadster, and Wilbur sported a new pocket watch with a gold-plated chain. They gradually came to spend less time pulling moss and more time going to the factory. Frequently they crossed the Bridge, supposedly going to the factory, without enough moss to pay for their gas. No one said anything, but it was becoming obvious they were into another business, a business that probably was not acceptable to the law or to their Creek neighbors.

One Saturday, George Fairbanks was walking home from frog hunting at about 4:30 A.M. and saw a big touring car, driving slowly and without lights, cross the Bridge and continue east. Everyone agreed that no game warden would have access to such a fine automobile. Tom Morrison heard what he thought could have been a car coasting past his place, but since the first wind off a September storm was beginning to blow, he was not sure. Later the following morning he noticed a set of tracks made by new tires leading off the main road and into the hammock road that led back toward the Hutchenson place. He assumed the moss pullers had bought a new set of tires and said nothing more about it to anyone. Clyde drove through about eleven o'clock, and everyone assumed Wilbur was sleeping in the rear compartment. Tom Morrison was on the lake and missed seeing Clyde pass in the Hutchenson Model-A.

That Sunday morning the clouds were moving low and fast over the Creek, foretelling a late summer storm moving in our direction. With the wind up, no one could fish, and several of the men, including Mr. Hutchenson, gathered on the Bridge to speculate on whether we were going to get a major blow or just a few squalls in its wake. Neither George Fairbanks nor Tom Morrison were at the Bridge, and none of the other men knew about the strange vehicle that had come through in the early morning hours.

There has always been a high sensitivity to the moods of the weather at Cross Creek, and the anticipation of an approaching storm often created an exhilaration associated with high adventure. On that morning a feeling of camaraderie developed among the fishermen and young'uns gathered on the Bridge. An Essex sedan chugged out of the woods approaching the Bridge from the west side, initiating a general discussion as to who could possibly be coming to the Creek, especially when the weather was on the verge of turning mean. Then everyone simultaneously recognized the county sheriff in the unmarked olive-green-and-black automobile. He drove to the center of the Bridge and climbed out, exchanging greetings with all his old friends. Mr. Hutchenson was introduced as an accepted member of the Creek community. Then there were the usual inquiries about wives and children, and eventually the reason he was visiting so soon after an election.

"It's nothin' important enough to come all the way for," the sheriff said, "but since I was already in the vicinity I thought I would come on down and see how everybody was doin'." Everyone said they were glad he did. Then there was an awkward silence. "I just wanted to know if anyone could of seen a new Buick sport sedan with a white canvas top come through the Creek early yesterday." They all shook their heads no. Marcel Ferguson asked, "How come, Sheriff?"

He spoke as if he was not sure it was worth telling the whole story. "Well, we been having some burglarin' up around La Crosse and Alachua. Tools, tires, and stuff like that. Except Friday night, somebody—and I can't say it was the same ones been doin' the tool stealin' anyway—two men stole a new maroon Buick, had a white canvas top and big chrome headlamps and light brown leather seats, from a timber man up by High Springs. And then they broke in a fillin' station in the edge of Alachua, took two cases of NeHi orange soda and two packs of ready-roll cigarettes and two quarts of oil, kinda like what a young'un would steal. A deputy that's half-blind seen them at the station when they was leavin' in a big car, but he didn't know if they had stole anything and let 'em get away.

"Well then, a city policeman in Gainesville ridin' on a motorcycle seen this big touring car come hell fer bust out on East University Avenue and figured it was somebody runnin' liquor. He took chase right through the middle of town and would of caught 'em, 'cept that big car took them rough streets like they weren't full of holes. When they got out toward the Palatka road he was in shootin' distance when the pavement run out and he damn near lost his motorcycle in the sand ruts. That all happened about four o'clock."

The sheriff's casual demeanor changed as he came closer to his point. He pushed his hard felt hat up from his forehead. "That would of been the end of that, 'cept the turpentine still boss at Phifer sent me word this morning a big car just about run over one of his gum loaders that was goin' out before daylight in a two-mule wagon to pick up a load of gum on the grade road comin' this way." The sheriff's audience on the Bridge was captivated by the narrative and especially by hearing it first-hand from the high sheriff. They waited with bated breath, but the story had ended. The sheriff fell silent.

"That's all?" Pete asked.

"It is for now, unless some of you seen it come through the Creek, 'cause they ain't no way it could of gone back without bein' seen, and the River Styx is flooded." He covered the last possibility. "Whoever it was could of hid it in the pine woods, but if they did the turpentine woods riders will find it in a couple days."

Everyone began to talk at once, saying they couldn't see how it could have gone through to Island Grove. My dad said a strange car at that time of night would have had his dog barking and raising hell. The Rawlingses didn't have any strangers visiting so everyone agreed the Buick couldn't have come through Cross Creek.

A fine mist from the approaching storm was beginning to swirl down and across the Bridge. The sheriff said he knew the people out at the Creek wouldn't put up with a thief, but he just thought he would check. He climbed back in his car and invited them to stop in his office for a visit when they were in town. Then he backed his big Essex off the Bridge, turned around on the narrow fill, and drove back the way he had come. Everyone watched intently as if their sharing such important knowledge with the high sheriff made it proper and necessary to give him their undivided attention until he was out of sight.

There followed an immediate exchange of "Now ain't that the damnedest thing," and "If I stole a big classy Buick I wouldn't try to hide it at Cross Creek." An old fisherman said, "It's hard enough to hide a seine." Mr. Hutchenson was first to leave, probably to avoid getting wet and aggravating his rheumatism. The rest followed, each taking his perplexity home with him to sit out the oncoming storm.

The storm intensified throughout the afternoon and into the night, not dangerous but strong enough to blow the fronds on the spherical cabbage palmettos downwind, like green weather vanes reeling back and forth on long, flexible poles. The rain came intermittently, torrents of water slashing across the surface of the hammocks, followed by a calm and steady downpour. The citrus, still green, hung heavy on the trees and whipped back and forth on the branches. Half of it would be bruised and drop from the trees before it was ripe. On Monday night the rain slacked to a drizzle, and the wind calmed.

Tuesday morning the sun came up on a soggy world. After breakfast Dad went down to Mamma's garden to see what could be salvaged. At the gate he noticed that the piece of tin normally left there to protect garden tools had blown against the wire. Some of the tools that had been there on Friday were missing: a shovel, a spade, a grubbing hoe, and his double-bit ax. The only reason he could imagine for their removal was Henry, our grove man, borrowing them to do something at his house.

Dad wished he didn't have to tell Mamma what the storm had done to her garden. The rain had washed sand over most of the plants and carried the rest down the rows and into the debris at the lower end of the garden. As it was, he didn't get a chance to tell her. Tom Morrison was waiting at the back steps. "I think we have a situation that needs lookin' into," he said. He had talked to George Fairbanks, who had not been on the Bridge on Saturday when the sheriff was there, and George had told him about seeing a car fitting the sheriff's description cross the Bridge without lights. Tom had then remembered how he had seen the new tire tracks leading down the hammock road on Saturday morning.

Dad told Tom to wait until he got his good hat and they would go down to the Hutchenson cabin and see what was going on. While they were walking, Dad asked what chance there was of someone coming out of the Creek in a car like the stolen one during the storm.

Tom said, "None. If they tried to go when it was rainin' hard, they couldn't see to drive. They would end up out in the woods. And if they had come out when the rain was light, they would surely have been heard." He had obviously thought it through. "The place where the road passes the slough would have bogged down even a mule and wagon if somebody tried to drive through it before the water had time to run off." That assumption was confirmed when they reached the low area where the water was still draining across the ruts. In addition, a large sweet gum tree had fallen across the road. A quick examination revealed all the sand and marl had washed out of the crevices under and around its taproot, which meant the tree had uprooted in the beginning of the storm. It would have been impossible for a car to have come out over it.

When the two men neared the Hutchenson place, they fell silent. Nothing like this had happened at the Creek before. They felt shame on behalf of the community, where thieving was unacceptable. The Buick would have to be returned, and the law could have the thieves.

As they walked into the clearing, they expected to see the big maroon Buick parked in the edge of the woods, but there was nothing. The only sound came from a redbird singing in a wild plum. Standing next to the door was Dad's shovel; the spade, grubbing hoe, and double-bit ax were leaning against the old shanty. The shovels were bright from recent use. NeHi soda bottles were strewn around the yard, some with a few drops of orange liquid in them.

The Hutchensons were gone. Dad went inside the open front door. Half a can of pork and beans sat open on the crude table, providing a feast for black ants. Old guns stood in the corner beneath some clothes hanging from a nail. The kerosene lamp had burned until it was out of fuel, leaving the glass shade black with smut.

When Dad came back out into the yard, Tom was walking out of the hammock on the side toward the prairie, clearly puzzled. "The A-model is back here in the edge of the woods. Looks like it was set on fire, but the rain must of put it out. He removed his hat and fanned himself in the humid heat. "They ain't no sign of that Buick. The rain has washed everything until it's hard to see any sign, but on the other hand the woods is so thick it would be impossible to get a automobile far."

Dad said if they didn't go out by the road the way they came in, the only way would be down to the edge of Right Arm Prairie. They couldn't have got it far enough out into the marsh to more than cover the wheels before it would have been stuck in the muck.

Dad sat down on the steps, and Tom hunkered in the shade of the shanty and whittled. They looked at the tea-colored rainwater still running out of the grove into the hammock. At the same moment both of them looked at the recently used shovels and then tried to reject the mutual, amazing thought—surely the Hutchensons didn't bury a new Buick?

They walked back into the hammock without speaking. George Fairbanks came into the woods wanting to know what they had found. Dad said, "Nothing," and he joined the search. In the afternoon several more men joined, and though all agreed they could not believe the three men could have buried the Buick, they stomped and jabbed the ground in the open spots looking for soft disturbed soil. The leaves and natural debris had washed into piles, leaving most of the hammock floor suspect.

That night on the Bridge everyone was asking, "Where is the Hutchensons?" No one believed they would hide in the woods. What would be the point? It was unlikely they would attempt to walk out past all the yard dogs and then through Island Grove, or cross the creek and walk to Micanopy. In either case they knew they would surely be seen.

Someone suggested one slim possibility that could have been feasible if the old man was strong enough. They could wade across Right Arm Prairie, cross Burnt Island, and then wade the marsh on the east side to the railroad water tank south of Lochloosa Station. There they could hop a freight and be long gone.

There was the question "Why run if they actually buried the Buick?" But no one wanted to say they believed that, even though there was more evidence to indicate they did than they didn't.

In the weeks that followed some claimed they were hunting bee trees in the hammocks east of the Creek. Others laughed, trying to make a joke of going Buick hunting, and went into the woods with sharp sticks to probe the ground.

Nobody ever saw the Hutchensons again. As the years passed, the

Creek folks either tired of the mystery or felt a little embarrassed they had ever believed the Hutchensons actually buried the Buick. If no one else was around, they would talk about it, and when they did they would tell the story as fact. If an outsider came while they were telling the story, they would refer to the whole episode as a yarn that was not worth telling.

My friend W.C. and I spent many hours searching for that big maroon Buick with the leather seats and the big chrome headlights. We had a pact: if we found it we would dig it up before we told anyone, and we would drive that fine automobile out of the hole—of course we visualized it in mint condition. I fantasized about driving it down to the Bridge on a Saturday afternoon when everyone at the Creek was there. I never came up with a reason why our mothers would be there, but in my dream they were. W.C. later told me he had the same fantasy, except *he* was driving the Buick. Of course when I grew up I realized how preposterous the story was. Still, to this day I cannot resist probing around in soft places in the ground, just in case.

Eight. Henry

AT THE Creek grown folks talked a lot about trouble. Maybe they thought if they talked about it enough it would go away. Aunt Martha Mickens was always talking about trouble. We even sang about it:

> Trouble, trouble, trouble,
> I had it all my days.
> It looks like old trouble
> Gonna follow me to my grave.

I didn't know much about trouble back then, but I sure learned something about it on the New Year's Day when I was twelve years old and all hell broke loose, right in front of our garage.

I could jump in when the shooting started and try to explain what happened—but that's the way Mrs. Rawlings always did, and when it came to that kind of thing her way just added to the trouble. Dad said, "That woman likes to go way back when she's writing, but she jumps in past the middle when there's a mess to straighten out." And that's exactly what she did this time. She came home to the Creek from a trip, jumped in, and turned a simple catastrophe into a downright disaster, or at least that is the way it appeared to me.

When I was twelve years old, everything that happened at the Creek seemed to have started wa-a-a-ay back. Our New Year's Day disaster was no exception. I say "our" because before it was over, we all had trouble one way or the other.

The best explanation would have to begin with my earliest memories of Henry Fountain, a huge black man who lived at Cross Creek and worked for my family and the Brices. It would be impossible for an outsider to understand what happened if they didn't know something about my friend Henry. I was saddened then and still am that his love for his family and his desire for self-respect was the cause of all the trouble that descended on him.

Henry had a way of speaking that made each sentence sound profound, and it usually was. He told me, "The truth of anything depends on how much you knows about it." I asked him what that meant. He looked around for an example and selected Old Kate, one of the mules hitched to the wagon. "Most folks would say the mule pulls the wagon, but them what's hitched 'em up knows Kate pulls one end of the chain and the other end pulls the wagon." Then he paused, "What's the first thing you hears when a wagon's a-comin'?"

I said, "The mules and the wheels."

"That's when you ain't listen good." He gestured as if he were straining to hear. "Way off, 'fore anything else, you hears them chains clinkin'. Little man, you got to listen for the clinkin' in this ol' world. You remember what Ol' Henry tol' you."

He always ended one of his philosophical discussions with "Now, I's got to get back to work."

He was right about the clinking of the chains. I still associate that sound with the Brices' two-horse wagon and Henry Fountain. Late in the afternoons I listened for that rhythmic clinking and waited to see Henry coming around the curve, standing behind the seat with the reins hanging limp in his huge hands. He didn't drive the team. He spoke to the mules with sincere respect, softly telling them what to do.

To me he looked like a giant bronze god in his chariot, urging on his team. As he passed, he gave me a darting glance and tipped his ragged hat. His twelve-hour day would not end until the mules were fed and penned for the night. That simple encounter evolved into a pleasing ritual for us, and my friendship with Henry was one of the strongest bonds I had with anyone at the Creek. I would watch the wagon after it passed until it turned into the lot on the south side of the Brice place. Then I began a vigil that would last until Henry came back, walking home. The wait was interminable, but it was always worth it.

Henry shuffled his huge feet when he walked, like a little young'un trying to wear his father's shoes. The soles of his worn-out brogans were sometimes tied to the uppers with hay wire to make them last another year. They barely cleared the ground with each step, which would have given the impression of a man who was exhausted if Henry hadn't stood so straight.

I would stand by our gate as Henry approached, pretending to be unaware of him walking on the grass along the other side of the narrow road. He would also pretend not to see me until he was just about to pass. Then he would stop abruptly and look in my direction. With an expression of absolute surprise, complete with gestures, bordering on shock, he would say, "Well sir, if it ain't young Mr. Tom. I thought you was your daddy, you gets more like him ever' day." (I liked being compared to my dad.) "I bet you been up to somethin'. What you been doin' all day?"

Now it was my turn. "Ah, nothin'."

He would counter, "Come on and tell ol' Henry what it is you been doin'. You got sumpin' you has done?"

Back when we first started the game I would have an object I had whittled out of wood or made with string, but as we perfected our routine, the pictures I drew on Mamma's ruled tablets were his favorites. I would act as if I didn't think what I was holding behind my back was good enough to show to the public, and he would insist on seeing it. Finally I would give in and show him the picture I had drawn. This was the best part. Henry would be absolutely spellbound. He'd hold it up to the light and hum, then turn it to a different angle and hum again, amazed by its unbelievable beauty. Then he would pretend to be seized with doubt and assume an air of disbelief.

"You did this?"

"Uh-huh."

"Your mamma or daddy ain't helped you to do it?" At that point I would desperately attempt to convince him that I was truly the artist that had created the masterpiece. He then moved into the peak of his performance. "You is smart! You gonna be smart as your daddy. When I get to the house I'm gonna tell Sissie about what you done." (By that time I was eight feet tall. I had to take a deep breath to keep from getting dizzy.) "I'm goin' straight home and tell Sissie what it is you done. Don't you lose that. You go straight and give it to your mamma so she can keep it safe. That's gonna be worth a lot someday."

A friend recently asked me what first inspired me to become an artist. I fumbled for an answer then, but I might well have said, "One of America's great art critics, who lived at Cross Creek."

When I was growing up, the only thing I disliked more than fooling with Dad's cows was being trapped into doing piddling jobs for Mamma. My sister, Marjorie, usually did the things Mamma gave me to do, and if I held out long enough Henry would do most of the grove work. My dad was constantly exasperated with my excuses. I would claim that I couldn't find the hoe or that a handle on the pruning clippers was broken or that I would have worked but I just didn't know what he wanted me to do. He put an end to that excuse with one of his typical solutions. "If you don't know what to do when you are supposed to be working, don't sit down. You dig holes and fill them up until I get there."

Henry was my best source of escaping my dad's efforts to teach me the virtue of good hard work. To avoid being assigned a job by my folks, I would announce before breakfast that I had to help Henry in the grove, which usually drew the comment, "You mean kill time with Henry, don't you?"

Working with Henry was life at its very best. Sometimes I did actually work, but it was more like visiting than work. In the summers we pruned and hoed the trees. In the winter we picked the fruit. The old seedling trees that had been nursed back from the roots left after the Big Freeze were thorny and required a thirty-foot ladder to reach the tops. Henry wouldn't let me climb them. "I don't want you takin' no chance of gettin' hurt," he would say. Of course when I was not supposed to be working, I climbed the tallest trees in the hammocks.

During the hot summers he would say, "Ol' Henry don't want the bear to kotch you." (By this he meant sunstroke.) "You jest better work over there in the shade." Consequently I sat in the shade and asked him thousands of questions, everything from what color baby he and Sissie were expecting to what it was like on the chain gang. (My dad had said he thought Henry was in the gang when he was young.) He always gave me a clear answer. He thought a long time on the chain gang question.

"It be's like the devil done took you and shet you off from any folks what cares a drap 'bout you. Even when they lets you out you feels that place tryin' to pull you back." He paused. "I still wakes up believin' them chains is on my legs. Sometimes when I is walkin' I feels them shackles and hears 'em rattlin'. Sho nuff." He looked me straight in the eye. "Little man, you listen good. Don't never get in one of them places. They's worse than being dead. Now, I's got to get back to work."

Frequently Dad came down into the grove to see how we were doing and to plan the work for the next day. Henry indirectly warned me by saying, "Well sir, I believes I see yo' daddy comin', looks like he gonna pay us a visit." I would jump up and become a model of industrious energy. Dad would talk to Henry about the work, then he would ask, "Henry, is that boy helpin' you? Is he worth anything?"

It was times like that when you knew who your friends really were. Henry tried to be convincing. "I don't know how I could get along without him. He is smart. They ain't nobody like him at the Creek."

Dad would say, "You got that last part right."

When my dad was safely out of sight I was magnanimous in my gratitude. I told Henry, "When I get grown I am going to have all kinds of business drawing pictures and make piles of money." I even promised him a job as my assistant.

He laughed and said, "Then's when I is gonna sit in the shade and watch you work."

❦ With the exception of Henry, Aunt Martha Mickens decided who among the blacks at Cross Creek worked for whom and where they lived. She was the matriarch of the black families at the Creek because half of each couple was her offspring. Although Henry's wife, Sissie, was one of Martha's daughters, he kept his distance and stayed independent of Martha.

Martha's oldest daughter, Estelle, lived at the Creek until I was nine, then moved with her husband to Hawthorne. Adrenna (called by everyone Drenna), another of Aunt Martha's daughters, periodically left the Creek and invariably returned with a new husband. She was small and skinny, with large eyes, a high-pitched voice, and the open, friendly nature of her mother coupled with a devilish laugh that seemed to imply something wicked. During the time she was at the Creek she worked for anyone who needed help, doing house or field work with the same lackadaisical ineptitude. Dad teased Drenna about leaving with one man and returning with another. She said, "When I gets ready to leave I takes the man closest to the door." Then she squealed with her trademark laugh. "Men's like shoes. You got to try 'em on to see do they fit."

In 1939 Drenna was sporting a new man named B.J. Samson. I was twelve years old that year, the water in the lakes had been high and low, Mrs. Rawlings had wrecked her car, and Charley had been on his annual drunk; everything was about normal. I reasoned I would be thirty before anything would change at Cross Creek. That assumption proved false on Sunday, January 1, 1940.

My folks didn't celebrate New Year's, and there was no church that Sunday. It was just another quiet Sunday morning. I was tinkering with a bridle for my horse on the worktable behind our garage when an explosion jarred the Creek. It came from the direction of the Brices'. I thought, *Hot dog! Somebody's got fire crackers,* and raced around the corner of the garage just in time to see Henry shoot B.J. Samson with a Remington twelve-gauge shotgun for the second time. The impact knocked B.J. backward, and Henry shot him again. Samson fell.

It was like a nightmare. Limoges china was strewn down the center of the road all the way from the Brice house to the Rawlings house. Drenna was at the end of the trail of broken plates, jumping up and down like she was a yo-yo, screaming louder than anyone I have heard before or since. Henry didn't move. He stood holding the shotgun in the same position as when he pulled the trigger the third time. B.J. lay face down on the shoulder of the road; he didn't move either. Drenna continued to scream, down in front of Mrs. Rawlings's house. Her squalling didn't seem important. Henry was looking toward me, but his eyes were focused miles away. I don't know if we all remained in that state a few seconds or several minutes.

The slamming of our front screen door broke the spell. My dad ran out of the house, through the gate, and down the road toward them. Henry ran to meet Dad. He changed ends with the shotgun as he ran, holding it by the barrel and offering the safe end to my dad. His voice was not the voice of my friend Henry. It was loud, coarse, staccato. He was crying uncontrollably. "Mr. Tom, I woulda shot him till the sun went down if he hadn't a-fell. What he done to me, I'd druther be dead."

My dad answered, "You've played hell, that's what you've done!" He ran past me to where B.J. was lying. Henry followed him quietly. Drenna was still jumping up and down and screaming, like a perpetual echo. Dad bent down over Samson and rolled him onto his back, then yelled to my mamma, who was out on our front steps trying to comprehend what had happened. "He ain't dead! Get some quilts to cover him."

"What?" she answered.

"He ain't dead! Get some blankets! And Henry, you get my pickup truck."

Running across the yard, Mamma shouted, "Tom, I can't hear you."

Dad finally realized that Drenna was still screaming. He stood up and shouted, "Drenna, hush!" She didn't stop. He waved the gun over his head and yelled a second time. "Dammit! If you don't hush I am goin' to shoot *you!* You come back here and help get your man to a doctor."

She screeched, "Lord, I can't, Mr. Tom, I can't, I's skeert! He gonna DIE!"

My dad was exasperated. He shouted back, trying to make himself understood; she was more than a hundred and fifty yards down the road. "If you can sleep with him you can damn well be close to him when he dies. Get back here, now!" He turned and repeated the request for blankets to my mother.

The pickup shot out of the gate with Henry at the wheel, slinging dust and sand in every direction. Dad jumped back to avoid being hit before the truck skidded to a halt only inches from B.J.'s head. Dad said, "Dammit, you've already just about got him, and I sure as hell don't want to be your second victim today."

Drenna had ventured closer and stood about fifty feet from her fallen Samson. She was twisting and swaying back and forth as if she was in a trance, saying, "He gonna die. I's skeert of dead people. He gonna die-e-e-e."

Mamma came with quilts and blankets. Henry dutifully helped my father roll Samson in a heavy quilt. His anger seemed to have dissolved with the last shot.

Dad said, "Let's lift him in the truck."

Henry reached for B.J.'s head. Dad yelled, "No, Henry! On second thought, you handle his feet. I'll take care of that end."

Drenna was still swaying back and forth. "He gonna die. I's skeert of dead people."

Henry, with some help from my dad, lifted the body into the back of the truck and covered him with another blanket. "I expect you better ride up front with me," Dad told him, then pointed to Drenna, "You get in the back with your husband or whatever you call him and keep him covered."

"No sir, I can't do that," she wailed. "He gonna die."

My father's patience was gone. He held up his hand to command silence. "Drenna, if you don't get in that truck with that man, I am going to have Henry throw you in it." She immediately climbed in over the tailgate and squatted in the back corner as far from B.J. as possible. Dad climbed into the cab. "I'll be back as soon as I take Drenna's man to the hospital and Henry to jail."

He switched on the engine, and Drenna started screaming again as if she had been wired to the ignition. They did a U-turn and headed

toward Gainesville with Drenna hanging out over the tailgate straining to get as far from B.J. as she could without falling out. I could still
hear her wails echoing in the hammocks a half-mile away after they
had crossed the Bridge and were on the grade road racing toward
Gainesville.

I stood in the same spot where I had stopped when I saw Henry
shoot B.J. It had all happened so quickly and still it seemed like hours
had passed. Reality dawned on me gradually. Henry was on his way to
jail.

I had introduced myself to B.J. and talked to him only three or four
times when Drenna and he were passing on their way to and from
Mrs. Rawlings's place. He talked differently than anyone at the Creek
and seemed to look down on everyone, including Drenna. I remembered my dad asking one night at supper who "this one" was, meaning
Drenna's latest catch. I felt important to be asked such an adult question. I told him, "Drenna didn't bring this one. He says Mrs. Rawlings
brought him from New York."

"Not just for Drenna!" Dad retorted.

"No, sir, he's a yard man, or that's what he tells everybody."

"He's trouble, that's what he is. Miz Rawlings should know better
than to bring anybody from the city to Cross Creek, especially a
Negro, into Martha's clan."

When B.J. was shot and lying on the ground I felt sorry for him.
Afterward, when I thought of the consequences for Henry, I felt nothing but anger toward the outsider. Then I began to cry.

As usual, I had to wait for answers to my questions, and while I
waited the list grew. After the longest New Year's Day I had ever
known, my father arrived back from Gainesville at first dark. I raced
to open the gate for the truck, hoping to get some answers before
Mamma insisted he eat first and then talk. Normally I got my information about serious things by eavesdropping on their conversations, but
this time my dad surprised me. Before he got out of the pickup he said,
"You all right, son?"

"Yes, sir," I answered. "What did you do with Henry?"

Dad said, "I think me and you should have a little talk. First, let me tell your mother what the situation is and then we'll take a walk down to the Bridge, okay?"

"Yes, sir." I was confused at being treated like a man. Normally when he said "let's have a little talk," it meant he had found out about something I had done wrong. This was different. For a moment I forgot my anxiety about Henry and B.J. I demonstrated my new adult status by suggesting we eat and then walk down to the Bridge.

Supper was simmering on the wood stove. While my dad washed his hands and Mamma put the food on the table, I set out plates and silver for the four of us, unprompted. My mamma looked at me with amazement.

At supper Dad sipped his coffee and said, "Well, Miz Rawlings's Negro is in the hospital, and Henry's in jail." He continued, directing his comments to my mother, "If that city Negro lives it will be because the good Lord won't let him die. He's got enough shot in him to sink a tussock."

"What will happen now?" my mother asked. "Sissie's the one who will suffer the most. She has a new baby and there's no one that can give her full-time work."

Dad said, "I suppose everything depends on whether Miz Rawlings's Negro dies or not." The more I thought about the situation the more my prejudice against B.J. grew. No one around the Creek liked him. He had been thrust on us, and now he held all of us hostage. His fate would determine whether our lives at the Creek would ever return to normal.

After supper my dad and I took our walk. We talked about how bright the stars were in January and about the peculiarities of fishing in the winter until we reached the Bridge. I remembered Henry telling me, "When somethin's important you wait for the tellin'." We sat in silence for several minutes. The turmoil of the morning seemed distant and unreal.

My dad said, "Well, you had a New Year's you won't soon forget. When something happens that is so important it will affect your life and the people that are around you, a man needs to get out and study it over until he has a clear picture of the whole situation." He paused and then continued. "I know you and Henry are big buddies so I figure you're entitled to know everything about the whole mess. You know Miz Rawlings has gone to St. Augustine. Well, last night B.J. or whatever his name is took Miz Rawlings's old truck and started out with Drenna to go jukin' over around Boardman on the other side of Orange Lake, and Drenna can't let well enough alone so she insisted to Sissie that she and Henry had to come too. They made Henry sit in the back, said it was too crowded in the front. B.J. stopped on the River Styx bridge to drink some 'shine. He made some advances toward Sissie deliberately to provoke Henry, and it did. B.J. then pulled a switchblade and cursed Henry, called him a ignorant nigger. He forced Henry away from the truck with the switchblade and drove off with Sissie and Drenna.

"Henry walked back to the Creek. He must have been crazy mad. Anyhow, he knew Will Brice was gone to Gainesville so he went in his house and took his shotgun, knowing B.J. and Drenna would come by on their way to work. He waited for them out there in Brice's driveway. When they came along Henry stepped out from behind them old lilies with the shotgun. Drenna had a bunch of Miz Rawlings's dishes she had borrowed and was carryin' back before Miz Rawlings came home. Henry told her, 'Drenna, you be gone,' and started shootin' B.J." Dad laughed. "Drenna must have set a world record down that road scatterin' dishes like her ass was on fire and she was plantin' peas at the same time."

"What about Henry and B.J.?" I asked.

He said, "Well, I took the one that Henry shot to the hospital. I drove through every red light going through Gainesville because I was afraid he would die before we got there. It was perfectly safe with Drenna in the back flayin' her arms and screamin' louder than any siren the police had. Then I had a hell of a row with that fool woman that runs the county hospital. She wasn't going to let me bring him in unless I promised to pay his bill. I told Henry to help me, and we took him in and put him on the table anyway. I told her he was just as much hers as he was mine, but if she could get him back on his feet, I would see that he paid his bill. I walked out with Henry and left her still runnin' her mouth."

"What happened to Henry?"

"I took him to the jail and told them to lock him up. Because it is Sunday there wasn't anybody around except the jailer. I have to go in and tell the sheriff what it's all about as soon as everyone here at the Creek agrees on what should be done."

"What do you think that will be?" I asked.

"It will do Henry good to set in jail until we see if B.J. lives or dies. The odds right now are that he won't live more'n a day or two. If he dies we'll have to have a trial, and the court will decide. If he lives Henry should have to come back to the Creek and support his family and Drenna, though she ain't worth it. Then he will have to work out that hospital bill."

"That don't seem fair," I said. "That old B.J. ought to pay his own bill. He caused it."

Dad said, "I agree. Knowing Henry, I would say B.J. might as well have shot himself when he decided to bully Henry, but on the other hand Henry is a grown man, and he made the decision to do what he did knowing when a feller makes his bed, he has to lie in it."

We walked home without speaking, lost in our private thoughts. When we got to the door, Dad said, "Just before Henry went in the jailhouse he said he was sorry you had to see what he did and to tell you not to worry."

I rushed past my dad and into my room. I couldn't handle too much of being grown up in one day. I considered B.J. the villain rather than the victim and I hated him—although I desperately hoped he would get well, only because I wanted Henry to be free as soon as possible.

Word came from the hospital that B.J.'s condition was critical, and then the situation at the Creek got worse. It was Tuesday before Mrs. Rawlings came back from her cottage in St. Augustine. My dad went to tell her what had happened. When he came back he told my mamma, "She's on her high horse again and is determined to make bad matters worse. She talks like Henry attacked her personal property."

He shook his head. "She started yellin' about justice, whatever she thinks that is."

Two days later the hospital reported that B.J.'s condition was slowly improving. In the meantime Henry sat in the county jail. I was haunted by my melodramatic vision of him bound with clinking chains in a rat-infested moldy cell. My dad said that was not the case. Nevertheless, the image would not go away.

When I came home from school one afternoon, Dad said he wanted me to go with him to Gainesville. My first thought, that we were going to get Henry out of jail and bring him home, was partially correct. Dad had talked with a friend who was a deputy in the sheriff's office earlier that morning and decided we had to do something with Henry. Mrs. Rawlings was raising hell and would eventually discover Henry had not been charged with anything. If she then swore out a warrant, it would be impossible to get him out.

We arrived in Gainesville in our pickup shortly after sundown. Henry was waiting at the curb in front of the jail. It was the first time I had seen him since the shooting. He had on the same clothes he was wearing when he left the Creek. I slipped to the middle of the seat so he could get in on the passenger side. He said, "I shore is glad to see you all."

"Me, too," I told him. We drove out through the north edge of Gainesville on U.S. 441 past the La Crosse road. Dad pulled over on the shoulder, and we sat there until it was dark. Then he said, "Well, Henry, this is where you are on your own."

Henry answered, "Yes, sir, this will do fine." He got out of the truck and stood by the door.

Dad gave him some money and a piece of paper. "Here is the address of my wife's sister. Her name is Waver Werthington, and she will give you a job on her farm. It's a long way, but you got in this mess, and it's gonna take some time to get you out. We'll take care of Sissie and your young'un. You stay off the main roads and walk at night. If and when the time comes to clear this mess up, I'll send for you."

Henry said, "I sho' thank you" and then put his huge hand on my shoulder. "You take care, little man." He crossed the ditch and disappeared into the darkness. I was amazed he didn't even look at the address Dad gave him, he just lit out. Aunt Waver's place was more than two hundred and fifty miles away in Decatur County, Georgia.

Two weeks later Mamma got a postcard from my aunt. She said they were having plenty of rain and had a new man to help on the farm.

Mrs. Rawlings swore out a warrant against Henry on charges of assault and attempted murder. For the first and only time, I was mad at her. Everyone at the Creek, including the blacks, tried to talk her out of doing it. For someone from the Creek to swear out a warrant, especially against anyone else from the Creek, was to be in league with the government against us. I do not believe Mrs. Rawlings knew what a breach of local code her warrant was. Ironically, a few years later that same code would be cited in her defense.

The trial date was put off several times, then finally set for the end of summer. In the interim the nurses said they shook bird shot out of the sheets from B.J.'s bed every morning, but he gradually got better. Two things saved him: his heavy shirt, denim overalls, and denim jumper, and the fact that Mr. Brice had gone bird hunting before leaving and had not replaced the birdshot in the shotgun with the more deadly buckshot that Henry assumed was in it. One morning a nurse making her rounds discovered B.J. was gone. Another patient had seen him slip out during the night. He apparently didn't want any more to do with Cross Creek or the local justice Mrs. Rawlings was insisting upon. To my knowledge he never returned to Cross Creek.

Mrs. Rawlings continued to pressure the judge to prosecute Henry. I met her occasionally and avoided any talk about the trial. I was a little uncomfortable with her because I didn't want to be disloyal to Henry and Sissie.

I came in from school one afternoon and noticed the side door to our garage was closed. That was unusual, since we normally left it open for the dog. It was also unusual to find my dad sitting in the kitchen talking with my mother that early in the afternoon. "Why is the garage shut up?" I asked.

My folks looked at each other with indecision that turned into smiles of agreement. Dad said, "Can you keep something under your hat?"

"Yes, sir," I answered.

"Then why don't you go out to the garage and look for yourself."

I charged out of the house and raced to see what the surprise was. I do not remember what I expected, but the first thing I saw inside the dark garage was Henry. We had a joyous reunion, and I brought him so much food he said he would have to walk back to Georgia just to keep from being called Fat Henry. Eventually I was forced to stop visiting and do my chores. Dad said it would give Henry's ears a rest. A poor excuse, I thought.

At supper I learned the trial would be held in two days in the Gainesville courthouse. The warrant for Henry was still valid, but the sheriff said that if he showed up for trial it would be okay since he had not been served or arrested. Dad told me he wouldn't speculate on the outcome of the trial until after the meeting. I didn't have an opportunity to ask what meeting, with whom, and why before Aunt Martha and Sissie with her baby, Junyus (for Junior), and Drenna came in.

Even though we all saw one another frequently, Aunt Martha made any meeting seem like the Second Coming, and she was the Messiah. "How is you all? My, you is looking good. I thinks 'bout you folks all the time." She rolled her eyes up toward the ceiling. "Sho' as I loves the Lawd, he loves you. I brought you some guava jelly."

I was busting to find out if Martha and Sissie and Drenna knew Henry was back. I should have known when Dad suggested Drenna sit in the chair by the pantry door and Martha and Sissie sit near the stove, where it was warm. I knew he was not normally concerned with details like seating arrangements. They talked about all the usual things: the weather, insects, babies, poverty, and religion.

When I was sure I couldn't stand it any longer, Dad said, "Y'all know Henry's trial is day after tomorrow?" They all nodded. "How do you want it to come out?"

Aunt Martha and Sissie both spoke at the same time. "We wants Mr. Henry back."

Drenna was caught between a rock and a hard place. It was obvious she was Mrs. Rawlings's only hope of support in prosecuting Henry, and she had sworn to help do the job. Dad looked at her. "Drenna, what do you think they ought to do to Henry?"

She twisted on the chair and looked left and right several times without moving her head. The room was silent. When she finally spoke, her voice was even higher than usual. "I don't wants to be the cause of more trouble. But Henry, he shot my husband B.J. and it caused me to be older than I is, and he—"

Dad interrupted her, "Why don't you tell Henry all that stuff yourself?"

All of us saw the pantry door open except Drenna. She turned to see what had attracted our attention. When she did, her face was only a few inches from Henry's. She shrieked and jumped straight out of her chair, then screeched without catching her breath, "How is you, Mr. Henry! I is so glad to see you! Us all sho do love you! I been hopin' you was comin' home! I is got to tell you again, I is glad to see you!" She managed to stumble backward and get behind Martha.

Aunt Martha said, "I am glad to see you, Henry," and she meant it. It was apparent that Henry and Sissie had met earlier in the day, but she evidently did not know he was in the pantry when they came in.

My dad said, "Drenna, what are you going to tell that judge day after tomorrow?"

She answered, chanting the words, "I is gonna tell him we wants Mr. Henry back at Cross Creek. That old B.J. Samson done caused it all."

Aunt Martha gave her the same look she would give a child she was simultaneously encouraging and reprimanding. "Praise the Lawd, I knows that's exactly what you is gonna do!" The issue was settled. Martha and her daughters said good night and filed out, Martha humming one of her spirituals. Henry slept on our old army cot in the garage.

The next day was torment for me, because my folks decided not to allow me to stay home from school and visit with Henry.

The situation could not have been more complicated. The lawyer said he wanted us to take Henry back to the Gainesville jail so he could turn himself in the night before the trial. But my sister's junior-senior banquet was that night, and she had to be driven over to the high school in Hawthorne. Since the Bridge was out and it would be necessary to go around through Hawthorne anyway to get to Gainesville, Dad reasoned that we could all go in the pickup, stop in Hawthorne for my sister to enjoy her banquet and make her speech, then all of us would take Henry to jail.

Marjorie was the salutatorian of her ten-member class and was supposed to make a speech wearing her first formal dress at the grand affair, to be held in the Hawthorne City Hall. The dignitaries invited included the county sheriff, the school trustees, and Howard E. Bishop, the county superintendent of public instruction. Marjorie liked Henry and was sympathetic to his plight, but she didn't want to go to her special affair with the entire family, including me and Henry. (The banquet was for students and school officials only, not relatives.)

"The banquet is the most important thing that will probably happen to me in my entire life," she pleaded with Dad. She said it was not fair that her classmates were all going to Gainesville to see Charles Boyer and Irene Dunne in a movie after the banquet while she would be taking Henry to jail in a pickup truck. Looking at me, she exclaimed, "Something will go wrong. I just know it."

Dad was in a conciliatory mood, and he said we would take her to the movie after we dropped Henry off at the jail. He promised Marjorie and my mother, who was beginning to sympathize with Marjorie, that he would make me behave, and he reminded them that Henry never bothered anyone. I, of course, thought this was a great plan. It would be the first time the family all went to a picture show together and I would get to ride in the back of the truck with Henry. For the life of me I couldn't understand why Marjorie would want it any other way.

On the big night Marjorie put on the evening dress Mamma had made for her. We all except Marjorie thought the neckline was too low. While Mamma made some alterations, I got Marjorie's corsage (sent to her by some boy in Hawthorne) out of the icebox. She wouldn't put it on, preferring to carry it so it wouldn't get crushed in the truck. Henry and I were already sitting in the back when Marjorie came out, holding up her skirt.

We were late, and everyone was already inside and seated when we got to the banquet. Dad parked toward the back because there would be less mosquitoes away from the lights. In retrospect, I am sure Marjorie forgave us for being late and didn't really mind us parking out back the whole time. I was proud of her, and any other time I would have slipped up by the windows and listened to her speech. But I knew she would understand I didn't want to miss being with Henry just when everything that was really important was about to happen.

My folks waited in the cab while Henry and I sat in the back. He told me of his trip to Georgia, and why he liked Cross Creek better than Georgia. I asked him if he was scared to go back to jail. He said, "It's like takin' medicine to get well. I's goin' in so I can get back out."

When the banquet was over, we drove the eighteen miles to Gainesville. It was cold, and Henry and I snuggled together without talking. I remembered my dad saying, "You don't ever know how a trial is going to turn out. In spite of the evidence, a judge can always find a law to fit the decision he wants to make." I didn't want to think about Henry being sent to the chain gang, but the thought wouldn't go away.

When we arrived at the jail, ground fog lay like a cloud around a single electric light bulb over the only door to the box-shaped brick building. I always link crime and punishment with my memory of Henry at the jail on that cold February night. My dad asked if Henry wanted him to go in with him.

Henry said, "No, you is done more than enough." We watched him shuffle toward the door. He waited there a few seconds, then the door opened, and the inside light flicked out into the darkness like a serpent's tongue before it disappeared along with Henry.

None of us enjoyed the movie. Marjorie cried, whether about the picture or Henry or just some of those things girls got flustered about,

I didn't know. When it was over, we all crowded in the cab to go back to the Creek. I said, "The theater was cold." Everyone agreed.

At school the next day my teacher talked about sentence structure while Henry was being tried. When I finally arrived home, Dad said, "They turned Henry loose." It was like Christmas, Thanksgiving, and the last day of school all rolled into one.

"What happened?" I asked.

He gave all the details of the trial in his calm, factual way. The judge asked where B.J. was, and no one knew. He asked Mrs. Rawlings where she was when all the alleged charges occurred, and she answered "St. Augustine." He told her to step down, and she got mad. She tried to argue with him, and he threatened her with contempt of court. He asked Sissie and Drenna what happened, and they told him that the night before the shooting, B.J. had threatened Henry with a knife and told him he would "get him later." The judge asked Bernie Bass what he knew, and Bernie said he had heard B.J. threaten Henry prior to the day of the shooting. The judge apparently had heard all he wanted to hear and threw the whole mess out of his court. To her credit, Mrs. Rawlings offered to shake hands and forget the whole thing.

The next day was Saturday. I announced at breakfast that I thought I should help Henry in the grove. I found him down in the back picking oranges. I asked him what he thought about the trial. He said, "I found out I sure has got some good friends here at the Creek. You know ol' Henry has done told you a heap of times. When you sees old *trouble* coming don't jest stand there. You tell yo' feet, 'Feet! You get me out of here.' Now, I's got to get back to work."

Nine. Bigger Young'uns

THE YEAR 1939 was an eventful one for me. I celebrated my twelfth birthday, and I was no longer considered a little young'un. The additional freedom that came with my age was wonderful, although I would have preferred to skip the added responsibilities. Life for me was a grand adventure: hunting, fishing, exploring, visiting friends, drawing, and a new interest, girls. The problem with girls was there weren't any, at least not at the Creek.

Our family was prospering. In 1937 Dad had bought a new pickup even though my mamma objected to him spending so much money, almost four hundred dollars. He told her he had decided to go into the fish business. He had noticed that the prices the Creek fishermen received for their fish had been lower than they should have been. Worse, when the fish were running at their best, the local buyers would say the market was glutted and refuse to buy.

Dad was convinced he could do something about the low prices and undependable market. He told Mamma, "People in Georgia love to eat freshwater fish so much, there ain't enough fish in Florida to ever satisfy them." He drove to Valdosta and Macon, then back to Columbus and Albany. When he returned he was whistling. He told the fishermen he would immediately raise the price of fish—and if they sold exclusively to him, he would promise to buy all the fish they caught. The wholesale fish business flourished from the beginning.

When time allowed Dad built new cypress houses on property he had purchased near the Bridge to rent to the increasing number of families who sold their fish to him.

Our orange grove had grown to maturity and finally produced a small annual profit, even though the State conjured up reasons to restrict the small growers from marketing citrus in north Florida. We hauled our organically grown fruit across the Suwannee River on a rickety ferry in the middle of the night and sold the oranges in south Georgia.

As my family's finances improved my folks added some work-saving devices that didn't require electricity, although modern conveniences were slow in coming to the Creek. First they bought a gasoline-powered washing machine that usually required as much labor to start as doing the washing by hand. Then Mamma bought a gasoline iron that had to be pumped up with air. It caught fire frequently and had to be thrown into the yard until it burned out. Nevertheless, it eliminated the need to have a fire going in the wood stove all day Tuesday, which was ironing day. In 1940 Dad bought a kerosene refrigerator, and for several months we had ice cream frozen in the ice trays every day. After that we returned to the old hand-cranked churn because the ice cream was better. Without electricity, we were forced to heat water for clothes-washing in an iron pot in the backyard. I complained when I was given a new job: hand-pumping water into a cypress tank elevated on fat lighter-wood poles in the backyard. The tank provided water pressure for a new indoor toilet and kitchen sink. Dad said my labor was free while motors used gasoline and were even harder to start.

In addition to the modern conveniences, he and my mother began purchasing land along the shore of Right Arm Prairie and new acreage west of the creek. Their commitment to own land was as strong as ever, and they sacrificed many of the pleasures they would otherwise have enjoyed toward that goal. Dad reasoned that land was a good investment and anyway, private ownership would be necessary if we were to remain in the cow business when closed ranges inevitably came to the county. I didn't admit it then but that time could not come too soon for me.

Starting the year Dad arrived at the Creek, he added a few cows annually to his herd and bought more on speculation from small farmers. (We never used the word *ranch* at the Creek. Ranches were cow pastures owned by city people.) Every Monday, if I had finished my chores, I went with him to the livestock market, sometimes to buy and sometimes to sell.

A perspiring, overweight auctioneer at the market sized up our cattle, wiping a flood of sweat from his forehead in the shimmering heat that was permeated with the odors of cowshit and parched peanuts. He pounded his gavel for the hundred or more farmers sitting in the arena, and especially for the dozen meat packers lounging down front in the cane-bottomed rocking chairs reserved for buyers. While a bunch of mean-looking range cows charged into the pit, he chanted, "Nooooww gentlemen, we have here twenty head of Tom Glisson's gen-u-wine, thoroughbred, Cross Creek web-footed cows, all fattened on saw grass at Tom's muck-and-mud swamp ranch out there in Cross Creek. Wherever that is. I am told they were never on dry land until this very morning. Nooooooooow gentlemen, what am I bid?" Designed to get the buyers' attention, the auctioneer's witticism was also a friendly jest directed toward my dad, a friend and a regular seller at the Monday auction. Dad's concept of cattle raising was to breed cows that could make a living without human help. Although the hammocks and flat woods did not provide enough food to support a herd through the winter, cows willing to wade into the marshes among the alligators and cottonmouth moccasins could stay fat throughout the year. In fact, my dad preferred stock that showed a distinct dislike for human beings, reasoning that the meaner they were, the harder they would be to steal.

Dad gave me the title of cow chaser, not to be confused with cow puncher or cowboy. It was, like all my Creek titles, bestowed without my consent and not to be refused. Originally all our cows were free on the open range, which made it necessary to keep them from grazing along the railroad that ran east of Lochloosa and through Island Grove. The only way to herd them back nearer the Creek was on foot. This gave the cows the same advantage as the fishermen had when running from the game wardens—they could choose where they wanted to run.

I dreamed of having a horse and sitting tall in the saddle while driving our cows wherever I pleased. Dad said a horse would be impractical in the palmettos and would be worthless chasing cows in the marsh, although years later I learned he was afraid I would get killed trying to ride in the palmettos and scrubs. I reminded him of the stories I had heard him tell of his driving cattle with a horse when he first moved to the Creek, and I continued to use any excuse to persuade him to get me one. He had bought me a mule when I was ten that was so small the fishermen made jokes about him. I suggested selling the dwarf mule, thinking the transaction would pave the way for me to get a horse, but this scheme proved unsuccessful.

Every few weeks we got word our cows were straying too near the railroad. Dad would take me in his pickup to the area where they had been seen and drop me off. He would laugh and joke, "J.T., you can come home anytime you choose as long as you bring our cows." I sincerely liked him, but his humor at such times did not amuse me. I pointed out that he only said "our" cows when they were in the wrong place.

Tracking was easier in the early morning and after a rain, which meant I ended up wet to my neck whether the cows were in the marsh or feeding in the ti-tis and palmettos soaked with morning dew. In the summer the deerflies were bad, not to mention the snakes crawling in every direction. The Bible has high praise for those who showed love and responsibility while tending their father's flocks. The Bible notwithstanding, those paragons would have fallen short of such praise had they tended Tom Glisson's herd.

My strategy was to track the cows by chasing them until they wearied of being run back and forth across the woods and marsh. When they saw me coming, they immediately recognized me and knew I had come to drive them home; they acted as if they had never seen a human being before and pretended to panic, always running in a direction away from home. The only way to convince them they had no choice but to return home was to run them hard, keep them moving no matter what direction they were going by not allowing them to stop to rest or eat. That meant running out into ponds, into thick hammocks, and through scrub palmettos, a good way to take a census of the snake population. After two or three hours their self-elected leader, usually the meanest one in the bunch, would suddenly go directly out to the road with the herd following and head for home. A casual observer would think they were as docile as a herd of dairy cows. From hard-earned experience I knew they were only getting their breaths before attempting to make a second escape.

Instinctively they knew which terrain I would least like to follow them in, and so chose the marsh and swamps in winter and the scrub oaks in the heat of summer. The lead cow was always a convincing actress. With no warning, she would shy backward like a wild horse bitten by a ten-foot rattler and bolt, throwing her tail in the air and charging across the woods. The entire herd would stampede after her. It was on those occasions I learned to cuss with precision and clarity. I never asked God to forgive me for that profanity since only he and the cows were privileged to hear it, and they all knew I genuinely meant every word.

Once the entire herd ran into a patch of scrub oak and palmettos that was nearly impenetrable. My frustration was overwhelming; black bass were schooling on the lake, and I was spending the day chasing cows. I picked my way on my stomach beneath the knurled highland scrub oaks and found myself face-to-face with a cottonmouth as big around as my leg. By the time I killed the snake, the cows had moved into another thicket. I went in after them, and by an accident of fate I saw the lead cow, the instigator of my torment, hiding with her line of sight obscured behind the palmettos. It was a chance to get even if I could only catch her tail.

Luck was with me. I moved as close as I dared and charged toward her. The brush was so dense she stumbled trying to escape and I locked onto her long bushy tail. She bleated and went crashing through the scrub with me hanging on for dear life. When she could not dislodge me in the thick brambles, she cut out into the open pine flats, kicking and bellowing. She lost control of her bowels and spattered me with green cowshit. Then she ran into a fallen pine top and stumbled, giving me a chance to twist her tail into a kink with the hope I could break it. At that point it became clear I had gone too far. She tried to turn on me, lowering her horns and snorting like a bull. I no longer had the option of turning her loose—now *she* was after *me*. Finally, when both of us were exhausted, she slowed for an instant, giving me a chance to let go and skitter for the protection of a small pine tree. The fracas was over. She headed straight for the road that led to the Creek, the rest of the herd following.

My folks were eating dinner when I got home. My clothes were wet and torn, and I was scratched and bruised from head to toe. Dad said, "Why did it take you so long?" and my mother complained that I did not show any respect for my clothes.

I asked, "If I frog-hunted and made enough money to pay for a horse, could I buy one?"

Mamma answered, "What on earth for?"

Dad said, "Pass the cornbread."

🌿 Dad's hog business was similar to all his other enterprises: totally unorthodox. The pigs were a byproduct of his fish business, fed entirely on scrap fish, muds, suckers, shad, and the heads and entrails discarded when the fishermen dressed catfish. It was one of my jobs to haul the scraps to these hogs, and Dad sold over four hundred head a year without buying any feed. Still, when my agriculture teacher in the ninth grade at the Hawthorne high school told me I had to have a project, I neglected to admit we had a large herd of cows and seventy-five or so hogs penned up west of the Bridge. (Although the last thing I wanted to do with my life was farm, I had enrolled in agriculture courses because they earned one-and-a-half credits a year and were practically impossible to fail.) "Something like a family garden or a farm animal to care for while you learn to keep accurate record books of your profits and losses," the teacher suggested. I didn't want my mamma's garden involved with the school, because that would give her cause to expand it. In addition, it was my policy to avoid any connection between my parents and school.

The general opinion in Hawthorne was that Cross Creek was nothing but swamps and poor folks, so the first year the school didn't press me for a project they assumed my family could not afford. The second year the teacher announced he had bought me a pig and I would have to raise it. He loaned me the two dollars the pig cost, to be paid back when it was sold at a profit. I suggested it would make a good class project if we constructed a pen on the edge of the school ground, where the waste from the school cafeteria could be fed to the animal until I could arrange to borrow a truck to haul her to the Creek. He agreed, and my popularity immediately fell to an all-time low when my fellow students were forced to help me build the pen.

Quite naturally, when the pig had a proper pen and the cafeteria was feeding her, I was in no hurry to pick her up and feed her myself. The end of the school year forced me into action. After being fed for six months, the pig was a grown hog and weighed more than a hundred pounds. I paid the teacher his two dollars with frog money and faced the problem of explaining the existence of my hog at home.

I opened my story by telling my dad I needed to use his truck to bring a hog from school. He said he was aware the State had recently guaranteed free textbooks to all students but hadn't heard anything about hogs. He asked a lot of questions about how I had come to own a hog purchased and fed by the school system. I tried to answer as vaguely and evasively as possible, implying that such was the way of modern education. My plan was to keep her in the open woods. He didn't like the idea of me having a hog running loose when everyone had started penning them. I assured him that I planned to sell the hog immediately after I finished the record book I was keeping of my hog project. I hauled the hog home without exactly getting his permission by volunteering to pick up a load of ice from the ice plant in Hawthorne for the fish business; I stopped at the school and brought the hog home sandwiched between the three-hundred-pound blocks of ice. Back at the Creek, I stopped on the curve just south of Mrs. Rawlings's house, opened the tailgate, and yelled, "Sooie!" The sow jumped out and ran into the woods.

Blue seemed like a good name for her; I liked it because it was short, like Flag, the deer in *The Yearling*. I didn't see her again until four months later, when she passed our house with eleven little pigs all the same size she had been when my teacher originally purchased her. That hog turned out to be a pig factory, regularly producing more than two litters of at least ten pigs a year. Blue nursed them until they were big enough to make a living on their own, then she taught them to forage before she delivered the next litter. When they were fat enough to butcher, I sold them off, keeping old Blue to raise the next crop.

Normally I received only a small portion of the sale price, since I borrowed money and sold futures sometimes two litters ahead of old Blue's production. My sister, who by then had grown up and lived in Gainesville, my mamma, two teachers and the principal at the school in Hawthorne, plus three of the Creek fishermen had nonvoting stock in my hog, all without my dad's knowledge.

When old Blue was first at the Creek she scavenged the hammocks, feeding on hickory nuts and acorns as well as bulbs and worms rooted from the edge of the marsh. The first sign of problems began when she started feeding along the creek. The complaints at first seemed frivolous because her behavior was quite natural for an industrious sow. The fishermen's wives complained that Blue ran their dogs away from their plates and also ate their chicken feed. The husbands didn't admit they were upset over this because it was embarrassing to own a dog that would run from a hog. I apologized and intimated that if Blue didn't behave, I would sell her.

Blue began spending less time foraging in the woods and more time around houses, doing more and more damage. While one family was carrying groceries from their old cut-down car into the house, she got into a sack that fortunately was all canned goods and scattered them over the yard. They said they had to eat guess-whats for two weeks because she rooted all the labels off trying to get into the cans. The friendly attitude I had always taken for granted from my neighbors began to slip away in direct proportion to how often Blue visited them. Even on the Bridge I was confronted with the exploits of my hog. To complicate matters, news of the sow's reputation was beginning to reach my dad.

"I will not have that high school hog ruining everyone's life at the Creek," he said. "J.T., you do something to stop it, or I will."

I pleaded for more time, not wanting to give up my chief source of income. I even stooped to suggesting I was considering being a farmer, knowing that would please him. If I had been totally honest I would have said I planned to complete a glorious tour of duty in the military and after the war become an artist supported by a patron brood sow.

I was breathing a little easier, feeling that everyone was beginning to put up with Blue's shenanigans, when the inevitable happened. C.J. Calton parked his boat at the landing near the Bridge and went to eat breakfast before skinning his catch of catfish. When he returned, Blue was in the boat helping herself to his hard-earned fish. C.J. chased her, swinging a boat oar, mad enough to kill her. The two-hundred-pound sow got hooked in his trotline and dragged it off into the hammock before dislodging the hook. Later that day she rooted up Mr. Martin's worm bed of night crawlers before retiring to the hammock.

I began to feel like a parent with an errant young'un. I promised the fishermen I would cover the damage as soon as I had more pigs to sell. Time was running out before my dad would learn what a truly destructive menace was running through the Creek. Looking back, it was a credit to my friends' loyal discretion that Dad had not discovered how destructive Blue was long before he did.

The climax came when Dad and I returned home after hauling a load of cows to the market. Mr. Brice's new field hand (a man named Henry Woodward but called Preach), who had moved into a tenant house sat in the grove across the road from our garage, came running to meet us. "Mr. Tom," he said, catching his breath, "I wants you to come see what done happened in my house."

"Tell me what it is," Dad said, "and then maybe I will want to see it."

Preach raised his arms and voice: "No, sir, you got to see this'n firsthand."

Dad got down from the truck and reluctantly followed him, with me bringing up the rear. Preach led us around to the kitchen door on the back side of the house and shoved it open. Looking into the darkness of the shanty we were confused; splashes of white powdered the walls, and the floor was snow-white with swirls of red ooze running in every direction. Dad said, "Damn! Preach, it looks like somethin' blew up, or you've had a hell of a fight in there."

Preach's voice rose in pitch. "Hit wan't neither. While I was workin' in the grove, it was that hog, Blue. She done busted in the door and turn over my corn meal, then she got my twelve-pound sack of biscuit flour and chewed a hole in it and slung it all over the place shakin' it out of the sack. Then the only thing else I had left to eat was a gallon of sugar-cane syrup I fetched in Micanopy befo' I come to the Creek, she busted the lid off and strung it all over my house." He seemed desperate to finish his story without being interrupted.

I wished he hadn't started.

He caught his breath and continued, "When I come in to my dinner that hog run slap over me with her head hung in my syrup bucket and took out through the front door and down through the grove yonder."

I thought about saying Mr. Preach should keep his doors locked, but when I looked at my dad I decided to forget that suggestion. He was breathing hard through his nose. In a calm, soft voice he said, "You clean up your house—and then come over to mine—and I'll give you some groceries until we can replace yours. We will also give you a half-day's pay for the time you've lost." I didn't like the sound of that "we."

I said something about needing to work in Mamma's garden and left immediately. It surprised me that Dad didn't mention Blue's raid on Preach's kitchen when we ate supper, even though I tried to keep a running conversation going in the event he did. Sometimes crises lost their steam if they were left alone.

Two weeks later I came home from school and found Dad sitting on the front porch looking as if he were waiting for me. I tried to rush past, but he said, "Just a minute, son, I want to see you."

"What did I do?" I asked.

"Nothing," he answered. "I did something for you. Today I got you out of the livestock business at Cross Creek." He took his billfold and handed me some bills held together with a paper clip. "I sold that renegade sow of yours and the shoats and paid Preach. You can write in that record book whatever you write when you go out of business. I think it's called selling out, or closing out."

After paying off my stockholders and creditors I was delighted to discover I had money left over. Then Mamma decided I should buy a $17.50 war bond that would not mature for ten years. My career in agriculture had ended.

❧ The end of the 1930s brought better times, even though the Creek was only remotely dependent on the national economy. The price of fish and frog legs quadrupled those paid in 1932 and 1933. As beef and pork rose in value, Dad increased the size of his herd, pasturing cows on the newly acquired property bordering the north end of Cross Creek and continuing north along the west shore of Lochloosa. My contribution to the cattle management shifted from running them on foot to building fences and clearing land with a pulpwood saw. I was not sure which I would have preferred if I'd had a choice.

The only marked change in our standard of living came in the form of a two-week vacation in the Big Scrub at Salt Springs. Before the 1940s we went there only for the day, on two or three Sundays each summer.

Salt Springs consists of several springs (also called buils) that are the terminus of an underground river pouring millions of gallons of pure seventy-two-degree water up into the Florida sunlight. It flows out over eroded limestone and across patches of white sand surrounded by emerald ribbon grass, into the St. Johns River. Mullet and crabs that had migrated more than a hundred miles upstream from the Atlantic by way of the St. Johns River mingled freely with Cracker swimmers.

Before air conditioning, the natural springs were our only sanctuary from the sweltering heat of summer. The water in the creek and in our relatively shallow lakes became warm from the blistering sun as the summer progressed, leaving us to dream of the cold water pouring up out of the ground down in the Big Scrub. In addition, at the springs there were those wondrous creatures called girls who wore what the older women called "skimpy" bathing suits.

At the Creek we considered the last two weeks of August the hottest of the summer, so that was the time chosen to go to Salt Springs. Each summer Marjorie and I asked if we were going to the springs for a vacation, and Dad would say, "I don't know for sure. It all depends on whether we've got enough work done when the time comes up."

Marjorie said, "If God decides to put heaven at Salt Springs, He couldn't find a better place." I agreed.

I learned to swim in the springs and dance at the juke located at the head of the springs. The juke was in reality the post office, ice house, grocery store, and restaurant. A portion of the rough lumber floor was set aside for dancing with a juke organ that was silent only between three and six in the morning. We swam and danced there during the day, and at night we told our parents we wanted to fish or go crab gigging in the run and then headed back to the juke. I was grown before I knew my parents were always aware of exactly where we were.

Even though the preparations for our first full two-week vacation at the springs had begun months before, on the day of the departure it was late afternoon before we finally got under way. Dad said, "Pearlee, you've got enough groceries to carry everybody at the Creek through the whole summer." After we passed over the Oklawaha River and entered the Big Scrub, the remaining trip was along sand and clay roads. Marjorie and I sat huddled in the back between boxes of Mamma's canned preserves and a variety of cakes, pies, and cookies "to tide us over the two weeks," as she put it, plus bedclothes and Sunday clothes to wear to church if she could get anyone to go. My personal baggage consisted of fishing tackle, a bathing suit, a toothbrush and a sketch book.

We arrived after dark, and although I tried to escape, Mamma commandeered everyone to unload and set up camp in our primitive cabin. When we finished it was past bedtime. I crawled into bed dreaming of the two weeks we would spend in paradise.

In the first light of dawn I slipped away from the camp and headed for the springs. There was no one in sight, although the smell of coffee emanated from the old Civil War–era packet that had long since given up plying the St. Johns and lay permanently aground just below the springs. This derelict boat was the home of Mrs. Griggs, one of the most pleasant women I have ever known. I didn't like the taste of coffee, but I sure enjoyed the smell that drifted out across the springs in the still morning air.

All was well in the world and at Salt Springs. Calm clear water swirled over the boils and moved off lazily down the seven-mile run to Lake George. Hundreds of fish swam in asymmetric colonies; schools of silver mullet moved over the ribbon grass like flights of migrating ducks.

Someone had attached a rope swing from a high limb in a hickory growing from a bluff that leaned over the spring several feet above the water. A diver could swing out and drop into a small hole where the sand bottom was more than five feet beneath the surface. I caught the rope, pulled it up the bank, and sailed out for my first drop into the springs. The water at that hour was only three or four degrees cooler than the morning air, and the exhilarating freedom of that glide through the air was like nothing else. I ran up the bank to swing again and again. I flipped my feet up and dove head-first into the clear water, being careful to pull up quickly so as to not hit the bottom. Each time I repeated the dive I imagined myself more and more a champion.

After a dozen dives I saw a girl with black hair, about my age, standing across the springs watching me. What more could I hope for than a beautiful young maiden admiring my extraordinary feats of daring? I swung out and dove again, trying to look as graceful as a fourteen-year-old boy could with legs that looked like ropes with knots tied in them. When I came up she was still watching. I thought that on the next dive I would come up facing her and say hello and something clever that I would think up in the meantime.

Trying to be nonchalant, I pulled the rope up to the bluff, backed as far as possible, and swung out over the glittering water, intent on making every move illustrate the perfection of a seasoned champion. It was probably that total concentration that caused me to miss the hole and come down head-first in less than a foot of water. There was a crunching sound in my neck, followed by a sharp pain up the back of my head. I couldn't see, and began to crawl in what I hoped was the direction of the shore. Gradually I regained a little sight in the extreme periphery of my vision. I heard someone saying, "Are you all right, son?" It was Mrs. Griggs. "Are you all right?" she repeated. Half of my vision remained blocked by a twelve-foot black spot with a purple ring around it. I tried to see the black-haired girl past the edge of my blind spot. She was walking away. Mrs. Griggs came near and asked again, "Are you hurt?"

The thought occurred to me that if I was hurt my folks would race me to Ocala to a doctor and that would be the end of the vacation. I told the kind lady, "No ma'am," and staggered in the direction of the camp, the big purple spot preceding me. Behind me Mrs. Griggs called, "You go straight and let your folks know what happened."

The spot went away in a few hours; however, I spent the rest of the week trying to avoid my folks. When they noticed me twisting my shoulders to look to the left or right (because I couldn't turn my head), I mumbled something about having a crick in my neck, probably caused by sleeping in a draft.

Four years later I was being examined for induction into the army when a doctor began to probe at the vertebrae in my neck. "How did you break your neck?" he asked. I told him I had not. He ordered an X-ray that showed one vertebra had been crushed down on one side. I insisted I had not been in a car wreck and was never treated for a neck injury. He said, "Think back, somewhere you had a fall or possibly dove into shallow water. Surely you knew when you broke your neck!" Exasperated by my ignorance, he waved me on. "You're damn lucky you can move any part of your body, but since it didn't kill you then it is not sufficient cause for you to be rejected now."

❦ At long last, when I was fourteen years old, my dad came home from the stock market with a long-legged, decent-looking stud in his truck. I ran to the gate exclaiming, "You got me a horse!"

He said, "No, son. I only want to pasture him until he puts on a little more weight and then sell him to a feller with a family over by

Orange Springs that needs a horse." I later realized the whole story was a hoax. He knew that the temptation to ride the horse would be too great and that I would certainly try it. If he had said it was okay I would have spent the entire summer breaking him. Since I had to sneak around to do it, I could not neglect my work without the risk of Dad knowing what I was doing.

I decided to name the horse Dynamite, hoping he would be the fastest thing at the Creek.

As it turned out, the least Dad could have done was tell me the horse was not broken before I tried to ride him. Dynamite let me climb up on him and sit, but when I nudged him with my heels, his back dipped for a split second before it sprang upward as if the jaws of an eight-hundred-pound bear trap had been released exactly where I was sitting. I went up in the air, and Dynamite moved over just enough so I wouldn't touch him on the way down. Although it knocked the breath out of me when I hit the ground, I swore I would ride him if it killed me.

I was not strong enough to break him the conventional way, and even if I had been, I didn't have a saddle. The next week I was totally preoccupied with how I, a ninety-pound weakling, could break what I had begun to think of as my horse. Drawing from my cow-chasing experience, it occurred to me he could not buck if I led him out into the marsh in muck and mud up to his belly.

The following afternoon I slipped out of my mamma's garden, where I was supposed to be hoeing sugar crowder peas, and caught my horse. He resented the only bridle I had, one made for a mule with side blinders, but finally submitted to the bit after biting me on the shoulder. I pulled off my shirt and britches so they wouldn't get muddy, led the horse out into the marsh along the edge of the creek to a place where the mud was well above my waist, and tied him to a cypress. Two sacks filled with sand provided ballast for his spring-loaded back. When I attempted to swing them up on him, he rolled his eyes toward me, anticipating what I planned to do. He reared back, trying to break loose from the tree, throwing mud and water in every direction. When he couldn't break the rawhide line, he bucked, creating a commotion that scared all the gators in the north end of the lake.

The muck and tangled water plants did the job. He tired in a few minutes, making it possible to throw the sand bags across his back, which sent him into another frenzy. Half an hour later I climbed on, and he threw me off, head and ears, into the muddy water. I came up and spit mud in his eye. That was enough for one day, and I released him back to the pasture.

The next day, I caught him again and led him back to the tree out in the marsh. I added more sand and succeeded in staying on, but I was afraid to release him from the tree until we had repeated the routine three days in a row. A week later I was able to ride him up and down the marsh, forcing him to wade in the mud away from shore. Each time I rode, I waited for him to tire and then ventured into shallower and shallower water.

After three weeks of hoeing peas at breakneck speed and then sneaking out to wade naked in hot mucky water saturated with leeches and gator fleas, I rode him out onto dry ground. I stayed on. I had me a horse.

I suspected Dad knew what I had been doing, but I was reluctant to ride Dynamite where he could see me. In addition, Mamma would make me explain where I had found the time to break a horse. I chose a fifth Sunday, one of my favorite days because neither the Methodists nor the Baptists had church that day.

For the first time, I didn't tire the horse in the marsh because I didn't want him muddy when I showed him off on my inaugural run. I planned to ride him past our house and down near the Bridge to a spot where the fishermen congregated on Sunday morning when the sun was too hot on the Bridge. After they had admired my horse, I thought I would go down to Bernie Bass's house so his family could see me. The finish of my coming-out exhibit would be to ride past Mrs. Rawlings's house and let her see the horse firsthand. I was sure it would be a day to remember.

Dynamite seemed much taller out on dry land. I had to climb up on a gate to mount him. He was frisky and pranced and snorted while I struggled to stay on. After twenty minutes he calmed down, boosting my ego and confidence. The moment of victory was at hand. I rode him up the lane and out onto the highway between our garage and the Brices' place across the road. At that crucial moment, Mr. Brice's ancient mule mustered up a spark of life in her sterile genes and became amorous with my horse.

The old rusty lot fence had fallen to the ground in the years that had passed since the mule had been able to do a day's work, but she knew where the fence had been and was content to spend her remaining years within its previous boundaries. Or had been, until she saw Dynamite. She frisked over the fallen wire and came snorting and swishing her tail toward us. There has never been anything more unwelcome to me than that old mule at that moment.

The Brices were away, and I knew it was my neighborly responsibility to put their mule back and prop up the fence. With great things to do, however, I elected to tend to this duty after I had completed my equestrian exhibition. I thought surely the twenty-eight-year-old mule would not try to follow, so I ignored her and turned my horse toward the Bridge.

I was unaware that a conspiracy had been contrived by my dad and all the fishermen. Dad had known all along I was breaking the horse. In fact both he and the fishermen had enjoyed spying on me. Knowing I would be anxious to show off the horse, they had connived to act as if they didn't notice the animal no matter what I did. I should have been suspicious when I passed in front of the house without Dad appearing to notice, but I was distracted by the old Brice mule. I rounded the curve and saw all the fishermen hunkering in front of Mr. Gillis's house. It was perfect. All of them would see me at the same time. I crossed the pavement to their side so that they would have to move back to allow me to pass. As I approached, they continued to talk, pretending to be totally engrossed in a story Mr. Gillis was telling. I passed within a few feet and said, "Howdy." They all raised their hands and mumbled howdy, barely audibly. I rode the horse down to the boat landing, insulted and angry.

The devil is the instigator of sudden impulses, and at that moment he laid one on me that was guaranteed to get their attention. I turned the horse around and aimed him squarely in their direction. I had scarcely enough skill to ride bareback on any high-spirited horse, and I certainly was not ready to allow Dynamite to run. It was of little or no importance, as it turned out, whether the devil or my anger made me do it. I kicked Dynamite in his sides, and he nearly shot out from under me. I remember thinking I didn't know a horse could run that fast. We sent the fishermen scrambling in panic to avoid being trampled and crossed the pavement literally flying back in the direction of my house. Halfway around the curve we met the old Brice mule still trying to follow us.

Seconds after I passed the mule I saw Mrs. Rawlings coming toward us in her new light-green hydromatic Oldsmobile, driving full speed as usual. I actually managed to raise my hand for a split second to say hey, as was mandatory in the country. She waved back as she shot past, and behind me came a crashing sound that reverberated through the quietness of the Creek. I looked back. The mule was coming over Mrs. Rawlings's car upside down, with broken glass flying in every direction. Fifty yards up the road I slowed my horse enough to jump off. I always assumed that when something bad happened I would automatically be blamed. In this instance I assumed I would be hung within the hour.

Mrs. Rawlings emerged from the mangled car alternately wringing her hands and throwing her arms over her head. The mule lay partly on the back bumper and partly on the road, belly up, her neck twisted in an impossible configuration. I stopped a safe distance away.

"Are you all right, Miz Rawlings?"

She looked up. "Get your father. Tell him to bring his gun and shoot the poor animal."

I assumed she must have hit her head and was addled, since a two-year-old kid could see the twenty-eight-year-old mule was dead. I answered, "Miz Rawlings, that old mule is dead."

She shouted back, "You get your father to come, *now,* and put the poor thing out of her misery. Dammit! Do it! This instant!"

I pleaded, "Miz Rawlings, that mule is dead as she can get." Coming from behind me, the voice of my dad calling to us was a welcome relief. He had heard the crash and was running down the road in our direction. She shouted at him "Tom, get your gun and shoot this poor animal."

Assessing the situation, he slowed to a walk. "Marge, I ain't gonna waste a bullet on that old mule's carcass. Hell, she's been dead for ten years and just waitin' around tryin' to find a place to fall."

Mrs. Rawlings insisted. "Tom, are you sure?"

"Of course I'm sure, and I know you're upset, but I ain't goin' to shoot no dead mule."

I followed in his shadow, feeling safer once he was there. While he asked if Mrs. Rawlings was hurt, I looked at the condition of her new car. The mule had cut across the road directly in front, and then jumped square into the vehicle when she saw she was going to be hit, smashing the hood, the windshield, the top, the trunk lid, and the rear fender. Water was trickling from the radiator through broken glass, running down beneath the mule. While Mrs. Rawlings assured my dad she was not hurt, I peeked into the car and was horrified to see a lady lying crumpled on the floorboard. I yelled, "There is a woman in the bottom of this car!"

Mrs. Rawlings gasped and ran around to the passenger door, pushing me away, and jerked the door open. The poor woman was white as a sheet and out cold. Mrs. Rawlings lifted her by her head and shouted, "Julia! Julia, wake up!" The helpless woman rolled her eyes, clearly not knowing who or where she was. Then she tried to get up.

My dad pushed aside Mrs. Rawlings, who was still holding the lady by her head, and said, "You better let me help." He lifted the woman into a sitting position and asked if she was okay.

Disoriented, she nodded and whispered, "Yes."

Mrs. Rawlings was still concerned about the status of the mule. "Now, Tom, I want you to have your men"—she motioned toward the fishermen who had heard the crash and were gathering to see what happened—"properly bury that poor unfortunate mule."

Dad was becoming impatient. "There ain't no damn way I know of to properly bury a mule and as a matter of fact, that's what we've got buzzards for."

She turned to the fishermen. "Will you do it? I will pay whatever it costs." They nodded yes, grinning sheepishly and looking down at their feet.

Dad said, "I think we had better be concerned with that woman there in the car and get her up to the house rather than worry about that wore-out dead mule." Mamma arrived and helped the lady from the car. She was weak but able to walk with Mamma's support on one side and Mrs. Rawlings's on the other. Dad asked one of the fishermen if he would get his Fordson tractor and drag the car out of the road and then drag the mule to "wherever it is y'all plan to bury him." He emphasized the "y'all," stifling an urge to laugh.

At the house Mamma inspected the few scratches and bruises the ladies had and said she was sure it would not be necessary for anyone to go to the doctor. Mrs. Rawlings said she was afraid she had neglected to introduce her guest: "This is my good friend Miss Julia Scribner from New York. Her father is my publisher." Dad said he was glad to meet her and bet she would be glad to get back to the safety of New York City. Mrs. Rawlings praised me for being so helpful. I didn't quite understand this, because all I really did was bring the mule to the scene of the accident. Maybe she was trying to clear me of any blame. An hour later, after they had regained their composure, Mamma drove them back to Mrs. Rawlings's house while I retrieved Dynamite. My horse had been instrumental in the crash, but I was thankful neither he nor I was accused. Justice always was an enigma at the Creek.

No one inquired as to exactly how the mule was buried. However, for the next three or four days a large flock of buzzards circled over the hammock a quarter of a mile from the place where the wreck had occurred.

Ten. Trap Fishing

*M*Y FRIEND Bernie Bass was the best trap fisherman at Cross Creek. He once told me fishing is like gambling for a living: "You can't see 'em until you catch 'em, and then you ain't really sure there's any more down there until you catch some more. You just have to believe they're there and guess where they'll be on a particular day. Then if you're right, you have to guess when they are going to be hungry and what they'll want to eat." He laughed. "Now that I think about it, I don't know why I ever started fishing."

The State annually sold us commercial fishing licenses with full knowledge that trapping and seining were the only methods we had to catch enough to make a living, and both these methods were against the law. It then committed itself to catch us when we did it. It's not surprising that young'uns growing up at Cross Creek had a weird concept of government.

Trap fishing was different than seining (fishing with nets) in two particulars. First, it was done by a single fisherman, and second, the traps (cylinders of poultry wire which the fish could swim into but not out of) had to be fished regularly. I enjoyed nothing more when I was a little young'un than fishing traps with my dad. I would sit on the back seat of the boat and dream of big oceans and marvel at the world of nature around us. Dad placed his traps in and around the patches of bonnets—lily pads—or the clear water grass, depending on what

species was active and the particular time of year. He paddled our trim, homemade cypress boat from one trap to another without sound, stopping the bow directly over each trap. He knew the exact location of each of his 100 traps. He would extend the handle end of his wild-mulberry paddle down into the water and hook the trap within an inch of its center, even though he had left nothing to mark where the trap was located. Slowly he would lift the trap. It was not possible to estimate the contents because the swimming fish exerted no weight until the enclosure reached the surface. For me, opening the trap was like opening a present. If it held a large number of fish, a great fluttering noise would break the silence as the trap came out of the water. Some of the traps had only scrap fish, while others might have as much as twenty-five pounds of bream. Once, when Dad lifted a trap loaded with speckled perch, he winked at me and whispered, "It's like dippin' up money."

There are always some who do not believe any knowledge is essential to catch fish. They often fish with hooks bigger than the fish's mouth and use unappetizing bait. When they don't catch any fish immediately, they are sure someone else caught them all. Who better to blame than the commercial fishermen? It is only natural to think that if there were no commercial fishing, there would be more fish for the sportsman. This is not necessarily true. The scrap fish are never caught on sports tackle, so there is no way of knowing how many of these predators feed on the eggs of edible varieties. Even the State has come to realize the need for limited commercial fishing to keep shad, suckers, and other species of scrap fish from dominating the lakes. Still, all the Creek fishermen agreed that as the number of sport fishermen increased there would be more pressure on the State to curtail trapping, even though at that time a sportsman could catch all he could use with only a little time and skill. Right or wrong, that premise was the primary reason for keeping trap fishing, or anything connected with fishing, at a low profile at the Creek—that and the fundamental Cracker belief that what people don't know about your business won't hurt you.

Long before my family came to Cross Creek, probably when the first two fishermen put fish traps in the lake, it was decided by the community that each Creek family would have an exclusive territory for trapping fish. In a place that prided itself on personal freedom this rule served the cause of peaceful coexistence through all the years before and after I was born. Without the territories, fishermen would have put all their traps in the same place or mistakenly fished their neighbors' traps.

Every family who moved to the Creek could ask for a territory. It was theirs just as if they were property owners. There was no deed registered in the courthouse, but the people at the Creek would defend the right of ownership of fishing territories as they would their homes. A family's territory in Orange or Lochloosa Lake was a source of security and pride. Anyone could put out a cat line or fish with a pole anywhere, and naturally sport fishermen were welcome, but no one other than the territory's owner was allowed to place or fish a trap in that area. Some territories had been in the same families for three or four generations. Others changed hands from time to time as families moved to and from the Creek. On the few occasions when there was no vacant territory for a new family, a community meeting was called on the Bridge and each family agreed to reduce the size of its territory to make room. The effect was similar to slicing the pie into slightly smaller pieces when company came.

While the territories were as near the same size and productive capability as the community could divide them, they were not equal. Some families worked like good farmers to improve their territories. They moved traps around to catch the scrap fish when the eatable fish weren't running, in the same way a good farmer pulls the weeds from his field.

🌿 My dad's fish business was not a business in the normal sense of the word. It was a Tom-Glisson, Cross-Creek-style business. We built huge fish iceboxes of cypress boards, the outer box six inches larger than the inner. Sawdust insulated the area between them. The interior of the smaller box was lined with galvanized tin. The entire box held a thousand pounds of fish, including ice to preserve them until the trucks from Georgia came to pick them up. We hauled three finished boxes to the landing at the back of our property and set them beneath a live oak. Dad confiscated Mamma's three washtubs (she immediately bought new ones) and punched drain holes in the bottoms; the fishermen used these to carry their fish from the boats to the iceboxes. He hung a pair of cotton balance scales from a limb of a tree and as the finishing touch nailed a gallon syrup bucket to the trunk. In the bucket he put little receipt books that the dime store sold two for a nickel and wrote the name of each fisherman on his own individual book. He called the bucket "the office."

The fishermen would weigh their fish and ice them in one of the big boxes. Then they would write the number of pounds and the date of their catch in their ticket book and keep the carbon copy. Dad said he trusted all the fishermen at the Creek, and that trust proved to be well-founded. In all the years that followed he was never short. Mamma picked up cash to pay the fishermen when she went to town for supplies. On Saturday mornings they gathered at our house, a festive occasion for me, and she paid them out of a little wood Kraft cheese box—*her* office—where she kept her copies of the tickets and cash.

The wholesale truckers bought their fish from the iceboxes, which meant they had to take the fish out of the box, shake the ice off, and reweigh them. This system meant Dad did not have to touch the fish. However, much to my chagrin, he told the truckers, "My boy will be glad to help you weigh out and load." He also told the truckers he would prefer them to come for the fish at night because, as he put it, "If everybody knows your business, you won't have any very long."

Later, when his business was secure, he enlisted the help of one of the fishermen at the Creek and built a fish house using cabbage palmetto logs. I asked why he did not pour a cement floor and make the building big enough to have the scales inside. He said, "Son, don't advertise your successes. The only thing you'll get for it is competition."

With the exception of a homemade wheelbarrow built to haul fish from the boats, the log house was the last improvement he made to his fish business during its twenty-five years and hundreds of thousands of pounds of fish bought and sold. It brought him a substantial income and left him free to look for "another place to dig."

🌿 Sometime in the late 1930s the local game wardens came around and said they were being ordered to cut down on trapping and maybe

stop it all together. This of course changed the carefree way we had traditionally trapped. Although we never fished the traps when a strange boat was in the vicinity, apart from that we fished any time of the day we chose.

An elaborate set of rules for the interaction between the local fishermen and game wardens had developed over the years. One of these rules was for the definition of a "fair catch": The warden had to physically tag the fisherman in the act of either fishing or escaping.

Two new and overzealous wardens, incapable of making a fair catch, claimed to have seen through field glasses two teenage boys fishing a trap. They were fishing because their father was too ill to fish. The wardens then violated all the unwritten codes that existed between game wardens and fishermen. They made the boys go to town with them with their old rusty fish trap tied to the radiator and marched them into the judge's office as if they were a couple of desperadoes.

The judge was so enraged by the wardens' behavior that he ordered them to take the two brothers home with the traps and apologize to their family. The mother, who had been worried when the boys did not return from the lake, turned on the wardens with such fury that they left in full retreat and were not seen on the lakes again.

While the game department increased the pressure to catch the trap fishermen, the fishermen polished their skill and equipment in order to elude them. They fished at night or when the weather was bad, and they fished with pole and line in their territories for awhile before they hauled up their traps, to make sure a warden hadn't hidden in a tussock. The boats underwent a few modifications. Lids were removed from the live wells to make it easy to scrape the fish out with a paddle and reduce the boat's weight, making the boat faster in a chase. (It was also hard to accuse a man of fishing traps if he had no fish.) Boats with sides higher than the bonnets and grass growing in the lake were cut down to make them less visible. My dad and Bernie Bass often fished their adjoining territories at the same time so one could warn the other of suspicious noises or changes in their territories. Dad and Bernie were developing a problem neither could avoid. They had never been tagged. Their reputation for continuous trap fishing while eluding the wardens was becoming legendary among the fishermen. Nothing could have caused the wardens to try harder to catch them.

❦ Around 1937 one of the wardens came to the fish house to collect license fees for the coming year. He called Dad aside and said, "Tom, I don't know if you know it, but a couple of politicians were fishing in your territory and said they couldn't get a hook in the water without hooking a trap. They moved down south, apparently in Bernie Bass's territory, and said the bottom there was covered with traps too. The way I heard it, they told my boss that you and your friend Bernie have got enough chicken wire in Orange Lake to fence it." He paused. "They bragged they caught three times the bag limit."

Dad laughed. "Like hell they caught them fish. They stole 'em out of six of my traps. Then they mashed the traps flat and threw 'em across the water. I found 'em by probing the distance a man could throw a trap."

The warden said, "They want to make something political so they are putting the pressure on all the way to Tallahassee. The boss up there ain't against you people out here but his job is political, and he's got to do something when the pressure is on. They want to get you because you ain't never been tagged and because you buy the fish the other trappers catch."

In the months that followed, the wardens seldom came on the lake. Dad said he would feel better if they were probing around the way they normally did. He wanted Bernie to be careful. "They are bidin' their time. They'll be here when they think we least expect them."

The Bass and Glisson territories were at their peak productive level; fish were spawning there in greater quantities than in other areas of the lake. When fish are on the bed it is good news to all fishermen. From the first quarter of the moon to the full moon, from April to the end of July, bluegills followed by shellcrackers bedded in the clear-water bonnets. We located the beds by the odor first. Then we looked for what we called "bonnets knocking"—fish in high concentrations were forced to bump into the stems of the bonnets, making the leaves shake above the surface. The final positive proof that you were over an active bed of fish was the presence of fine, white, hairlike roots rising to the surface, brushed from the bottom of the lake where fish fanned out places to lay their eggs.

When the word went out that the bream were on the bed in the Glisson and Bass territories, the inhabitants of Cross Creek all gathered at the beds by sunup with cane poles and bonnet worms, there to enjoy the fishing and reap the rewards of an annual festive ritual. This was a family affair; young'uns five years old could pull the fat bluegills into the boats. The old and young women, who seldom went on the lake, were all there wearing large straw hats to shield their skin from the summer sun. Mothers nursed their babies and caught fish at the same time. There was friendly joking when a small fish was caught and a congratulatory cheer when an unusually big one was pulled in, especially when the fisherman was a little young'un.

Dad was proud that his territory had the best beds on the lake, because it implied he fished it efficiently. Although he enjoyed having everyone fish there, success brought its disadvantages. He could not put his traps in the middle of the beds because the folks fishing with poles and lines would hook into them, then either break the line or pull the trap to the surface to unhook it. This caused the fish to stop biting for a few minutes. In addition, we never fished traps when other families were around, so all our traps had to be fished late in the afternoon and at night.

The wardens kept a low profile through the summer. Dad said he hoped some political change had caused them to leave the fishermen alone, but his gut feeling was that they were waiting for the fishermen to lower their guard.

I will never forget the night that soft voices roused me from a deep sleep. I rolled over and saw a thin line of light shining beneath my bedroom door from the living room. I opened the door and saw Bernie Bass looking as if something was wrong. My mamma was sitting in the stuffed chair nearest my bedroom door. When she looked in my direction, I realized I was not wearing the pajama top she had forbidden me to sleep without. I was trying to retreat back into my room when she said, her voice breaking, "You poor thing—sleeping and your daddy probably laying out there on the bottom of Orange Lake." She reached out and hugged me with tears flowing down her cheeks. I looked at my sister, who had been crying, and then at my older brother sitting in the dining room, looking blankly at the floor. I turned to my friend Bernie. His clothes were wet. "What's happening?" I asked.

He answered as if it pained him to speak, "J.T., your daddy is lost on the lake. Me and your brother went back out there about two-thirty and we can't find him." He shuffled his feet and looked away. "When it gets daylight all the men from the Creek and some from Island Grove and Citra is gettin' up a search party to look for him."

Bernie added without expression, "Some of the Townsends are out there now. I come back in to organize the search when it gets daylight."

I was suddenly angry. "Why didn't somebody wake me up? I would have gone and found him myself."

My mamma said, "J.T., it wouldn't have done any good. We didn't worry until after one o'clock when he still wasn't home."

I walked outdoors, trying to grasp the situation, and was surprised to see cars parked out by the garage. A pickup coming from the direction of Island Grove illuminated several men milling around in the darkness. I sat down on the steps and waited.

🌿 The previous afternoon my dad had refused my request when I asked to go out on the lake with him, saying Carlton was going to help and he would be out too late for me to be up on a school night. He had finished fishing his traps about ten o'clock and sat waiting for Bernie to pass through our territory on his way home. Bernie pulled his boat alongside Dad and Carlton and joked quietly about Dad having his son chauffeur the boat around while he fished. They discussed the possibility of there being wardens on the lake, and both agreed it was unlikely, although they had been uncomfortable about a woods fire burning behind Seventeen Sisters, because the wardens had used woods fires to silhouette fishermen in the past. Dad asked Bernie if he would mind taking my brother and the fish in with him because Carlton had some work to do the following day. Bernie said, "I'll be glad to have him any time, so long as he is willing to help paddle." They sacked Dad's fish in burlap bags and transferred them to Bernie's boat. Carlton stepped into the back, and the two disappeared into the darkness.

Dad went about his task of replacing his traps, thinking it was a shame a man couldn't whistle because of the wardens. The solitude of the lake at night was particularly pleasant. The sky was slightly overcast, obliterating some of the stars and making it difficult to be sure of his usual pinpoint locations. A light wind was increasing as he replaced the last trap, and for the second time since dark a great blue heron squawked along the shore tussocks. One occasionally squawked because an alligator was trying to grab it as an extra meal, but it was unusual for this to happen twice. Dad dismissed it as an oddity and bailed the water that had collected during the night from the bottom of the boat.

Several weeks before, he had treated himself and bought one of the new single-cylinder outboards from Western Auto to use when he went bream fishing. The little two-horsepower kicker lay under the rear seat of his boat. He never intended to use it when he was doing anything with his traps because the noise could be heard for a mile. However, since he had finished with all the traps and the wind was coming from the direction of the Creek, he thought for one time only he would enjoy the luxury of riding home. He fastened the motor to the stern of the boat, adjusted the throttle, and pulled the starting rope. The little engine ran for two or three seconds and stopped. He had forgotten to turn on the gas. Before he could attempt to restart it, a giant outboard roared to life in the direction of the mouth of the creek. Then two boats came from the area where the blue heron had squawked earlier and still another from the direction of Seventeen Sisters.

Game wardens. *Lots* of game wardens.

He ripped the little kicker off the back of the boat and pushed it under the seat, then made his way to the front, keeping low. Brilliant lights were sweeping in every direction from the wardens' boats. Dad realized they did not know exactly where he was. He knelt in the bow and paddled deeper into the bonnet patch. The lights swept over him while three of the boats ran up and down between him and the shore; the fourth boat began to systematically circle the bonnets. It was no time to figure why or how four boats with game wardens were trying to tag a single trap fisherman, but one thing was sure—they weren't local wardens. It was the boss from Tallahassee that the local warden had warned Dad of. They didn't care about fair catches. They would tag him and then probe until they found a trap and swear they had seen him fishing it.

Dad muttered, "Okay, Mr. Big Shot, you may get me but it ain't going to be as easy as you think. All I want is for you to make one mistake and I'll be gone."

The boat searching the bonnet patches was concentrating its light on three or four tussocks and passed over his low-sided boat tucked in the bonnets. It was running too fast to search thoroughly. One of the boats ran alongside a warden guarding the shore tussocks and signaled him to join the search in the area where Dad had been moving his traps. They were confident that if they kept him cut off from shore it would be only a matter of searching the bonnets and tussocks until they had him tagged. They also assumed he would use the little motor when he made a break for shore. The warden in another of the boats running along the shore mistakenly thought the lead boat meant for him also to join the search and charged out into the open water.

Within minutes boats were running in every direction. Dad thought there would be one chance in a thousand for him to make it to the shore tussocks and escape across the marsh. The last thing anyone would expect him to do would be go toward the center of the lake. And that is what he decided to do.

The boat that appeared to be the lead boat stopped a hundred and fifty yards north of the place where Dad had paddled into the bonnets. One of the wardens was holding his searchlight on his partner, who was standing on the bow waving to the other boats to come alongside. Dad thought this was probably his best chance to make a run for it. Staying low, he paddled silently the length of the bonnets and turned abruptly out toward the center of the lake. After paddling across twenty-five yards of open water, he reached the thin strip of grass that surrounds the deep center of the lake, the area we called "clear water." Beyond the grass there was open water for seventeen miles from north to south and four or five miles across to the other side of the lake.

Behind him all four of the boats had cut off their motors. The warden in charge was raising hell. He shouted to the others, "Dammit! He's right here in some of these bonnets. He can't get away as long as we got him cut off from shore. He may have sunk his boat, so go through the damn bonnets until you find him. Now get it done!" One of the lights passed right over Dad as the three motors recranked and moved out. The warden directing the operation was probably not paying any attention, because he swept on in a different direction.

Dad slipped his little boat thirty, then fifty, yards out, moving directly toward the center of the lake. He knew that every foot he covered would make it harder for the wardens' lights to reach him. The problem was, eventually it would occur to someone that he was running toward the center of the lake. In the meantime, all Dad wanted was more distance. One thing was sure, these were not local wardens. They were running too fast and seemed to have no system for searching thoroughly. Over his shoulder he saw they had spread their search area farther up and down their side of the lake.

Suddenly, a new hazard loomed. Directly in front of Dad's boat thousands of coots and ducks were roosting on the water. If they flew up it would be like sending up a flare saying, "Here he is." To turn back was the same as giving up. Dad let the little boat slow until it was moving half as fast as a man could walk and murmured under his breath, "You fellers let me through, and I'll never eat one of you little rascals again." The waterfowl swam to the left and right, opening a narrow corridor for him. It was a nerve-wrenching situation to paddle slowly, trying to escape boats moving twenty miles an hour, knowing that if one of the ducks panicked, a thousand would take to the air in a clamorous roar of wings and quacking. The coots complained, threatening with a staccato clucking sound as they reluctantly moved aside.

One of the wardens made a run along the clear-water grass, pointing the boat lights back in the direction of the shore. Dad continued to ease through the ducks; he was still only two hundred yards out in clear water and had covered a mere fifty yards in the last ten minutes. One of the boats flashed its lights out toward the open water. Dad slipped down low in the boat. They were coming directly toward the open water, pointing the light off to his right. Dad thought, *The big man has figured out what I did and I won't stand a chance in torment out here.* He sat waiting for the light to pick him out of the darkness.

As soon as the lights hit the clear-water grass, ten thousand ducks took to the air, soaking Dad in a deluge of water. Coots were running on the surface, kicking to attain flight, and ducks flapped their wings against the water, pushing their bodies up and free to fly. Dad looked back into a cloud of ducks and droplets of water caught in the breeze. One of the wardens yelled to his partner, "There ain't no way he come out here with all these ducks." The wardens turned back toward the Glisson territory.

My father moved back onto the seat and continued paddling toward the other side of the lake. After all the effort they had put into catching him, the wardens would tag him anyplace they found him, claiming they had never lost sight of him since he fished the last trap. He wanted to get away clean. It was a matter of pride.

The wardens' motors continued to drone along the east shore of the lake, and on one occasion one of them circled about a mile out into clear water. By that time Dad was nearing the grass along the west shore.

He whistled through his teeth as he made his way to shore: "The moon shines bright on pretty Red Wing. . . ." Once he found a place he could get out without wading, he sunk his boat with the little motor

and covered it with water lettuce. There was no reason to take a chance; as frustrated as the wardens were, they would take the boat just to make him ask to get it back. And he didn't want to give them the satisfaction of knowing how he got away.

Dad didn't know it but he had landed at Samson Point. He found a narrow road running north and west and followed it, hoping it would lead to the Dixie Highway and a friend's home near Boardman. Once there he could ask his friend to drive him around the lake and back home. He was passing a packing shed beside the Atlantic Coast Line Railroad tracks when a Model-A came rumbling down the road toward him. He was still determined to get home without being seen, so he stepped behind the railroad platform. Instead of passing, the car pulled up parallel to the loading platform and stopped. The passengers climbed out, jumped up on the platform, and sat with their legs hanging over the edge. Dad stepped under the four-foot high platform and hunkered, waiting to see if he might approach them for a ride home.

He didn't have to wait long. One of the men said, "This has got to be the most damn foolish deal I ever heard of. Counting us, the boss has thirteen men down here to catch one trap fisherman. Eight on the lake plus six of us supposed to tag him on the hill if he gets by them."

The other said, "I hope he gets away. The man from Tallahassee calls hisself showin' us ignorant local wardens how to do our job."

Listening, Dad learned they were from up past Columbia County and had been ordered down for the bag chase on short notice. The chief had slipped the four boats on the lake through an orange grove on the south end of the lake before daylight and stayed hidden all day. The two wardens on the platform had been drinking beer in a local joint until it closed, agreeing they would not be lying about not seeing anybody fishing traps, if they hadn't been on the lakes. After not hearing the outboards for an hour they decided to go home, assuming the wardens on the lake had caught the man or had given up. Dad walked in the direction of his friend's house.

❦ I sat on our front steps contemplating the possibilities. Death was so strange to me. I went back in the house and put on my britches and a warm shirt, then to the kitchen and filled my pocket with biscuit pudding. I decided I was going with Bernie. If anybody could find Dad, Bernie could. Outside, I was surprised to see daylight breaking. There were more men out in front of the garage than I had ever seen gathered at the Creek. Bernie was drawing a map of Orange Lake in the sand to lay out the search plan. A car motored up behind them and stopped in the road. I presumed it was some other men who had heard Dad was lost on the lake and had come to join the search.

Dad stepped out of the car on the passenger side and walked toward the gathering of men. Everyone looked at him as if he was a ghost. "Howdy fellows," he said, "it's awful good to see y'all got up so early to come out here to look for me. At least that's what I assume caused you to come, or did you all plan to have a hangin'?"

They all laughed in a burst of relief. Fred Tompkins from Citra said, "Looking for you beat the hell out of what I had planned to do."

Dad invited everyone to breakfast, but they said if they weren't going to have a good time on the lake they would go to their usual work. Dad thanked them and nodded to Bernie to come in.

I ran ahead shouting, "Dad's home!"

He told the story of what had happened while Mamma fixed an unusually fine breakfast. When he was finished eating, he leaned his chair on its back legs. "If the wind had not been out of the east y'all would have heard all them motors and known there was a chase. Pearlee, I would have let them tag me if I had known you were going to be so worried."

She turned and shook her dishcloth in his direction. "If you had, I would never speak to you again."

In the afternoon Carlton and Bernie crossed the lake and brought the boat and the little kicker home. I walked with my dad down to the Bridge after sunset asking questions about the details of the chase, ending with, "Why does life have to be so complicated?"

He thought for a minute. "Most everything is chased by something. Bugs are chased by frogs, and frogs are chased by fish, and gators chase fish, and finally gators ain't got nothing to chase but each other. I suppose people are the same way."

Eleven. Fishermen and Game Wardens

WE DIDN'T play cowboys-and-Indians at Cross Creek. We played fishermen-and-game-wardens—our own real-life drama that had grown out of the necessity to protect one of the ways we made our living, commercial fishing. My dad bought all the fish caught by Cross Creek fishermen and wholesaled them to companies that trucked them to Georgia.

It's ironic that the Cross Creek fishermen started the whole thing when they asked the State to regulate commercial fishing on Orange and Lochloosa lakes. In the early 1900s, outsiders from the east coast came through the middle of the state, fishing the larger lakes with huge salt-water nets capable of destroying the Creek's main source of food and income. In a move they later regretted, some Crackers petitioned their local legislators to regulate seining by outsiders; of course they never expected the laws to affect their own trapping and seining. Thirty years later, the old fishermen said that for a short time the self-imposed regulations served their intended purpose. However, the State gradually came to view the regulatory laws as existing specifically to restrain all commercial fishing, including local trapping or seining. The difference in the Crackers' and the State's interpretation of the regulations was the beginning of a row that would last half a century. When I was growing up, the old Crackers were in agreement on the circumstances that had ultimately led to the "game." Everyone swore their family had not been a part of instigating any government involvement in local affairs.

The State recruited as wardens men from the surrounding area who were respected and familiar with the local ways. They even hired some men who had fished traps and seined for a living. A competition was created between honorable men who shared the same standards and goals, the perfect ingredients for a great rivalry. A Cracker's primary measure of a man's honor was his word. He would suffer any loss rather than renege on a verbal commitment, even if it was with the government. Among the Crackers there were only two classes of men, those whose word was "good as gold" and "white trash" whose word wasn't "worth a damn."

The object of the game for the fishermen was to catch enough fish to make a living while eluding the wardens. The goal of the wardens was to catch enough fishermen to retain their jobs. Over the years rules were made and agreed on by both sides. One of the basic rules required the warden to actually put his hand on a fisherman while he was fishing or during the time he was trying to escape. We called it getting "tagged" (I never heard the word "arrest" used by either side). Only if a man was tagged properly was it considered a "fair catch."

When, in the opinion of the fishermen, it was not a fair catch, the fishermen asked Sigsbee Scruggs, a Gainesville attorney and champion of the Creek people, to defend them. Because of his loyalty to the Creek folks, his knowledge of the law, and his uncommon powers of persuasion, he never lost a case. Nevertheless it was to the credit of both sides that they generally conducted themselves like good sportsmen with only an occasional loss of dignity and self-control during the competition. As the years passed, the rivalry became a fundamental part of our culture.

The last time I visited Mr. Gillis, one of the first fishermen I ever seined with, he was old and ill. We talked of the old days when we pulled seines on the lakes. Eventually we both drifted into our individual memories and sat silent. When he spoke again, it was like he was changing the subject. "A man is mighty lucky to get a chance to make his living fishing, and then to top it all, ducking and dodging them game wardens was the most fun I had in my whole life," he said. I agreed.

My favorite stories when I was a child were about "chases," the attempts made by the game wardens to catch the fishermen. I do not remember a single time when the men stood around talking on the Bridge that someone didn't tell some story about a chase on the lakes. To me these were the ultimate adventures, narrow escapes as a result of a brilliant maneuver by a fisherman, or tales of the honor or persistence of a particular warden. There were heroes and villains on both sides, and the good guys (usually the fishermen) always won.

I dreamed of the day when I would participate in the Creek's most prestigious sport, and as with most things I wanted to do, obstacles arose. The first hurdle was the fishermen. Tradition demanded that I wait until they asked me to be a part of a pull. With all due respect for tradition, I was certain that if my dad passed the word implying his approval, my good buddies the fishermen would ask me to help.

Getting my dad's approval meant overcoming an even more formidable problem—my mamma. The first time I suggested I wanted to help pull a seine, she recited a long list of objections. They began with "You're too young" and moved on to "A person has to be a fool to want to stay out all night in the mosquitoes and weather," ending with "You should be interested in your education, rather than pulling a net on the lake." Her weakest point was one that I had heard the fishermen discuss many times. She approached it with a tactic designed to prevent my dad allying with me: "Even though pulling a seine is considered all right here, seining is considered illegal by outsiders." I seized the opportunity to argue that point, implying that my answer was original: "If Jesus walked on the water to help Saint Peter pull his net and even told him where to lay it out, rules made by some outsider ain't worth talking about." I was so proud of my ready answer I became overconfident: "I would willingly bet a quarter that when Jesus comes back he would be glad to help us pull a seine on Lochloosa."

With Mamma, gambling was a sin. "Now you are betting on Jesus!" she exclaimed. I was forced to drop my campaign for more than a week. When it seemed safe I slowly renewed the pressure but was careful not to challenge Mamma on holy ground.

While I waited for Mamma to cool down I visited the most respected seiner at the Creek, Mr. Story, at his camp on the west side of Lochloosa, across the lake from Burnt Island. Mr. Story was a dapper old man who sported a handlebar mustache and lived in a camp that had a real touch of class. Although it had a dirt floor and was made of tar paper, it was immaculately clean and neat. Everyone called him Mr. Story, as if Mister was his first name. No one asked where he came from, and he never said. While we ate baked sweet potatoes and squirrels and rice cooked on his open campfire, I told him I wanted to help pull a seine. With the ever-present twinkle in his eyes he said, "I just might speak to your dad about that when the time is right."

My persistence was finally rewarded. Dad agreed to let me be a "sitter," the least prestigious task involved with seining. It consisted of sitting and keeping watch at one of the places where the wardens might launch their boats and gain access to the lake. The job, in my opinion, was as unrelated to actual seining as bee tree hunting was to shooting ducks.

The wardens' job was not easy. There were only a few places on the lake where they could launch their boats. In addition, everyone at Cross Creek (with the possible exception of Mrs. Rawlings, who didn't know what was going on) felt it was their civic duty to sound the alarm (two shots fired in the air one minute apart) if they discovered the wardens anywhere in the area.

I would sit hidden in a boat near the mouth of the Creek, watching for wardens who by some devious maneuver might have slipped past the vigilant families around the Creek. Mr. Story told me, "All you need is your eyes, your ears, and your dad's old twelve-gauge to give the signal." From a distance of three miles the signal would give the pullers time to save the net by pulling it from the water. Even though sitters had been responsible for saving nets and it was pleasant listening to the night sounds while the stars drifted toward the horizon in the west, I wanted to be near the action. I also knew the fishermen had a second watchman out in the lake between me and the place they were pulling the seine. I sat there all night three or four times, and no one came past. It seemed logical that if I sat without complaining the fishermen would eventually recognize my maturity and dependability.

My first adventure in the real world of fishermen-and-game-wardens came unexpectedly in late November of my thirteenth year. It began with a soft whisper outside my bedroom window, "Wake up, J.T., we're fixin' to pull tonight. And you're gonna help us." I was wide awake in a second. My folks were in the next room, and I was sure they had heard. I waited, but Mamma didn't say anything. I thought, *Hallelujah! Tonight is the night!* and rolled out of bed. I managed to get my legs in my britches, grabbed my shirt and shoes, and headed out of the house.

My dad stood blocking the door to the front porch. "Hold on, son. You can go with them, and you can be a watchman on the hill or the lake, but don't get near the seine. You know if you are less than twenty-five yards from the seine the wardens can tag you the same as if you were pulling."

I said, "Yes, sir," and tried to squeeze past him.

He stopped me a second time. "And another thing, if the wardens come, don't hesitate to put your behind in high gear and get the hell out of there."

I said, "Yes, sir," again and ran by him and out the front door.

Mr. Story was waiting at the gate. He whispered, "Put your clothes on, boy, the skeeters will eat you 'fore you get on the lake."

I fell in behind him, still dressing myself, relieved to be getting farther from our house and the possibility of my folks changing their minds. We crossed the road and cut through the tangerine grove, angling toward the old Slater place. I stopped and tied one shoe, then rushed ahead catching up, then stopped and tied the other. I decided I would leave my shirttail out, since the only reason I ever put it in was because Mamma and my sister Marjorie complained if I didn't.

Fortunately, my eyes were adjusted to the darkness because I had not taken the time to light a lamp. I looked up. The November sky was clear, and stars flickered through the openings between the rows of trees. I knew it was about ten o'clock. We would have two hours before the moon would rise and make it easy for the wardens to see us crossing the open water in Lochloosa to the seine hauls along Burnt Island. Although the weather was unseasonably warm, I shivered with excitement. I could not imagine anything that could happen during the rest of my life that would be as important as what we were about to do.

There is no sport that equals fishermen-and-game-wardens for excitement and plain fun. The game was not that simple; it required skill, daring, and an instinct for the backwoods. To be a winner necessitated a good game plan for offense and defense. We played the game in two different ways: trap fishing, which was generally one-on-one, and seining, which required several fishermen working as a team to pull a net in a circle and as many wardens as the Game Department could afford.

By mutual agreement the Creek families had established their own rules for conserving the resources of the lakes and held to the notion that Cross Creek's isolation excluded it from the laws that applied to the rest of the state. The Creek fishermen only used hand-pulled shallow-water nets, which only worked in specific places in the lakes, called seine hauls. The shallow-water take-up restricted the hauls to three or four acres along the shore that were clear of snags and water plants. In addition, it was necessary that the lake bottom be smooth to allow the net with its weighted lead line to drag across the bottom and prevent the fish from escaping beneath. There were only ten such places in Lochloosa and four or five in Orange Lake. The area of the lakes that could be fished with a seine was a minute portion of the total fishing territory.

Ahead of me, Mr. Story moved like a shadow. I was astounded by his ability to move so fast on his relatively short legs. I remember him saying, "A feller can't ever afford to get excited 'cause that's when you'll make a mistake, for shore." I was excited, and I didn't want to make any mistakes. At that moment the worst thing I could do would be to make some unnecessary noise and consequently lose face as a woodsman. I tried to concentrate on walking without making a sound.

When we were little young'uns we practiced moving through the woods at night. We learned to avoid stepping on sticks that might snap or leaves that made a crunching sound. The older boys told us, "Keep your feet close to the ground. Place each step as if you were trying to slip your toes under a rug."

We came to the north edge of the grove where it joined the hammock and turned east on the sand rut road passing the old Slater place. The pungent smell of hickories, gums, and magnolias floated in the night air. The sand rut road led us past Bernie Bass's hammock house and ended at the edge of the small clearing.

Mr. Story stopped abruptly. I copied his stance. We stood like two bird dogs on a point, silent.

A voice barely audible came out of the darkness. "Who you got with ya?"

"It's J.T. He's gonna help as a watchman."

I recognized the voice: C.J. Calton, Monk's brother. He was about seventeen and strong as any one at the Creek, except maybe Bernie or my dad. C.J. had earned adult status by demonstrating his willingness to work and his acute sense of responsibility. He still retained the carefree spirit of youth, though, and was a champion of the local young'uns. Tonight, as usual, he was shirtless and barefoot. He said softly, "We best get on. The others is already at the net."

We turned northeast and walked directly into the hammock. It was dark as a coffin. I felt comfortable walking between my two friends. My mind wandered. Wouldn't it be great if I could see in the dark like an owl or a wildcat? I could impress everyone by seeing the game wardens coming before they could see us. Suddenly I stepped on a dry palmetto stem. It cracked like a rifle shot. Both men froze in their tracks. I held my breath, expecting to be sent home, branded too young to keep my mind on such serious business. As suddenly as they had stopped, they moved off again. I was relieved, though chastened by their silent reprimand.

We made our way through the hammock to the edge of Right Arm Prairie. The spot they had chosen was perfect for racking and storing the net: a secluded clearing under a huge live oak surrounded on three sides by a six-foot wall of scrub palmettos and only a short distance across the marsh to the open water of Lochloosa. The Gillises and Charley Fields, boating the seine onto the pullboat, said howdy without stopping. Mr. Story assumed command. "J.T., you and C.J. get the water out of the watch boat. Y'all dump it—if you use the bail cup you'll make too much racket." He added, "Sop out the bottom with moss, 'cause some of you is gonna have to sit on it." I couldn't imagine why we would sit on the bottom of the boat, but did as I was told.

In the dark the seiners looked like animated black silhouettes moving efficiently about the job at hand without a sound. I thought the silence was the way it would be if a person was deaf. C.J. brought armloads of Spanish moss from where it had been gathered and piled. He placed it on the rear of an empty cypress boat until the size of the pile was even with the net piled on the stern of the pullboat. With a searchlight the two boats would look the same until a warden was only a few feet away. I knew from the stories I had heard that this was a decoy boat.

When everything was done, the fishermen gathered around Mr. Story. They all hunkered, took out their tobacco, and began to roll cigarettes, with the exception of me and Mr. Story. He filled his crooked-stem pipe with Prince Albert tobacco, using slow, exact movements as if he were following some ancient ritual. To this day I have never been able to hunker without rolling backwards onto my butt, and though I smoked for many years I could not learn to make a cigarette without the tobacco falling out of the flimsy paper, either onto the ground or, worse, sliding back into my mouth when I tried to light it. I knelt and sat back on my heels.

They lit their smokes by scratching their thumbnails across the head of a kitchen match cupped in the palm of their hands. The method concealed the flash and the subsequent flame. The only light came when they actually lit their cigarettes and the orange glow of the match illuminated their faces for an instant. The effect of watching them light up was comparable to flipping the pages in a family album. It was kind of like seeing the men in a different way for the first time.

They had two characteristics in common: they were good friendly men, and their eyes all glittered with the excitement and anticipation of schoolboys about to do something devilish.

Mr. Story outlined his plan for the night's pull. "We'll be using three boats—the seine boat, I'll paddle it to the haul, and the fish boat—hopefully we'll get enough fish to need it—and the watch boat." He gestured toward the lake. "I sent Winton on ahead in it, two or three hours ago. He'll probe around acting like he is gonna fish some traps. Winton'll be the watchman out in the lake. If they is wardens on the lake he may spot 'em before we get out there." He puffed on his pipe and continued. "Mr. Gillis, you'll paddle the decoy boat. J.T., you and C.J. and Charley go with him. You'll have to lay on the bottom of the boat, so the wardens can't see more than one man in it. They'll know we wouldn't take a chance on more than one of us gettin' caught." He chuckled, "Ol' Bud Skinner pulled with me before he took the warden job. He can look at the decoy boat and tell if it is settin' low enough in the water for the weight of a dry seine. Y'all have to make up the difference between moss and a net with a lead line and corks."

Mr. Story obviously was enjoying the mental picture of the unsuspecting wardens rushing out of their hiding places and catching a boat loaded with nothing but moss and four Cracker witnesses to tell how foolish they looked. "It'd be a good'un on Skinner and worth a night's fishing if he was to catch our decoy boat with you fellers all layin' in it." All of us jabbed each other with our elbows and stifled a good laugh, imagining such a situation.

The big moment arrived. Mr. Story rose and said, "All right, fellers, let's go seinin'. Everybody do his job, and maybe we'll all be rich in the mornin'."

We waded out, pulling the decoy boat (later to be the fish boat) into deeper water before getting in. After several attempts to squeeze all three of us in the bottom we gave up and let Charley sit propped up against the moss piled three feet above the back of the boat. He pulled strands of it up and over his shoulders and alongside his face to conceal his silhouette. C.J. and I assumed fetal positions in the bottom on either side of Charley's legs. I whispered to C.J., "Charley looks like he's got the biggest head of hair in Florida."

C.J. snickered. "He ain't near so ugly when he's all fixed up." Charley jogged both of us with his long legs. I tried to lie on my back and look at the stars, but there was not enough room.

I whispered to C.J., "How long will it take to get there?"

"A hour," he answered. There was nothing to do but lie staring at Charley's tennis shoe and listening to the night sounds of Right Arm Prairie. The combination of millions of insects chirping their high-pitched calls with thousands of rain frogs carrying the middle range, plus an occasional bullfrog singing bass, created a tranquilizing effect. I thought of the similarity to church singing in Island Grove when nobody came to play the piano.

Twenty minutes after leaving the seclusion of the hammock, we came to the line of mud tussocks that separated Right Arm Prairie from the open waters of Lochloosa. Mr. Gillis maneuvered the boat through a concealed passage between the tussocks, stopping just inches before the bow of our boat moved into the open lake. We sat without moving. If the wardens by some brilliant maneuver had gotten onto the lake and guessed the place we would enter, they had to be convinced that we had the real seine for the decoy to work. I was not sure what I wanted. It would be something to tell about if the wardens did come rushing up and caught us with a load of harmless moss. On the other hand, we would miss the pulling.

A long five minutes passed. Mr. Gillis paddled out from the tussocks, then turned north directly toward Burnt Island. If the wardens were waiting and had not seen us first, they would be in the open water. Once the boat came alongside of the island, we could jump out and run, hoping to lose them in the scrub palmettos on shore. I thought of the ridiculousness of what we were doing. We were trying to convince the wardens, who might be home in bed or might have been waiting in the mosquitoes for days, to catch us with a seine that we didn't have. We were pretending to slip by if they were there, yet making sure we didn't so that they would be tricked into catching us and not Mr. Story and his boat with the real seine. I snickered, remembering the new teacher in Hawthorne asking me to share with her and the class what we did at the Creek for recreation.

We made it to the island without seeing or hearing any sign of the wardens. That of course didn't mean they were not on the lake, waiting to choose their time and place to launch an attack. The wardens were Crackers too, and everybody agreed that only a fool would underestimate them. They could be hiding only a few yards from us on the island or a mile or more out on the lake, waiting until the seine and fishermen were in the water and would be more vulnerable. Charley whispered, "The decoy ain't no more use out here," and began to push the moss overboard.

It was a relief to sit up and see something other than Charley's tennis shoes. We passed the south end of the island, then Charley's camp hidden behind the lake cypress with their robes of Spanish moss. Mr. Gillis guided the boat toward the shore along the backside of a haul we called Minner Special. It was the first of three seine hauls on the west shore of Burnt Island. Someone said the haul's name originated because of the small fish usually caught there. Mr. Gillis drawled, "We'll check this place and wait for Mr. Story to catch up." We pulled in near the shore and stepped overboard onto the sand bottom. Mr. Gillis climbed out of the boat uttering the well-earned grunts and groans of a man who had paddled three men and a pile of moss three miles with no help. He gave his paddle to C.J. "You're the best there is at sounding fish. Go out there and see if they is any fish in this haul or not."

I had heard fishermen talk about sounding but had never seen it done. I asked Charley how would he know whether he'd found them or not. Charley said, "Sometimes on a clear calm night, like tonight, you can hear them all the way up here on the shore." We all stood silently, listening. I thought it would be nice if I knew what kind of sound I was listening for.

Behind us Burnt Island was a black space too primitive and wild even for the lightning bugs that brightened the darkness back at the Creek. I guessed it was about eleven-thirty. The lake lay calm, like a smoked glass mirror stretching to infinity. Millions of stars merged with their reflections across an invisible horizon. Charley leaned close to my ear and whispered, "It's like standin' on the edge of the universe and lookin' out into all that is or ever was." I nodded in agreement.

The seine haul was marked by an open space in the lake grass that circled the perimeter of Lochloosa. C.J. paddled to the south side of the haul, then turned and paddled to the opposite end. His paddle didn't make a sound going in or out of the water. He paddled back south a little farther out from shore. I heard nothing except the mosquitoes that had come out to greet us. C.J. came back to where we were standing. At the same time Mr. Story appeared, easing the boat loaded with the seine into the haul and stopping a few feet from shore. C.J. said, "There ain't nothing out there. Absolutely nothing." My spirits sank. I knew that this was what the fishermen called a dry haul. They all agreed that it was foolish to risk laying out the seine without knowing the fish were there.

"Well, let's don't stand around," Mr. Story said. "Let's check out another one." We moved up to Little Stump. C.J. meticulously sounded it; the result was the same as at Minner Special. We shifted to the only remaining haul on the island, the Point, the only one that backed up to a swamp instead of to the island's hammock. C.J. repeated the procedure while we all waited, straining our ears for the sound that would proclaim large concentrations of fish. I heard it simultaneously with the others: brrrrp, brrrrrrp, brrp. "Hot damn! They're out there, that's fer sure," Mr. Story whispered. Everyone was spitting, rubbing their hands together, and jabbing each other with their elbows.

C.J. paddled in. "You fellers hear 'em? There's got to be a ton out there. 'Course it could be scrap fish, shad, or maybe it's the first run of specks, I don't know." Charley said for certain it was speckled perch, "or there would have been scrap fish in the other hauls."

Mr. Story sucked on his cold pipe, unlit since we finished loading the seine. "Let's lay it out, fellers, and find out." He held up his hand. Deadly serious, he said, "Fellers, everybody do your job. We want to catch fish, ruther than get caught. Or have Skinner and his bunch catchin' our rig." He turned to me. "J.T., you take a stand back in the swamp, far enough so you can give the signal in time fer us to hightail it, that is if the wardens come. Winton, you be the lake watchman. Anchor about a hundred fifty yards out in front of the haul."

They all moved out into the lake and I turned to select my stand in the shallow swamp directly behind the haul. I chose a spot back among the cypresses about twenty-five yards from the edge of the lake. Then I changed my mind and moved closer, so I would be sure to see them if they passed by my stand. The problem would be to see them in the event they attempted to slip between me and the men pulling the seine. There was a possibility they would come in parallel to the shore along the outside edge of the swamp. I remembered them catching the Nagel boys by crawling along the shore on their hands and knees like a pack of gators, right past the watchman. The Nagels didn't know the wardens were there until one of them realized there were too many men helping with the net. Wilford was tagged before he could drop the anchor pole.

Selecting a stand was more complicated than I had anticipated. I moved a third time. One thing was in my favor. In the darkness of the swamp it was practically impossible for anyone moving around to avoid stumbling over the sticks and fallen limbs that lay tangled on the bottom. The water was butt-deep, with only twelve or fourteen inches of water above ten or twelve inches of soft muck lying on the sand bottom. The swamp became shallower as it neared the lake, with less muck. Our summer rains had ended in early September, causing the lake to drop five or six inches and exposing a sand bar three to five feet wide separating the swamp and the lake. Out in the haul Mr. Story and C.J. were already laying out the net while Charley held the anchor pole.

My dad often said, "A man that can't make a decision can't be depended on." I obviously was of no value as a watchman if I continued to move about. I settled on a stand ten yards inside the swamp, facing the lake with my back against a sweet bay tree. The sweet bay would obscure my silhouette when the moon came up and give me something to lean on during the four or five hours that would pass before the pull was completed. The choice was a good one, with only one problem. When the fishermen pocketed the fish, they would have the seine close to shore; if I was less than twenty-five yards from the net I could be tagged the same as if I was pulling it. The margin of error would be less than ten yards. If the wardens actually came, I would have to remember not to go closer to the rig. On the plus side, I could see the wardens if they came in along the periphery of the swamp or through it. In a wave of self-confidence I imagined Mr. Story or Mr. Gillis telling my dad, "That boy sure knows what he's doing. Couldn't no man pick a better stand than J.T."

I then remembered my dad saying, "When a feller gets too cocky he usually plays hell." I tried to settle down and do the job I was expected to do. That task immediately proved to be far more difficult than I had imagined.

The infamous Burnt Island mosquitoes had delayed launching their attack until I was forced to stand without moving. Now they moved in for the kill. Once when I visited Mr. Story at his camp, he told me, "Watching is like a man hunting a wild turkey. The one what moves first, loses. You can't see nothing much in the dark except movement. Any warden worth his salt knows once the net is laid out, the fisherman can't pull the circle, pocket the fish, and boat the rig in less than two hours. If the warden's smart, he'll wait and let the watchman get restless and move around enough so the warden knows where he is. Then he kin make his plan to get past, even if it takes a hour to move a few yards. It's a heap better to get bit by skeeters than for everybody to end up gettin' tagged."

After waiting what seemed like a lifetime, finally I was being trusted as the shore watchman. I was determined to endure anything to be a part of the game. When mosquitoes bit me on the face, I blew them away by contorting my mouth and lips so as to direct a puff of air to the spot. I wished I had taken a puff on Mr. Story's old rancid pipe. I could have breathed on them and killed them dead in their tracks. When it became absolutely necessary to remove a spider or a worm, I did it by sliding my hand and arm against my body like a snake until I reached the critter, then I thumped it away. I tried to crush the mosquitoes on my back by scrubbing back and forth against the bay tree. This allowed black ants to crawl from the tree and join the mosquito picnic in progress.

The tree stand also proved to be a bad choice in that the bottom sloped away from the tree, and I had to strain to avoid sliding down deeper into the water. It was amazing that all these factors I was learning about had never been a part of the exciting seining stories. I decided to ask why, if the night ever ended. Considering all the distractions, it was difficult to be sure a warden was not slithering by along with the other things that slither in a swamp.

The last-quarter moon rose in back of me, washing away the cool blue-gray starlight, replacing it with its warm amber glow. The objects around my stand came into clearer focus. Small beams found their way through the trees, creating abstract designs on a thousand textures singular to every Florida swamp.

Past the trunks of the shore cypress, I watched C.J. bring the end of the seine back past the anchor pole, completing the circle that encompassed the fish sounded in the haul. Charley was walking the lead line. Although I had never done it, I knew from all the seining stories that you had to catch your toes in the net an inch or more above the lead-weighted rope sewn along the bottom of the seine and hold it down onto the lake bottom. This prevented crowded fish from escaping beneath the netting as they were herded into the pocket.

Splashing broke the silence that had shrouded the lake since we began the pull. Silver flashes began to erupt on the surface as the circle of netting drew smaller and smaller, forcing the thrashing fish into the pocket.

"Hot damn, we're gonna get a bunch of fish," I thought, "and it's happenin' on the first night I'm in charge of shore watching." I was certain I would be considered a symbol of good luck. I intensified my watch, straining to see or hear anything that moved. Below an audible level I whistled Glenn Miller's current hit, "American Patrol." That tomfoolery ended with a scare that left me short of breath and embarrassed. Something bumped my leg below the water, and I jumped up in an attempt to lift myself out of the water. I thought it was a gator until I realized how short it was and knew it had to be a big cooter (our name for the local soft-shell turtles) trying to swim between my legs. I slipped and went under, head and ears, emerging with my hair and collar full of duckweed and puffing like I had run a mile.

The possibility of having given away my stand was compounded by a peculiar sound coming from the main body of the lake, although it was becoming impossible to hear anything except the fish splashing and churning the surface of the water. After the long hours of silence it sounded loud enough to be heard in Island Grove. Then I not only heard something, I saw it move! During the second that transpired before I could take a deep breath and shout the alarm, I realized what it was. A sow coon was wading along the sandbar at the edge of the lake. I muttered, "Thank you, Lord, thank you!" I would never have lived down shouting the alarm and causing the fishermen to run off like fools into the swamp and hammocks, leaving a net full of fish. No one raised at Cross Creek could live down mistaking a coon for a game warden.

I watched Mr. Story and Mr. Gillis lift the bottom of the pocket up and over the side of the seine boat. They pulled the top side of the pocket up and back, forcing the fluttering fish to the surface, then picked up each fish, dropping the good ones into the boat and crushing the gills of the trash fish before throwing them back into the lake. (Once I had asked Mr. Gillis why they did that. He said, "'Cause you wouldn't throw live weeds back in your garden, would you?" I reckoned not.)

Mr. Gillis sent me into hysterics when I heard him say, "Son of a bitch!!" followed by a splash fifty feet out from the boat. The worst thing next to game wardens that could happen when removing fish from a seine was to pick up a live moccasin. Occasionally a snake would swallow a fish that caused a bulge in its body and kept it from escaping through the net. It would become trapped with the fish and inadvertently picked up by the men clearing the pocket. Mr. Gillis's uncommon profanity left no doubt as to what had happened. Everyone laughed except Mr. Gillis.

It was a wonderful moment. With prosperity always a temporary condition at the Creek, all the families rejoiced when any of the fishermen made a good pull. I believed we were most certainly getting rich. With this haul Mr. Gillis could replace the money his wife had burned up in a mattress. Winton could chase all the girls in the scrub. C.J. could afford to marry Mary Lou. I tried to think of something Mr. Story or Charley would want but could not. The only thing they cared about was living in seclusion and fishing on the lakes. Eventually I decided maybe Charley could buy comfortable pews and donate them to the Island Grove Methodist Church. That would be a knee-slapper if there ever was one.

I tried to get my mind back to the reality of the moment. C.J. was out beyond the men in the seine boat, boating the wing of the net into the decoy boat. The others worked feverishly to boat the fish. A big catch was great, but it increased the time we were vulnerable to attack by the wardens. The tremendous catch would be worth more than the net and seine boat; the fish were more important now. The anxiety was becoming unbearable. I wished I could leave my stand and go out to help but promptly dismissed the thought.

The moon slipped behind a line of clouds moving in from the northwest. For the first time that night a breeze from the east stirred the tops of the trees, moving in soft waves over the swamp. The lake along the shore remained calm, but out farther the wind struck the surface, creating ripples and then waves. In ten minutes clouds covered the moon. The first cold front of the season hid the last stars near the horizon, leaving us in almost total darkness. I struggled to see but decided I could only listen for the wardens. There was one consolation. They would have to stumble and thrash through water along the lakeshore or the swamp without a light, and I would hear them.

Gradually fatigue and the need for sleep descended on me. Bernie had said, "Staying awake is what separates the men from the boys. You can't depend on a feller that can't stay awake when there is a need." I was desperate not to become drowsy. I tried biting my lip and wetting my face with swamp water. As a last resort I was leaning back against the sweet bay tree reasoning that nothing could keep me awake better than a few mean black ants, when all hell broke loose out on the lake. The swamp lit up like the sun in August. The glare out toward the lake was blinding. In a crazy way I thought the lights were making the thunderous noise. They came blaring, shrill, ruthless, like ten sections of the "Orange Blossom Special" all coming across the lake together.

It was outboard motors! Big kickers! *Game wardens!*

Charley, Mr. Gillis, and Mr. Story stood staring at the lights for several seconds. Out beyond them, C.J. was desperately paddling parallel to the shore, allowing the portion of the net he had loaded on the boat earlier to slide back into the water across the lake side of the haul.

Although I originally was convinced there were several boats of wardens, it became obvious there were only two, powered by enormous outboard motors and coming faster than anything I had ever seen on water. The noise and blinding light made it hard to move or think. For some bizarre reason Mr. Story stood in the seine boat waving his arms at C.J. Mr. Gillis and Charley were plowing frantically toward shore looking (as my dad would say) like two wild bulls shot in the butt with birdshot. The pass separating Burnt Island and Allen Point was less than two miles wide. The wardens had paddled to the middle before they cranked their monstrous motors. In seconds they were approaching the haul. In the bedlam I ran to meet Charley and Mr. Gillis. When the seine was all out of the boat, C.J. raced toward shallow water and the shore.

Mr. Story continued to stand in the seine boat, facing the oncoming wardens, looking like one of those granite Confederate soldiers that stand on pedestals in front of southern courthouses. Finally, when the two wardens' boats reached the outside of the haul, Mr. Story jumped over the side.

Like a dream that seems to drag on and on, the situation lost any semblance of reality. I remember Mr. Story's hat floating on the surface in the glaring lights. He didn't come up. Charley and Mr. Gillis ran past me. I was shocked because they were smiling as if they were enjoying the whole predicament. Charley said in his usual calm way, "Come on, J.T., it's time to go."

I yelled at their backs as they disappeared into the swamp. "Mr. Story didn't come up. He's hung in the net! He's gonna drown!"

I looked back at the lake. The noise stopped. Water flew into the air. The two big searchlights mounted on the boats flipped down to create small circles on the water as the boats hit the net, then swung up, flashed across the sky, and came back down, glaring on three men flying through the air, arms and legs everywhere, like rag dolls thrown by a child. They reached the summit of their trajectories and fell like watermelons dropped from the Creek Bridge. One of them no sooner hit the shallow water than he was back on his feet headed for shore, trying to cut C.J. off. C.J. sprang out of the boat on the opposite side of the warden and raced for the high ground beyond the swamp with the warden less than ten yards behind him.

The two remaining wardens sat on the sand bottom with only their heads above the water, dazed and confused. Their boats had come to rest with one of the lights pointing straight up into the sky. The other light was shining down on the water and reflecting back up into the trees directly over my head. I just stood there paralyzed, waiting for Mr. Story to reappear. One of the wardens looked surprised to see me still standing only a few feet away. Suddenly they remembered their duty and lunged toward me. One of them promptly fell face down, while the other cursed the netting tangled around his gun and holster.

In the excitement I had gotten too close to the net. For the first time since the commotion began, I knew what to do: run. I didn't think about the best direction, I just lit out running down the sand bar along the edge of the swamp. Although I could hear someone coming behind, I didn't look back. I ran for all I was worth, expecting to be tackled any second. At the south edge of the swamp I cut away from the lake into the scrub palmettos, stumbling over logs, bogging, falling, and running again. Finally I ran into an open area clear of palmettos and cypress knees. I knew I was outrunning the warden and felt that wonderful confidence of being a winner. At that moment a bamboo vine caught me across the chest and neck. My feet kept running until there was no slack left, the vine yanked me backwards,

and I crashed to the ground, flat on my back. As I scrambled to my feet my pursuer bolted into the clearing and blinded me with his powerful flashlight. I was about to be tagged. I hurled myself back into the palmettos, running with total disregard for their razor-sharp sawtooth stems that tore my clothes and raked my arms and legs. Behind me I heard a thud, and the light went out. The warden had run into the same vine that had brought me down.

Once we were back in the palmettos, his light was useless. By the time he unsnarled himself and resumed the chase, I had opened the space between us and was continuing to increase my advantage. When I was a little young'un, I had learned something useful: when you are running in scrub palmettos, step high. Now I ran high, tripping, falling, and getting up and going again.

Without warning, someone tackled me around the legs. We tangled like two wildcats until he pinned me face down into the palmetto roots. As suddenly as he had tackled me he jumped up and ran. I rolled over just in time to miss being stomped in the face by the warden, who unknowingly ran over me chasing whoever had thrown me to the ground. Completely baffled, I muffled my hard breathing in my shirt sleeve for fear another warden might hear me. As I fell back exhausted into the security of the foliage and darkness, it dawned on me that the man that tackled me was not wearing a shirt. So it had to be C.J.

For a moment I savored the sweet relief of having escaped, until it occurred to me that another warden might be lurking nearby, waiting to tag me. I decided I'd stay there a month before I'd move and get chased again. Tired and scared, I lay on the ground, my arms and legs stinging from the cuts from the palmettos and bamboo vines. I did not like fishermen-and-game-wardens anymore. I could not bring myself to think of the possibility of Mr. Story drowning. It seemed certain that if he didn't drown he would have been tagged, which seemed a shame after eluding the wardens for years. Especially on the first night that I was a real part of a pull. I yearned for my room with its big poster bed and the clean sheets that smelled of being dried in the sun and my pillow stuffed with wild duck down. For the first time in my life it dawned on me that just for my comfort Mamma and Sissie ironed the sheets and pillowcases with flatirons heated on the wood stove. I remembered my mamma's admonition: "A person has to be crazy to want to stay out all night in the mosquitoes and weather." At that moment I agreed.

Surely everyone at the Creek had heard the wardens' big motors, especially when they hit the seine and ran wild. They had set an all-time record for noise. I knew all the families were lying in their beds staring into the darkness, wondering who got tagged or if anyone was hurt. The loss of the seine would not be worthy of attention until everyone was safe. My thoughts wandered back to the many times we young'uns had played fisherman-and-game-wardens, running from one another, laughing and cavorting through the woods, both sides winning. The real thing was certainly different.

When the onslaught had started, all the night critters had hushed. The island lay quiet. Then way back in the swamp, someone began to shout and swear hysterically. "You low rotten bastard, I have took off my gun and took off my badge. If you'll come back I'm gonna whup your butt till your nose bleeds!" Whoever was shouting sounded like he was going violently berserk. It had to be a warden because none of us had a gun. One thing was sure, no mamma at Cross Creek raised any young'uns stupid enough to go back and pick a fight with someone they had just outrun.

I wondered about Charley and decided he had probably made it back to his camp on the south end of the island and pictured him sleeping in his shack or maybe writing a poem about the whole mess. I wished I had not come. Tomorrow, tradition held, the fishermen and game wardens would meet on the Cross Creek Bridge to reminisce and joke about the chase. I had no intention of facing my adversary the next day or ever.

Back up the island at the Point haul I heard the wardens loading our seine. The clouds had thinned, though they still partially obscured the moon. Fog was gathering over the lake and island, tranquilizing the atmosphere. Finally I heard someone trying to start one of the big motors. After several attempts it caught and sputtered, then finally roared into life, sounding more like a twenty-foot gator bellowing than a kicker. Moments later the second motor merged with the first in an angry duet. The two moved off slowly, towing our seine and seine boat plus all our fish. The sound rounded the north end of the island, moving in the direction of Lochloosa Station. I sat listening to the din of the motors until they were only a murmur in the distance. At last, if Mr. Story was okay he could safely call us back to the haul.

I had recognized Mr. Skinner, the head of the local wardens, and was certain he would honor the tradition of meeting the tagged fishermen at their mutual convenience in the county judge's office. I pictured them like the two old friends they were. The warden and fishermen would amble into the judge's office and exchange greetings with him and anyone else who happened to be there. The judge would make polite inquiries as to the health and new additions of their families and ask if there was anything new at Cross Creek before getting to the business at hand. The most respected official in the county, he knew that both men agreed that the warden had made a fair catch or they wouldn't be together. The story of the chase was not heard as evidence but as a narrative of an exciting local event. Mr. Story would pay the usual twenty-five dollars and shake hands with Mr. Skinner and the judge. A rematch was inevitable. Life would go on at the Creek. Nothing would change.

Winton yelled from down at the haul, "Hey, fellers, it's clear." Someone rustled the palmettos less than ten feet from where I was hiding. My heart and tongue collided in the back of my throat. Not again. I felt frightened and angry.

"You might as well come on, J.T. That is, unless you plan on spending the night." Charley's voice was a welcome relief. He stood up, unfolding his angular body, and stretched. As if he were continuing a conversation that had been interrupted, he said, "You know you're perfectly welcome to sit in my part of the woods any time. But, J.T., the next time, even though it may seem unneighborly, I would just as soon you didn't bring that warden feller that was chasin' you." I was not in the mood for his dry humor and tried to ignore this comment. Undeterred, he continued, obviously enjoying himself, "I have never heard of two seiners that could swap places in the middle of a chase, especially without the poor wore-out warden knowin' you did it."

I asked, "Do you suppose that durn warden caught C.J.?"

"No. C.J. can outrun a rabbit in a briar patch. He's probably still out there taking a few laps around the island just to cool down."

"They got Mr. Story," I blurted. "Two of them had him trapped in the net when I ran." I could not bring myself to mention that I thought he might have drowned. We walked back to the haul in silence.

Winton and Mr. Gillis were sitting on the watch boat peacefully smoking. C.J. was wading along the shore, pulling the decoy boat back from wherever he had abandoned it during the chase. A faint odor of gasoline was the only evidence of the tumultuous invasion that had shattered the tranquility of Lochloosa less than an hour before. "Where's Mr. Story?" Charley asked.

"There ain't no use in him runnin' off if he was already tagged." Mr. Gillis spoke to everyone, including himself. "You don't suppose them long-legged, muckety-muck wardens Skinner had with him would of took him in like he was a criminal, do you?"

"No way," Winton answered. "There was two men in each boat when they came by me scaldin' the dog on the way in. And two in both boats goin' out. Mr. Skinner cut over by me when they was passin' and said 'cause it was so late they would meet us about twelve o'clock on the Bridge."

That was all I could stand. "Mr. Story's drowned and none of y'all stayed to save him!"

A reply came out of the darkness back in the edge of the swamp. "Not this old gator. Bud Skinner's new long-legged warden thought he had me tagged. When they come in and hit the net, three of 'em got throwed out between me and the shore." Mr. Story emerged from the swamp, sat down, and lit his pipe while we waited. (I hated it when he did that.) "One took out after C.J. and them other two seen J.T. While they had their attention fastened on him I slipped in behind their boat and hung on to that big kicker. One of the wardens went after J.T. and then Bud Skinner's new man waded back out to their boat to see what was wrong with his partner, the one that didn't get throwed out when they hit the net." Mr. Story puffed some more on his old meerschaum before he continued, "The poor feller that didn't get throwed out must of hit his head, 'cause Bud's man had a hell of a time gettin' any sense out of him. While the warden that came back to the boat was tryin' to tell the one that got knocked out where he was, I thought it would be a good time fer me to leave. I started easin' to the shore with jest my nose and eyes above the water, kinda like a gator fixin' to sink. The warden that was all right had his back to me. When I got up to where it was only about a foot-and-a-half deep, I stood up and tried to wade out nice and easy. I thought I might jest walk away without no fuss, but the first thing apparently that unconscious warden seen when he come to must of been me. He hollered, 'Look a-yonder!' I didn't have to look back. That new long-legged warden of Bud's yelled, 'Stop, dammit! Story, you're caught.' Just like that he called my name, and we ain't ever been acquainted." Mr. Story seemed more perturbed by the new man's ignorance of etiquette than by being chased.

"What happened then?" I asked.

"I commenced runnin' and got a fair jump on him while he was gettin' to shore. They wasn't no way I could outrun him fair and square, so I cut in along the edge of the swamp, where the cypresses join the hammock and scrub palmettos. They is a little bit of a trail if you can stay in it betwixt a lot of cypress knees an such. I hated to do it but he was gainin' on me every step with them long legs."

Mr. Story started to relight his pipe. C.J. and Charley both bellowed at him, "Tell the rest!"

"Well, about a year or two ago," he continued, "when my leg was stove up, I tied a wire across that trail about ten inches off the ground between two cypress, for a margin of safety, jest in case I got chased when I was fishin' my traps. With him shining his flashlight on my back and gaining more every second, I stepped high when I went between the two trees, hopin' the wire was still there. 'Bout ten feet on the other side I stopped and turned around waitin', 'cause if the wire weren't there he was gonna outrun me anyhow. Lord, that feller was a-comin'. It turned out worse than I expected. Poor man didn't have time to get his hands up before his face hit the mud and the dirt." The vision of the warden made the night's catastrophe worth it. While we laughed, Mr. Story said, "I run a few yards up in the palmettos and sat down and hid. I ain't never seen a warden lose his temper like he did. He called me some purty bad names. Course his feelings was hurt so bad I don't plan to hold it against him."

The chase was over. Winton took the decoy boat back to the hiding place on Right Arm. Charley went with him as far as his camp. The rest of us settled in the watch boat for the trip back to the old McKay Landing at the Bridge, Mr. Gillis and C.J. paddling. Mr. Story elected to come with us; he would sleep the rest of the night in the boat. I sat on the bottom, next to the live well. Mr. Story ceremoniously packed his pipe, then lit it, deliberately flaunting the open flame. A hint of a grin pushed the ends of his handlebar mustache up. He was old, but the fire of a youthful adventure was glimmering in his eyes.

I tried to unravel the events of the night. There were many questions I wanted to ask, but they blurred into an incomprehensible muddle. Thinking would have to come later. I drifted into deep restful sleep.

Mr. Story ruffled my hair, partially waking me when the boat glided beneath the live oak at the McKay Landing. "You better get home. Your folks'll be worryin'." It was breaking day when I slipped between the sheets I had yearned for a thousand miles away, on a planet called Burnt Island.

When I awoke, a single redbird was singing his territorial song outside my window. The sun was directly overhead. I was afraid I would miss the meeting on the Bridge and scrambled into my shoes and britches. My dad opened the door and read my thoughts. "It's just 11:30. Go wash up and put on clean clothes. You ought to look decent down there."

I did what my mamma called "a hit and a miss" at the wash pan and put on a clean starched shirt while I cut through the kitchen, snatching a piece of warm biscuit pudding on my way to the back door. Mamma lowered her head and peered over the top of her glasses. Her disapproval was obvious. I knew she would never understand the affairs of men. I ran out of the house, deliberately allowing the screen door to slam behind me, and headed through the grove to the Bridge. The meetings with the game warden after a chase were Cross Creek's most popular social occasion. I knew Dad wouldn't miss the meeting, but he would walk down at his own pace.

The fishermen were all waiting on the Bridge, hunkering in the shade of the trusses along the south side. I slowed to what I hoped looked like a casual walk. They all looked in my direction. I knew they were planning something. When I came onto the bridge, C.J. jumped up pretending he was going to run. "Y'all get out of the way, here comes the Burnt Island scared rabbit! You better look out, he's likely to run right over you." They all enjoyed a good laugh. That much was all right. I only hoped C.J. and Charley wouldn't tell the details of how C.J. had taken my place and saved me from the warden in the chase through the scrub palmettos. Once it was told, I would never hear the end of it.

Mr. Story came to my rescue. "Don't none of you joke J.T. He is the only one that stood facing them wardens waiting to see that I was in the clear." The comment was only partially true, but I appreciated it just the same.

"J.T., how come you thought he was drowned?" Mr. Gillis asked.

"They ain't nobody expected to wait fer a man to come up a third time in the middle of a chase." Mr. Story went on, ignoring him.

The subject was terminated by a cloud of dust preceded by a Model-A Ford coming from the west. Charley observed, "It looks like Bud brought his three cronies so they could get a look at us in the daylight."

Mr. Skinner pulled his tired old car to the center of the single-lane bridge and stopped alongside where we sat. Parking on the center of the bridge was as good a place as any, since it was reasonable to assume no other vehicle would come along until we had finished our visit. In fact, there was a good possibility there wouldn't be another all day.

Everyone exchanged howdies with varying degrees of enthusiasm. I was surprised the wardens as a group did not really look any different from my Cracker friends. Conspicuously stiff and sore, they emerged from the car. Mr. Skinner shook hands all around, then introduced his men, including the long-legged one who had recently been added to the district. His introduction included a résumé of the young warden's wife and children and who his folks were. The new man was originally from some place out in west Florida. The other two lived in the fringe of the Big Scrub.

They each selected a spot on the running board and fenders facing us, obviously intent on enjoying the meeting as much as we were. It seemed impossible that these friendly Crackers could be the same terrifying creatures who had invaded Burnt Island only a few hours earlier. Physically, they looked as bad as we did, scratched and black-and-blue. Mr. Skinner was in the best shape, although he seemed to be a little sore in the joints and had several cuts and scratches on his hands and arms. One of them, a skinny fellow, had a huge scratch across his neck and face that matched one I had acquired in the same place. His left arm appeared to be rigid beneath his long shirt sleeves carefully buttoned at the wrists. The other fellow from the scrub had a black eye virtually swollen shut, plus a goose egg in the edge of his receding hair line. Apparently he was the one that was not thrown clear of the boat. The new man looked like he had been hit in the face with a shovel and shut up with the wildcats. His nose varied in color from red to blue, and its puffiness extended across his face beneath both eyes. Of the four, he definitely had suffered the most damage. I couldn't decide whether he looked shy or angry.

We all stared at one another, momentarily unaware of the hush that had settled over the gathering. Then, embarrassed by the awkward silence, all of us laughed at the same time, pointing to the ridiculous appearance of the others. C.J. recovered enough to comment, "If you fellers think we look bad, you ought to see how skint-up we are with our britches off." Mr. Skinner said he had seen men look better after a free-for-all in the Eureka juke.

Something in the Cracker culture demands that enjoyment be delayed as long as possible. The discussion began with the present depth of the water in the lake, the snake population, and the cost of white bacon. I hated the ritual but had to admit it made the good part sweeter. Finally Mr. Story, deliberately casual, said, "We heard they was a chase over on Lochloosa last night."

Silence.

Imitating Mr. Story's inflection, Mr. Skinner drawled, "Yeah, it was at the Point haul."

C.J. asked, "Did anybody get tagged?"

Mr. Skinner answered, "Nooooo, but the State got them a new seine. It probably wasn't used more than twice." He was enjoying what he had accomplished. "Everybody in Chattahoochee and Raiford and all the State's institutions has got thirteen hundred pounds of speckle perch to eat." We all pondered the amount of fish we had caught and lost.

The skinny one from the scrub, obviously proud of their new equipment, said, "The State's got us some new fast kickers. I 'spect we're gonna be doing even better now."

Charley answered, "I live over that way, and I seen them things. They sure are fast." He added, "They looked like they stop quick too." I coughed to mask my laugh.

Mr. Skinner said, "I give credit to the man that pulled the end of the net across the lake side of the haul. It was a fair trick."

The new long-legged man said, "I don't care what y'all call fair and what not. There is one of you I intend to whup soon as I'm able."

Mr. Skinner looked his young warden in the eye and snapped, "Ain't nobody from the State gonna whup anybody!" Convinced he had made his position clear, he continued in his usual pleasant tone. "That wire was probably put there by some old stove-up man couldn't win in a fair chase." He made a quick grin. "But seriously, you fellers will all agree neither side ain't ever done nothin' that would intentionally cause a man to get hurt."

"A body can't tell who's liable to get whupped when two Crackers tie up. Sometime it's the old bull and sometime it's the yearling," Mr. Story said. "For my part, I don't know of but one wire anywhere around the lake, and your man there knows where it is."

My dad spoke for the first time, answering for the fishermen. "All of us has got families and our doings on the lakes ain't worth anybody gettin' hurt. I think we would agree they won't be no more trip wires and the people runnin' big kickers ought to be careful not to run over any man that might happen to be wadin' out in the edge of the lake." Both sides nodded their approval.

Without any loss of face the conflict was settled. After that ruling the clear but unwritten code of fishermen and game wardens deemed the use of trip wires unsportsmanlike conduct.

Every detail of the chase was discussed as if the fugitives were not present: how fast the new thirty-five horsepower motors ran, the way the three men looked and felt when they found themselves being thrown from their boats, and the foolish situation the two found themselves in when they fell into the net. One of the wardens told a joke himself. He had attempted to tag Mr. Skinner, his own boss, when the two met on the way back to the seine.

The skinny man from the scrub looked directly at me. "They was a watchman I put my light on, had eyes big as dinner plates. The further he run the faster he got, especially after he took off his shirt." He studied me with a certain amount of confusion and undeserved admiration. Euphoric with our deception, I braved a comment: "They always say you'll lose your shirt if you fool around a seine." Without discussion my friends had elected to allow the swap between me and C.J. in the palmettos to be a private joke on the warden, at least for the moment.

We visited until the shadows from the adjoining hammock moved across the Bridge, and I have never attended a meeting I enjoyed more. We wished one another good health and good luck. Mr. Skinner paused before climbing in his car. He looked up and down slow-moving Cross Creek. "I won't be seein' you fellers for about a month. It will take you that long to get a new seine hung in." They drove off toward Island Grove and the Big Scrub.

I walked with Mr. Story and Charley to their boat. Mr. Story seemed lost in his thoughts. "J.T., you know Mr. Skinner just give me a idea. We'll get your dad to finance two seines. We'll let the wardens catch one. Then while they are settin' back for three or four weeks we'll pull all we want."

Twelve. Bernie

CROSS CREEK'S most successful citizen was Charles Bernie Bass. In fact, he is the most successful man I have ever known. Bernie was born on a small family farm in the community of Bell in Gilchrist County, Florida, northeast of Gainesville. He was shorter than the average man, but hard work as a boy had made him powerfully muscular. His strong neck muscles made his head appear to merge with his shoulders as if they were one. He had black hair that tried to curl but thinned early. He told me everything he had always seemed to be misplaced. The tools he needed around the house were down at the landing in his boat, his winter clothes hung in front of the closet all summer, and the hair that belonged on his head was on his chest and arms.

When he was grown he left his family's unproductive farm, whose sandy land, like most in Florida, had little or no topsoil and was depleted of its nutrient value within a few years after being cleared. Bernie found a job in Gainesville at a retort plant, where fat pine was converted into creosote. The fumes caused permanent damage to his respiratory system, and he was plagued with shortness of breath throughout his life, although he never complained. He exuded an aura of genuine joviality. To paraphrase Will Rogers, who never met a man he didn't like, I can say unequivocally that I never met a man who didn't like Bernie Bass. I grew up feeling as comfortable with Bernie as if he were my father, brother, and buddy all joined into one person.

During my last year of high school I was desperate for money, especially after Dad sold my hog Blue. Bernie suggested I look for alligator nests because Ross Allen's Silver Springs reptile attraction was paying thirty-five cents apiece for baby gators. He said if I could find some eggs he would help me hatch them. He hadn't ever actually hatched any himself but had been told how to do it by a man who lived on the west shore of Lochloosa. I scouted the edge of the marshes, climbing trees along the shore to look wherever clumps of large vegetation grew among the grasses and lily pads—indications of areas shallow enough for a sow gator to build a mound above water to put a nest on. In excavating the muck to build the mound, she created a pool of water next to it, which we called a gator cave. The telltale sign of such a place was a plant alien to the marsh that had sprouted from seed dropped in the excrement of birds that had alighted on the mound. A small sweet gum, and especially a pine sapling, was almost a certain guarantee that a gator had been or was nesting there. On Bernie's advice I began my search in June after the gators laid, and I spotted a nest in mid-July in Right Arm Prairie off Buck Hammock.

I was a little skittish about wading out in a gator cave, although unprovoked attacks by gators were unheard of at the Creek. Tom Morrison said one ran at him once when he was stealing the eggs from her nest, and he stopped her by flaying the water with a homemade walking stick. No one else believed there was any danger.

I picked a clear afternoon and waded out through the pickerel weed and coontail to the thicket of buttonwoods and willows growing out of a maze of bladderwort and every conceivable variety of water plant. I tried to follow a straight line to the spot where I had seen two sweet gums sticking above the profusion of foliage. Near the two trees I discovered an open pool of water, possibly thirty feet across. The water was as clear as the water in Lochloosa. I entered the clearing only a few feet from a nest about four feet across and three feet high built by a gator on a mud flat.

For a moment I was frightened by the musty odor. I didn't know where the sow gator was, but I was certain she knew exactly where I was. Then, without causing a ripple, two eyes appeared above the surface near the center of the pool. They were about ten inches apart, indicating she was approximately ten feet long. I worked my way over to the nest and began to tear it open, digging through the layers of decaying foliage and muck; I found the eggs clustered in the lower quarter of the nest on a bed of fiber taken from scrub palmetto trunks.

While I kept a wary eye on the sow gator, I placed the three-and-a-half-inch oblong eggs into my croker sack. There were forty-one eggs. I eased out the way I entered, relieved to see that the old female hadn't moved. The instincts that would cause her to defend her nest against another gator twice her weight had not been stirred by my intrusion. It is a hard walk wading in the marsh, and I was exhausted when I finally made it back to shore. But Bernie had said it was important to rebury the eggs before they became cool, so I rushed home with them.

"We are going to be the only two-legged mamma gators at Cross Creek," Bernie said when I found him and showed him the eggs. "Let's go fix the nest." Following Bernie's instructions, I nailed a six-inch board to make a sandbox around the top perimeter of a three-by-six-foot table my mamma used to sun milk bottles and buckets in order to kill germs. Bernie said the table had to be in the sun all day to incubate the eggs. We filled the box with sand shoveled from the grove and buried the eggs halfway into the six inches of dirt. He explained that we needed to put the table legs in tomato cans filled with water to keep the ants from getting to the eggs, especially when the baby gators were ready to emerge from their shells. He called the cans "ant moats." When everything was complete, we wet down the sand with water from a rain barrel because it was warmer than water pumped directly from the well. Bernie told me to sprinkle our nest night and morning until the eggs hatched, about the time all gator eggs normally hatched, sometime during the third or fourth week of August.

"Hatchin' gators is more work than I figured," I said.

Bernie broke into one of his deep, infectious laughs. "It beats layin' 'em!" He said he had to get home before his wife, Theresa, came looking for him, although I knew the remark was only his polite way of leaving. Bernie teased his English-born wife, calling her "Old Lady" in her presence. He pronounced her name "Treeser." (He said southerners used a lot of r's just to be sure nobody thought they were from Boston.) The fact that they loved each other was obvious. "The best day's work I ever did was marrying Treeser," he would say.

Although his education was minimal, Bernie was an avid reader and what we called "good with figures." He spoke perfect Florida Cracker without apology. Mrs. Rawlings gave him a membership to the National Geographic Society in the late 1930s and renewed it each Christmas thereafter, which Bernie said made him the first in his family officially accepted in a society. The magazine was the only publication he received, and he read every issue cover to cover, apparently retaining all of what he read.

I am sure Bernie was the most disconcerting person that outsiders encountered at the Creek. They would at first assess him as simply another backwoods character, ignorant of the ways of the world. Then in the middle of a conversation, Bernie, drawing on his store of National Geographic information, would describe the distance from the Creek to Island Grove by saying, "It's the same as the height of Aconcagua, down there in the Andes, about 22,830 foot, but it's easier to get to Island Grove than it would be to get up that mountain." In other conversations he might compare the volume of water flowing out of Mongolia down the Liaohe in Liaoning Province, up there in the north part of China, to the volume of the Oklawaha.

Our gator hatching provided an excuse for me to go to Bernie's house more often and discuss our project while we drank Theresa's coffee and he played his guitar. Mainly I wanted to hear his stories. My favorites were the ones about hard times and nature. Some were original and others were old ones that would have been boring if anyone else was doing the telling.

One afternoon just before sundown I went to Bernie's house and found him chopping wood for Theresa's wood stove. One of the limbs was so crooked that every time he put it on the block it fell off before he could chop it. "J.T., look at that crooked stick. It reminds me of one a feller found in the woods up there where I come from."

It sounded to me like the beginning of one of his stories. "What was the feller's stick like?" I asked.

Bernie sat down on the chopping block, still holding the stick in his hand. "Well the pore feller had one of them ol' women that was a pedigreed, natural-born nag. The kind that's always complainin'. You know, couldn't shut up, had a tongue like a ice pick, grumbled in her sleep. Couldn't nobody please her no matter what they done. She got up one morning and started in on the poor feller 'cause she hadn't had no squirrel gravy. She claimed she had begged him to kill some squirrels for months and he had just ignored her. Truth was, she knowed she hadn't ever mentioned it before but knew he had give up contradictin' her the first night they was married. To keep from havin' to listen to her mouth runnin' and knowin' she wouldn't hush till he got her a mess of squirrels, he cut his breakfast short, picked up his rifle, and headed into the hammock.

"It was still mornin' and the fog hadn't lifted so it felt good jest to be by himself in the woods where it was quiet and peaceful. It was one of those mornings when nothing was feedin', the time of year after acorns has all dropped and before hickory nuts matured, J.T.— you know what I am talkin' about?"

I said yes as quick as possible, wanting him to go on with the story.

"So the feller kept roamin' deeper in the rough hammock. He'd move up and sit down and listen like you do when you know how to hunt squirrels. Well, he was hunkered under some water oaks when he heard a rustling sound off further down in the hammock. He listened hard but couldn't make out what it was. First he thought it could be wind. So he studied the high limbs of the oaks and was positive they wasn't no breeze. The fog was still layin' in the tops of the trees even though it was after eight or nine o'clock. He thought it sounded like a big ol' bear movin' through the palmettos, but it didn't get no closer nor no further away.

"The feller decided right there he had to find out what it was or

spend the rest of his life wonderin'. He made his way in the direction
of the noise the same as if he was tryin' to slip up on a old gobbler,
which you know can't be done. Finally he had to get down on his belly
and crawl like a snake through palmettos and bamboo vines and all
kinds of rotten limbs and stuff. After all the work he was puttin' in he
didn't want to spook whatever it was before he seen it. When he
stopped and listened, it still made the same sound, a soft thump-blap-
thump, followed by a low swishing sound. The feller finally made it to
the place the noise was comin' from and stuck his head real easy out in
the clearing.

"It looked like somebody or somethin' had swept the ground under
a big live oak clean as a widder's front yard. Even the tea weeds was
mashed level to the ground. Then down at the end of the clean spot he
seen it move on the ground."

Bernie paused, "J.T., you know what it was?"

Of course I didn't know what it was. That's what I had been listening all the time to find out. "What was it, Bernie?"

He laughed until he started coughing. "It was a stick that was so
crooked it couldn't lay still!" He began to laugh again. "It was so
crooked it had crooks inside and on top of and around the crooks." He
paused. "You know what kind I mean, J.T.? It was kind of like this
crooked limb I got here. No matter how it landed it would rock back
and forth and then roll to another side that was still not steady. Fact
was, they wasn't a steady side on that stick."

I laughed too, visualizing such a stick. "What did the feller do with
the stick?" I asked.

"Well now, that was the sad part of the whole thing. He eased up to
where it was flayin' around and swooped down and caught it. Course
it didn't try to wiggle soon as he picked it up. He stood there for a
while just holdin' and lookin' at it. He thought this could be the
crookedest stick in the whole country. 'Cause he shore hadn't ever
heard of one that rolled around until it cleared a patch out of the woods
just tryin' to lay still. Maybe it was the crookedest stick in the whole
world, or that had ever been.

"The feller hadn't been as excited since before he married his old lady, but he got so steamed up about what he had found, he lit out fer the house. Course, he was bein' careful not to let it get away. When he got in the backyard he hollered, 'Old lady, come out here and see what I got.'

"She come out on the back porch sulkin' and grumblin'. 'What's so all-fired important?' she asked.

"He said, 'Look at what I caught,' and he laid the stick down on the ground and sure enough it commenced to rock and flop around.

"She said, 'Where's the squirrels?'

"J.T., that feller was so put out he shouted at his old woman, 'Dammit, you old grouch, look at it! It's the crookedest stick you ever seen.' The stick rolled in a different direction. And the feller said, 'Now, ain't it sumpin'?'

"His old lady turned, goin' back in the house, and casting her eyes up, she started to grumble to God himself, 'Lord, see what I have to put up with. No squirrels and a fool of a husband that spent the mornin' traipsin' around the woods chasin' a damn crooked stick.'"

Bernie was as involved in the narrative as I was, changing his voice slightly to fit the participants. I was sure he was making it up as he told it and at the same time I believed every word.

"That pore feller's bottom lip dropped halfway to his knees," he went on. He took the stick and threw it in the corn crib and then latched the door, making sure it wouldn't get away. He was proud of it even if his ol' woman didn't appreciate it. That night the feller was layin' in the bed listenin' to the ol' woman grumble and snore when it occurred to him, maybe that stick was worth a lot of money. Somebody like Ringling Brothers might pay a fortune for it, haul it around with their circus and charge people to see the Crookedest Stick in the World. He imagined hundreds of people crowdin' and squeezin' each other just to see that stick of his, thrashin' around. He smiled in the darkness thinkin' how his ol' woman would sing a different tune when he sold it for a wagonload of money.

"The next morning he woke up to a commotion going on in the backyard, cussin' and fumin' and such. He jumped up and put on his overalls, taking only enough time to hook one of the galluses and run out the back door.

"The garden was beat flat on the ground. That stick had worked itself out a knot hole in the side of the crib and flattened two rows of okra, the squash, and all their black-eyed peas. His ol' woman was jumping up and down and choppin' at the ground with his double-bladed ax and cussin' loud enough to wake up everybody in the cemetery.

"He run out there and wrestled the ax away from her, but it was too late. She had already chopped his crooked stick into little bitty pieces. The feller went crazy mad. 'Look what you went and done, you mean-mouthed old woman! You done kilt it! It was the only chance I ever had to amount to somethin' and you kilt it.' She knowed she had gone too far, so she tucked in her big rear end and ran in the house."

Bernie's voice grew mournful: "The feller buried the pieces down in the edge of the woods. But he wasn't never the same. He was like he lost his will to live. They say he roamed around in the woods the rest of his life, hopin' he'd find another stick like that one. Course he never did."

Bernie burst into uncontrolled laughter while he held the stick that inspired the whole story. He said, "I got to finish cuttin' Treeser's stove wood before she starts raisin' sand at me." He held his crooked stick on the chopping block and chopped it into short pieces.

I know Bernie never intended me to believe his story, but when I walk through the hammocks and I see a crooked stick lying on the ground, I occasionally stop and watch—just in case it moves.

🌢 By the end of the last week in August I was sure my gator eggs were not going to hatch. Dad and the rest of the fishermen made all kinds of jokes. They said I should sit on my nest and not bathe so I would smell like a mamma gator. I decided to throw the eggs out and forget the whole thing. When I went down to Bernie's to tell him, he was patching a tire on his old cut-down truck. I told him how disappointed I was, especially after all the kidding from the fishermen. He said, "Some things just get off to a bad start. I been patchin' tires all my life. Now, J.T., if you think about it, when they invented automobiles they could have made concrete tires and had rubber roads." He laughed. There was not anyone who enjoyed laughing like Bernie.

He wiped his eyes and became philosophical, trying to cheer me up. "A feller comes here on this ol' earth, and in a short time he's gone. We are all lucky to have found Cross Creek, and what's more important is, the folks that live around here know it." He laughed again, although he was serious. "I do what I like best, and I live where I like to live. I got good young'uns. And even though we lost Alton, the rest of them has sure helped make up for it." He took a deep breath and exhaled, dispelling the memory of the loss of their third child. "Me and Treeser and the young'uns enjoy one another, and none of us has or ever will be lonesome. Some folks are lonesome all their life and some are hungry. We ain't ever needed to eat a Hoover hog since we come to the Creek." (Hoover hogs were possums.) He finished patching the inner tube.

We sat waiting for the patching cement to dry before he pumped up the tire. I told him I only had one thing I wanted right then. I wanted them dern gator eggs to hatch. Bernie chuckled. "Then you are probably the only person I know that wants less than I do."

"What do you want, Bernie?" I asked.

"Well, J.T., I already got the most important things. To begin with, I wanted a family, and I got that. Then, I wanted to get set to where I didn't have to ever worry where our next meal was coming from, and comin' to the Creek took care of that. I ain't rich but as long as I fish and frog-hunt, can't nobody fire me, and if it ever gets to where nobody's got the money to buy what I catch, we can eat 'em ourself. And then I wanted a house on my own land, and I got a deal going and I'm gonna get that." He paused while we contemplated his accomplishments.

He continued, "Before they throw that yellow dirt in my face, I got three more things I want. One, I want my young'uns to all get a education. Two, I want to go see the Grand Ol' Opry in Nashville, Tennessee. And three, I want a pickup truck that somebody ain't wore out before I get it."

I told him I had to get back to my house and asked what did he think I ought to do about the eggs. He said, "Give them some more time. You'll end up gettin' what you want."

Three days later I went out to sprinkle them. Ten feet away from the box I heard the familiar high-pitched grunts. The wet sand was moving in several places. I wanted to tell Bernie, but he was on the lake at that time of the morning. I brushed the sand back from a spot where it was moving. The shell had cracked and mostly fallen away from a white membrane that caused the little gator to look like it was in a plastic sack. He wiggled without success until the sun dried the membrane, making it brittle enough for him to poke his nose out, then his head, and finally the little rascal crawled out. I put my finger down to touch him, and he would have bitten it except I snatched my hand back.

I have never had a less enthusiastic reception than I got from Mamma when I ran into her kitchen to show her my glorious prize: "Get that thing out of my house—now!"

My dad's reaction was only a little better: "When you're hatchin' gators, what did you expect?"

Forty of the forty-one gators hatched. I dropped another one putting it into the sack, and my dog killed it. So I sent thirty-nine Cross Creek baby gators to Silver Springs by way of a friend of my dad's who regularly sold gators and rattlesnakes. Rather than the fourteen dollars I expected, my dad's friend returned with three five-dollar bills. He said, "Mr. Allen said they were worth more when he heard I sat on them and hatched them myself." I figured I got an extra dollar for the joking rights.

I offered Bernie part of the money, suggesting he take what he thought was right for his advice, help, and especially his support. He guffawed. "I wouldn't have helped you if it had been for the money." He said he would settle for a cold RC out of Dad's fish box, just so I wouldn't feel beholden to him.

It was the most money I had at one time since Dad sold Blue, and I kept it quiet because I didn't want to invest in more war bonds.

🐚 Mrs. Rawlings called at our front gate one night about an hour after dark. I hadn't heard her car and wondered why she was out walking that time of night. When I asked her to come in, she said, "No, I can

only stay a minute. I have someone I especially want you and your folks to meet." We all came out on the steps trying to see in the darkness with only lamplight from the living room behind us. Mrs. Rawlings said, "Mr. and Mrs. Glisson and J.T. Glisson, I want you to meet Mr. Wendell Willkie."

The large man shook my mamma's and my hand while I thought, *Why all the formality?* I didn't have the slightest idea who the man was. Then he shook hands with Dad, who said, "Are you the same Wendell Willkie that run for president?" He said he was, and Dad said, "We're glad to have you." Dad hesitated for a second. "I think I should be honest with you up front, Mr. Willkie. I didn't vote for you, but you're welcome here at the Creek."

The big man laughed. "You cannot imagine how glad I am to meet you, Mr. Glisson. I know a lot of people did not vote for me, but you are the first one I have had the opportunity of meeting." Everyone else laughed while I thought, *Oh, it's* that *Mr. Willkie.*

Mrs. Rawlings told us Mr. Willkie would be at Cross Creek for a day or so, and she would consider it a favor if I would take him bass fishing. I was happy for any excuse to go fishing, especially during the week, but was disappointed when I asked what time and he answered, "Oh, about nine o'clock." I knew Mrs. Rawlings had done enough bass fishing to know that nine o'clock was the time we normally quit, because they seldom hit after the sun rose high enough to make the lake hot and bright. She didn't say anything.

The next morning Mr. Willkie came strolling up the road about a quarter after nine. We walked together to the landing back of our place. He seemed interested in everything he saw. He was especially intrigued by the fish house made of palmetto logs and wanted to know if I liked to eat the heart or bud of the cabbage palmettos, the part we call swamp cabbage and outsiders call heart-of-palm. He certainly didn't seem to be a man "hopped up" on bass fishing. He asked who my friends were and if they were my age. I told him about Charley and Henry and especially of my admiration for Bernie. Out on the lake, the wind rose from the south, making it difficult to maneuver the boat. Mr. Willkie saw the difficulty I was having and suggested we try again the next day. I agreed and told him it was too late in the morning to expect much action anyway.

When we returned some of the catfishermen were "skinning up," dressing their catch, while my dad and Bernie swapped stories with them. Dad introduced Mr. Willkie to each man. Mr. Willkie emphasized his first name and made a point of being sure he got the pronunciation of the first and last name of each individual clearly. The two of us got the usual questions about what we caught, and I was thankful Mr. Willkie took full blame for our failure. Then everyone had suggestions as to where and how he could do better.

At that point Bernie asked Mr. Willkie if he could talk about his trip around the world. This was 1942, and we had all heard on the radio that Mr. Willkie had gone on a mission for President Roosevelt to more than a dozen countries, and that he had talked intimately with many of the world's leaders. The principal issue at the time was how the United States would assist other free nations to secure world peace after the defeat of Germany and Japan. Willkie told Bernie that there was nothing secret about the mission.

Bernie's questions were precise and appropriate. He asked about the future of the Middle East and the success of communism in Russia. He wanted to know about specific provinces in China. Mr. Willkie seemed to enjoy answering Bernie's questions while the men finished skinning their fish and went in the fish house to weigh and ice them. Bernie apologized for asking so many questions and said it reminded him of a feller that lost an arm in an accident: "The feller learned to get by with only one arm and had no problems dealing with his loss, except every time he met somebody new the first thing they did was ask how he lost his arm." Bernie began laughing, enjoying his story as much as his listeners. "Well, the feller got tired of tellin' all the details so he would tell the questioners that he would answer if they would first promise not to ask another single question about it ever. Naturally, they always agreed. Then the feller said, 'It was bit off.'" Willkie laughed loud and hard. Bernie then excused himself and headed home. "That is a remarkable fellow," Mr. Willkie commented. Dad said he was also one of the best fishermen at Cross Creek and suggested

Bernie take him on the lake the next day. Mr. Willkie asked if I would mind. I said not as long as it was Mr. Bass who replaced me, trying to sound formal.

For the next two days Bernie and his famous fishing partner spent long hours on the lake fishing and releasing what they caught. They came in at noon on the second day when all the other fishermen had finished with their catches and gone home. Only my dad and I were at the fish house. Bernie and Mr. Willkie said goodby to each other because he was leaving the following morning.

Willkie stood watching Bernie walk up the sandy road. Dad said he was sorry they had not caught a prize fish. "That was not important," Willkie responded, "but being with Mr. Bass was." He turned to my dad. "I have had the privilege of meeting presidents and kings and dictators, as well as philosophers and all sorts of distinguished individuals. That man has a fundamental understanding of mankind that is equal to the best of them."

That was something all of us at the Creek already knew.

Thirteen. World War II

A DIFFERENT wind was beginning to blow across the lakes and marshes in the spring of 1941. There had been some talk on the Bridge of a row brewing over in Europe and the possibility of another generation of Americans being sent back over there to settle it again. However, it did not appear to us to be as imminent a threat as the sudden wild proliferation of water lettuce that insisted on clogging our lakes and marshes.

During the summer of 1939 it had become practically impossible to pole frog boats across the marshes or fish traps in the lettuce-clogged bonnet beds. Without artificial methods of controlling nature's constant extremes, we were forced to endure the new pest until the Ol' Gal decided to subdue it in her own time and way. Tom Morrison, our local self-appointed naturalist, said if we had a manatee it would eat the lettuce faster than it could grow. Bernie Bass reasoned the manatee would have to be the size of the *Queen Mary* to keep up with the lettuce growing in his territory alone. And since none of the rest of us had ever heard of a manatee and Mr. Morrison had never actually seen one, the idea was discarded.

In the fall of 1940 the U.S. government conducted a lottery to determine the order that young men would be drafted into the peacetime army. John-Henry Bauknight was selected on the first call. We usually referred to John-Henry and his brother George collectively as the Bauknight boys, and no one could remember having ever seen one without the other. They were born on their family's property two miles west of the Bridge and grew up hunting and fishing. After John-Henry passed his physical, George took him to Gainesville and watched him board the bus to Camp Blanding for induction. We all thought it would be a waste of time for the army to teach John-Henry to shoot, since he was the undisputed best shot at the Creek. They didn't need to spend time getting him in physical shape either, since he was probably tougher and leaner than they were. George was proud of his brother. "John-Henry is the only man in this country that can outrun a rabbit in a briar patch, barefooted," he said, and everybody agreed.

A few years ago John-Henry and I were talking about the war. I told him I had recently been in Europe and wondered if I had visited some of the places where he had fought. He said, "I don't see how you couldn't have. I toted a backpack and a M-1 all the way across a bunch of them countries, including France and Belgium and I don't know where all. Then I toted it into Germany until it was all over and they told us we was goin' home. J.T., I seen all that country over there. We slept in them big churches and old castles and on the ground." He hesitated. "Funny thing is, I liked the Germans better than any of the rest." I was sure he had seen all of those places since he was one of the first to go and one of the last to come back. When someone talks about all the places that Caesar conquered, I think of John-Henry Bauknight from Cross Creek. I asked him if he would like to go back over, if only on a visit. He answered in a positive tone. "I didn't leave nothin' over there. No sir, I am stayin' right here at the Creek."

December 7, 1941, was just another quiet Sunday at the Creek. No one heard the news of the attack until we arrived at the church in Island Grove for Sunday night preaching. The reaction of the folks at the Creek surprised me, especially because few if any had ever heard of Pearl Harbor. They took the attack personally and were mad as hell. I had never heard issues of patriotism discussed on the Bridge, I suppose because it smacked of being in cahoots with the government. But the Japanese attack was different. It was all right to settle a row with a fight if you gave notice and met your adversary face-to-face. If it was local, you met on the Bridge; if it was between countries, you met on the battlefield and fought it out. But you gave notice. The attack by the Japanese was a cowardly act that demanded satisfaction as well as retribution.

The younger men from the Creek scattered like a covey of quail in hunting season, spreading across the country and to distant places they had never heard of. The skills developed to stalk wildlife and to run from the game warden appeared to meet the needs of the military. By 1944 physical and age requirements had been lowered until most of the young able-bodied men were gone; by the time the war ended, more than half the adult males at the Creek were in service. Marvin Townsend and his brother Preston fought in northern Europe; Preston was wounded in Belgium. Snow Slater served in the Philippines. Murray Zetrouer joined the navy and was sent to the Pacific. My brother, Carlton, shipped back and forth across the Atlantic in the merchant marine. Monk Calton was in the navy.

By the fall of 1942 the sky over Orange Lake looked as if we had a plague of orange mosquito hawks. Fifty to a hundred bi-wing training planes from bases in Ocala, Dunnellon, and Williston practiced spins and rolls over the fishermen that were left. The government asked for more and more fish to offset the demand for meat, while the men continued to leave.

In July of 1943 Norton Baskin, Mrs. Rawlings' new husband, volunteered for the American Field Service; he was accepted and immediately shipped to the Far East. Her anxiety for him caused her to be more restless than usual. When we met, we talked more and more about the war. On one occasion Norton was reported missing in Malaysia, and the Creek shared her worry, then rejoiced when he was located. Bernie Bass had told me, "When they call me, I'll go. It's up to them." He was good for his word, although he had a wife and four children. When he received his notice he went uncomplainingly. I thought every outfit should have a Bernie Bass. He could be the morale officer, because wherever Bernie was, there was laughter and jubilation.

Bernie is the only person I have ever heard of that was drafted into the army on Tuesday and came home on special leave to go fishing on Saturday and Sunday of the same week. A captain at the Camp Blanding induction center was so impressed by Bernie's fishing stories that he gave him leave and then decided to come home with him to bass fish on Orange Lake. Everyone at the Creek said, "Bernie shore knows how to make friends."

He was later shipped to Hattiesburg, Mississippi, where his military service again took an unusual turn. He was pulled out of basic training and became an instructor because of a unique skill that was not available to the army before Bernie joined it. The army was training an amphibious assault force at Hattiesburg and was unable to accomplish its goal because the soldiers could not crank the big outboard motors in less than ideal conditions. A search of the trainees' premilitary experience indicated Bernie was their man, with his many years of experience cranking cantankerous worn-out kickers without proper tools in the dark and in the rain. Bernie's new job was to instruct the assault team in the care and starting of outboard motors.

Bernie finally finished all his basic training, and he was just waiting to get on a ship and go overseas when the officer in charge of his outfit asked him how many children he had back at Cross Creek. Bernie told him four. The captain said if he had four children, he would go home. Bernie said, "You mean, I could go home now, if I wanted to?" The officer said with that many children, he could. Bernie asked him what he thought would be the right thing to do, "seeing the army has given me all this training?" The captain said he would still go home. So Bernie accepted an honorable discharge and came home to his family and the Creek.

As the war wound down in Europe I became frantic to get into service, any service. I would go to the post office in Ocala and sign up for every branch. Invariably I was turned down because I had been born with clubfeet, which of course was why I wanted to get in, to prove myself. I tried all the recruiting offices in Gainesville. Finally, they wouldn't let me in the door. I would have to go elsewhere to enlist. I was surprised and thankful for my dad's reaction. He said it was a waste of time, but he thought I should try if I was sure that was what I wanted to do.

I walked to Island Grove and flagged the Greyhound bus to Tampa and tried to join everything they would allow me to fill out enlistment forms for. They all rejected me. However, I learned that appearing too anxious was a handicap and changed my tactic. The next week I rode the bus to Jacksonville and told the navy recruiter the only reason I wanted to join was to keep from carrying a rifle and walking in the mud. I told the army that I wanted to join them because I didn't like boats, and the air branches that I would rather fly than walk. I reminded them I was coming up on my eighteenth birthday and they had to move quick or the draft would get me. At first I skipped the army and navy air corps because their physicals were the most strenuous, but on my second trip to Jacksonville I gave the army air corps a try and made it through the preinduction physical. The recruiter told me to obtain the necessary documents, including a character reference from someone who had known me over an extended period.

I returned to the Creek filled with optimism. It was a long shot, but it was further than I had gotten before. I went to Mrs. Rawlings, who had offered encouragement each time I had been turned down. She said writing the letter would be far easier than getting me through high school social sciences. The next afternoon she told me she had mailed the letter.

I reported for induction in Atlanta and, with a little deception and a lot of sincere praying, after passing the physical I was sworn in. A burly sergeant informed me that J.T. (which was my whole name, not just my initials) was not an acceptable name for the military. I changed it to James T. Glisson and was issued dog tags and a uniform. What's in a name, if it might cause a closer examination of rebuilt feet. In the reception center I was surprised with more physicals. The fear came back that someone might take a closer look at my feet and send me home, rejected. I remembered the World War I veterans at the Creek who had said I'd never have to go in the army. I had resented their remarks.

I stayed in the middle of the crowds, trying not to attract attention.

After three days I began to relax. Several hundred of us dressed only in dog tags and ten-by-twelve manila envelopes held modestly before us were getting immunization shots when a major—the equivalent of God at that stage of my military career—shouted "Glisson! James T. G-l-i-s-s-o-n!" I was certain I had been discovered. I knew I would be thrown out or possibly jailed in some dungeon until they processed the paperwork to bring about my dishonorable discharge. I saw myself arriving back at the Creek, shamed.

I walked toward the major, trying desperately to hold back the water that was clouding my eyes and maintain some degree of dignity. "Yes, sir," I snapped, while I attempted a salute I had not been taught to execute. I was relieved my voice didn't crack.

He said, "Follow me, soldier." We went into an eight-by-ten unpainted room furnished with an oak table, a straight chair, and an olive-green file cabinet. He sat on the edge of the table and motioned for me to close the door. I prepared myself. The key word would be *rejected.* I wondered why they didn't call it *shamed.*

He spoke in a soft tone, the likes of which I hadn't heard since I arrived at the reception center. "Do you know Marjorie Kinnan Rawlings?"

I didn't believe what I heard. I was hundreds of miles from the Creek, in Atlanta, Georgia, and a major was talking about my friend back home. I stammered, "Sir?"

His voice was unchanged. "Do you know Marjorie Kinnan Rawlings? Personally?"

I managed to say, "Yes, sir, I do."

The major said, "Relax, Glisson. This meeting is not military. I am a fan of hers. I loved every word of *The Yearling.* I have read it again and again. Cross Creek is as real to me as if I had lived there." He offered me a cigarette. I muttered, "No, thank you. Sir." "Tell me about her," he continued. "Do you see her often?"

I must have looked like the dumbest buffoon he had ever seen, standing there buck naked with my mouth hanging open. He frowned and said, "Are you J.T.?" I thought, *Oh, damn, he's read the part about the pathetic little cripple, hobbling down the road on his crooked legs. Boy, the army is thorough, they have me documented. Now they are going to throw me out for sure.* Anger began to creep up the back of my neck. I thought, *Throw me out but don't toy with me.* I snapped, "Yes, sir, I am J.T. Glisson. It is on my birth certificate!"

He put out his hand to shake hands with me. I hesitated, and he laughed. "It's okay, Glisson. It is an honor to meet someone who is actually from Cross Creek, Florida, and a friend of Marjorie Kinnan Rawlings." He pulled a letter from a file, laying it on the table, and spoke as if he were talking to himself. "I see hundreds of these. This one was written by her, and I have never seen a letter more perfectly written." He opened the personal-sized letter as if it were a fragile family heirloom. "My office is only a short distance from here, and I thought I would walk over and see if I could meet you personally." He put the letter back in the file and stood staring at the manila folder. "It is a shame a letter like that will be left to decay in the tons of military records. It would be worth a great deal to you someday."

The major assumed a military posture. "Well, Glisson, you're air corps now. You better catch up with your group. I wish you luck." All I heard was "You're Air Corps Now." Exhilarated, I dashed through the wrong door into a secretarial pool followed by twenty recruits who thought I knew where I was going. The fifty or more ladies seemed to enjoy it because they all broke up laughing before I collected myself and retreated.

The war ended abruptly in August of 1945 after the atomic bombs were dropped on Hiroshima and Nagasaki. I was shipped to Japan and stationed in Hokkaido. In my off-duty time there I built a boat and fished for trout and shot ducks on the Chitose River. In the spring of 1946 I hunted bear in the extensive forest around Lake Shikotsu. It wasn't the Creek, but it was a relief from the regulated life of the military.

Shortly after my mother's death in 1983 I found the letter the major had said should not be allowed to rot in forgotten military records. Apparently Mrs. Rawlings's admirer, acting under questionable authority, had sent it to my home address, where my mother had tossed it into her trunk. It was addressed to the Aviation Cadet Examining Board.

Dear Sir;

I am happy to recommend J.T. Glisson as a candidate for the Army Aviation Cadet Corps. I have known him all his life, and I consider him of precisely the caliber you desire for this program.

He has courage, poise, initiative, brains, adaptability and high integrity of character.

Very sincerely,
Marjorie Kinnan Rawlings

'I was not allowed to bask in my old friend's complimentary adjectives. When I showed the letter to my brother Carlton, he said it was no wonder Miz Rawlings got a Pulitzer Prize for fiction.

❧ The Creek had its own war in the early 1940s. It began shortly after Mrs. Rawlings published *Cross Creek* in 1942. Her close friend Zelma Cason, who lived in Island Grove, was offended by the description of herself in the book and filed an invasion-of-privacy suit in January of 1943 for $100,000, naming Mrs. Rawlings and Norton Baskin, as Florida law then required that the husband be included in legal action against his wife. The suit was not a surprise to any of us at the Creek. Mrs. Rawlings had been all too honest in her description of her neighbors, including some who had shared confidences with her they considered private.

Mrs. Rawlings had described her friend Zelma in a chapter called "The Census":

Zelma is an ageless spinster resembling an angry and efficient canary. She manages her orange grove and as much of the village and county as needs management or will submit to it. I cannot decide whether she should have been a man or a mother. She combines the more violent characteristics of both and those who ask for or accept her manifold ministrations think nothing of being cursed loudly at the very instant of being tenderly fed, clothed, nursed or guided through their troubles. (p. 38)

Everyone who knew Zelma agreed that the description was probably the most accurate in the book. In another paragraph Mrs. Rawlings referred to Zelma's special brand of profanity, which was a kind way of describing it. My dad characterized Zelma as an "old maid politician" who liked everybody except the damn fools who didn't agree with her. He added that Mrs. Rawlings and Zelma had more in common than either one would ever believe.

Most of the Creek liked Zelma and shared some sympathy with her injured ego. She was helpful and loyal to the downtrodden as long as she believed they tried to help themselves. Everyone agreed that if Zelma wanted to come to the Creek and curse Mrs. Rawlings out, that would be all right. In fact, they would have allowed that Zelma could have beaten hell out of Mrs. Rawlings or even shot her, but Zelma had violated a fundamental Cracker rule by taking the row into the court, and especially by doing it for money.

Shortly after the book was published, Zelma stopped my dad and asked him what he "aimed to do." He told her, "If that woman can come to the Creek and make a living writing about the people here, then I wish her luck. Friendship is worth more to me than any amount of money." Miss Cason was not pleased with his answer.

One afternoon Mrs. Rawlings stopped for a visit and joined my folks sitting in the big rocking chairs on the front porch. After the usual niceties, Dad said, "I understand Zelma Cason is suing you."

Mrs. Rawlings's reaction was a complete surprise. She said, "Yes," and her voice broke as she tried to wipe away a sudden rush of tears. "I didn't think she would take it the way she has. I had expected her to laugh, but she was clearly hurt." She recovered herself and asked, "Tom, what do you think?"

Dad had obviously given it a lot of thought. "You may have the best high-powered lawyers in New York and Jacksonville, but you ought to lose if you don't have any more sense than to go in that courthouse in Gainesville without a local lawyer." She asked who he would suggest and he said, "Sigsbee Scruggs." They both laughed, remembering that it was Mr. Scruggs who had defended Henry against her and B.J.

"I will have to think about that," she said.

I don't know why, but I always believed the suit would be dropped or thrown out of court. I was wrong—it outlasted World War II. It finally came to trial when I was overseas in May of 1946. I received clippings and letters that possibly kept me better informed than I would have been at the Creek. It was a great event for little Gainesville, putting the town's name on the national wire services' datelines and creating a carnival atmosphere for all to enjoy.

Although Philip May of Jacksonville was chief counsel for the defense, all eyes were on his co-counsel, Sigsbee Scruggs, the local favorite. Sigsbee was not only popular for his colorful and brilliant courtroom expertise, he had a winning record to back it up. More than thirty times the state game department had tagged Creek fishermen under circumstances that the fishermen thought were unfair according to our local rules. Sigsbee Scruggs defended every case and won them all. My dad said, "If they let Sigsbee select the jury, they might as well let him decide the verdict."

The plaintiff was represented by Kate Walton of Palatka, which created a unique situation—the defendant, the plaintiff, and the plaintiff's counsel were women in a court that at that time would not allow a woman to sit on the jury.

The publishers were in Mrs. Rawlings's corner, of course, hoping for more freedom to publish without fear of libel. Another faction saw the trial as a precedent setter that, if won by Mrs. Rawlings, would violate the right to privacy of the individual. Meanwhile, the defense was wary of the Creek folks, who were the predominant characters in the book and might think that if Zelma were awarded a large sum of money they should get theirs too.

Kate Walton was familiar with Crackers, knew how clannish they could be, and suspected they might come to the defense of one of their own, no matter what they thought of the book. She was right. Everyone at the Creek volunteered to be a witness in the defense of their neighbor. I do not believe anything in Mrs. Rawlings's lifetime touched her more than that act of loyalty.

After seven days of high drama and an inspiring summation by Sigsbee Scruggs, the all-male jury retired to decide a verdict. They deliberated only twenty-eight minutes, finding the defendants Marjorie Kinnan Rawlings and her husband Norton Baskin not guilty.

The victory was short-lived. Zelma appealed to the Florida Supreme Court, where the judges probably found the trial testimony entertaining but did not agree with the lower court's verdict, ruling that Zelma had indeed proven her case for invasion of privacy. They did not, however, sympathize with Zelma's claim for damages. The court ordered Mrs. Rawlings to pay all court costs and allowed her and her attorney to establish the amount of damage they would pay.

Mrs. Rawlings and Norton sent Zelma a check for one dollar.

❦ When I left the Creek to enter the army, it was assumed the war would include an invasion of Japan similar to that in Germany. The general consensus was that in a minimum of two-and-a-half to three years the war would end, and I would be discharged. If our luck at the Creek held, everyone would return, and life would go on much the same as always. However, that was not to be.

Murray Zetrouer was a tall, pleasant young man. He was better-looking than most and had a special understanding of the world we lived in. He catfished and pole-and-line fished for bream when they were biting on Orange Lake, helping to support his mother and sisters. Murray was a favorite of my folks, and they often talked with him about his plans to further his education after the war. Shortly after Murray entered the navy as an ordinary seaman, he borrowed money from my father for a small outboard motor to make it easier for his family to fish. He mailed the payments regularly to my mother until June of 1945, when the War Department notified his family that Radioman First Class Murray Zetrouer had been killed in action, his aircraft shot down in the Battle of Okinawa on June 12, 1945. Murray was twenty-one, and the only Creek boy lost in the war. No one at the Creek understood why the rest of the world needed such a sacrifice in order to get along.

Two weeks after the wire came, my mamma received a letter written by Murray three days before his death. He hoped everyone was well and looked forward to coming back and spending his life at the Creek when the war ended. A postscript said, "Enclosed is the last payment on the motor."

Fourteen. Death Comes to the Creek

AUNT MARTHA'S saying, "The faster it grows, the quicker it goes," was true at the Creek. With its abundance of sun, rain, and rich hammock soil, the Creek was definitely on the fast track. I knew that life could be cut brutally short, although I preferred to ignore that, and assumed we were all just short of immortal.

In the spring of 1939, huge log trucks began roaring through the Creek hauling the last of the virgin cypress from the Oklawaha River swamp to a sawmill in Gainesville. Each day they raced by at high speed, as if the thousand-year-old giants demanded immediate annihilation.

Dad stopped by the lumber company's office and told them, "If you don't order them truck drivers to slow down, somebody is going to get killed." The company seemed concerned and promised they would.

I was helping him build a fisherman's shanty less than a hundred yards from the Bridge one day when our attention was attracted to a truck coming from the river. The driver was coaxing every ounce of power and speed possible from the overburdened engine. When he came around the curve heading to the Bridge, he lost control and allowed the trailer to run off the pavement, kicking up a cloud of dust as he passed. We ran out to the road and stood helpless as the vehicle roared up onto the Bridge. The trailer, loaded with three giant logs, careened to one side and caught the steel truss that supported one side of the Bridge. The explosion ricocheted and echoed across the hammocks and lakes as the Bridge and the truck disappeared behind the abutment. When we arrived at the Creek, the Bridge lay twisted and tangled and mostly submerged. There was no sound. Even the crickets and katydids were hushed. Logs and oil floated unmoving in the water. The other end of the Bridge barely clung to the west bank. The crumpled cab of the truck lay mostly submerged on its side, supported by the huge steel trusses resting on the bottom.

An oily form slowly raised its head above the surface, looking more like an oversized cooter than a human. He looked around, stunned. I felt no pity. My dad's voice called from behind me, "Are you all right?" The man nodded and waved his hands, gesturing in despair at the destruction around him. Dad said, "I wished it had killed you." The driver began to cautiously pick his way through the twisted steel to the west bank. When he reached the abutment, he crawled up the side to the graded road that had been suddenly transformed into a cliff. We watched until he disappeared around the curve, walking down the dirt road toward Gainesville.

I turned to my dad. "You think he's all right?"

He directed his answer partially to me and partially to himself. "Yes. I meant what I said. He has played hell, and all of us here at the Creek is gonna have to pay for it." George Fairbanks came out of the hammock like a shadow on the west side and stood gazing at the destruction. Dad waved to him, and he waved back, the creek between them, suddenly dividing them. There was no reason to rush to a telephone and report what had happened. Nothing at Cross Creek was of any interest to the outside world, and everyone in time would learn of the disaster by word of mouth.

The end of the old Bridge marked the beginning of changes that eventually affected every aspect of our lives and ultimately the Creek itself.

We would live divided for more than a year. We had to go around through Island Grove and Hawthorne to get to Gainesville. No one was more impatient to have a new bridge completed than Mr. Baker, the rural mailman, who had to drive an extra thirty-five miles each day.

When construction finally began after three months, we learned that the replacement would be built with reinforced concrete set on creosote pilings. I considered it my duty to inspect every phase of the construction. It was, in my opinion, the biggest thing that had ever happened at Cross Creek, with the possible exception of Henry shooting B.J. Dad did not think my inspections were necessary, but I managed to get down to the Bridge nearly every day. As the work progressed, it occurred to me that I would like to be the first to drive across the new Bridge. The foreman said he didn't have the authority to guarantee that I could, but he would let me know. I told my dad about my idea, but I didn't expect him to be interested in such foolishness. I was twelve then and had only driven the pickup in the grove and pasture, never on the road. After a lot of thinking he said, "Okay. You watch, and when they get it to where you can get the pickup on it, I'll help you cross the thing."

In the excitement of possibly being number one in something, I rashly talked about it in my mother's presence. She immediately said, "Tom, how can you be a party to such a thing. In the first place, he is not old enough to drive, and secondly, I sure wouldn't want to be the first one to test something built by any government." Dad said it would be something for me to remember, and went out the door.

I kept a vigil for months. The new structure was four feet higher than the old one, which meant the construction crew had to haul in fill dirt to the west side to give their cement mixers and equipment access. At last the foreman told me the trucks would come the next day to create the ramp on our side. It would be necessary for the trucks to cross the Bridge and dump directly from it. When they had sufficient dirt, they would drive down our side and turn around to go for another load.

I was disappointed because I thought he was saying the trucks would be the first to cross. He confirmed my supposition, laughing at my childish desire to be first, and ordered his men to take the heavy timbers they had used in construction and build a ramp down to the old pavement on our side. He said he had to roll one of his cement mixers off that end at quitting time.

I ran home and told my dad what the foreman said. He handed me the truck keys. "You might as well drive down there. I'll go along, jest for the ride." When we got there the ramp was in place. The crew sat on the railings along the sides to watch the official crossing that would signify the completion of their months of work. They half-heartedly applauded as I drove up and onto Cross Creek's new gleaming white cement bridge and stopped the pickup in the center.

I waited for my dad to say something profound and suitable for the occasion. "It looks like a new tombstone in an old cemetery," he said to no one in particular.

I too was disappointed. Instead of the elation I had expected, I felt as nostalgic for the old Bridge as for a friend that had passed away. I suppose being number one was all right, but I would prefer the old Bridge and what it represented. A neat inscription on either end of the new bridge read simply, "1940." It was the same year that death began to enter my life.

Before I was thirteen I had never been in the immediate presence of death, although I remembered two or three occasions when a family had lost a baby. My dad had once pulled some of his boat cypress from storage and built a small casket while I held a kerosene lamp for his work light. Mamma padded the inside with moss and quilt batten, then sewed and fitted a lining, using antique satin she kept in the bottom of the large steamer trunk brought from Georgia. Watching wild animals had taught me that the weak die young and that only the strong have a chance to live out their normal lives. I assumed that was the way with humans, until it came to my friend C.J. Calton.

C.J. was a strong, handsome young man who loved life. He was unaware of his good looks and a pleasure to be around. His mother had died when we were all much younger; C.J.'s younger brother, W.C. ("Monk"), who was my age and my vine-swinging companion, had then moved to Gainesville to live with an uncle. C.J. stayed at the Creek with his aging stepfather. He married Mr. Gillis's daughter, and they had a baby boy that was as handsome as his father.

As an adolescent I seized every opportunity to go with C.J. on frog- and gator-hunting jaunts, and he was with me the first time I played in the real-life game of fishermen-and-game-wardens. On one particular gator-hunting occasion, C.J. spotted what he thought was a relatively small gator, about four feet, and decided to catch him alive. He signaled me to maneuver the boat into a position that would lead us directly to it while he kept the gator blinded with his headlight.

I paddled in the direction of the glowing eyes and allowed the boat to glide to the spot where C.J. could reach over the side and grab the gator. When it was only inches from the bow, C.J. realized he had made a mistake. The gator was over six feet in length, definitely too big to catch. It was too late to attempt to shoot it, so just for sport C.J. decided to see how long he could hold it, even though he knew it would be practically impossible, barehanded. He grabbed the hundred-and-fifty-pound gator by the back of the neck, attempting to lift it up against the side of the boat.

All hell broke loose. Water exploded into the air as the alligator lurched up and out of the lake, crash-landing in our boat on top of C.J. It busted the front seat and broke the headlight. C.J. was knocked flat on his back into the bottom of the boat with the gator upside down on top of him. I don't know anyone but C.J. that could or would have held on, wrestling with the gator in the dark until he finally got it over the side and back into the lake. I had climbed up on the back seat when the gator flipped in the boat and stood there throughout the fracas, prepared to abandon ship if the fight came in my direction.

Even though our equipment was smashed, we laughed for ten minutes, partly from the ridiculousness of the situation and partly because we didn't have any broken bones. C.J. wanted to know why I had not hit the gator with the ax. We always brought one to make sure a gator was dead before we boated it. I told him I would have been glad to if I could tell in the dark what was gator and what was him. That was the first and only time I remember that the aim in a gator hunt was getting a gator *out* of the boat.

Shortly after that hunt, Mr. Gillis came to our house and told my dad C.J.'s legs were numb and he could not stand. Dad called my mamma and the two went immediately to see what could possibly cause a healthy young man to lose the use of his legs. Although he didn't feel any pain and was in good spirits, the seriousness of his condition was obvious. Dad lifted C.J. into the pickup and rushed him to the hospital.

C.J. Calton died of polio the following day. At the cemetery I looked at my neighbors huddled together and realized that the small number of families that made up the Creek were in reality my family too. We enjoyed more common ties than I would ever have with our distant relatives scattered across the South. Like the destruction of the Bridge, the finality of death had become a reality in my life.

When Murray Zetrouer was killed in the Battle of Okinawa, I was a long way from the Creek, stationed in the South Pacific, and my heart ached at the loss of another member of our family. I returned home in December 1946, glad to be back. The citrus hung heavy on the trees, fish were more abundant than ever, and the scourge of water lettuce was decreasing. Bernie Bass and I agreed that even scrub palmettos, mosquitoes, and sandspurs looked good. I was looking forward to a return to normalcy, when suddenly death was back in our midst. Charley Fields was killed in the spring of 1947. Another leaf had fallen from our tree.

❦ Life at the Creek was beginning to change in fundamental ways. The State hired more game wardens and exerted greater pressure on the trappers and seiners. Gradually the families stopped trapping altogether, abandoning the territories that had been theirs for generations. They turned to catfishing rather than play the old game with the new wardens, who were mostly outsiders and had little or no feeling for the lakes and the people who lived on them.

During the war the military personnel stationed in north central Florida discovered the Creek because of the bases nearby and because of Mrs. Rawlings's books. After the war the ex-soldiers and a new generation of moneyed automobile owners became sport fishermen with leisure time to fish the lakes. The State paved the road from the Creek to connect with the Gainesville-Palatka highway, making the Creek easily accessible from the north. Change was everywhere.

When I arrived back at the Creek from my military service, I discovered my father had planned my immediate future. After a short greeting he asked what I intended to do, now I was out of the army. I told him I thought I would play around for a week or two and then enroll at the University of Florida.

He said, as if he were surprised, "You got that kind of money?"

I said, "No, not a lot of money, but I have seven weeks' paid leave coming, and I wanted to fool around and see some girls."

He laughed. "Well, then, if you will listen to me, you can go to school and go with the girls at the same time." He laid out his plan. "I figure you can put in a sport fishing camp on our land up there at the mouth of the Creek where it goes into Lochloosa. You can rent boats while you go to school, and you'll have some money to go with the girls and not spend what little you've saved." He leaned back in his chair and added, "Of course, seeing that you are grown now and all like that, it's strictly your decision."

The next morning I cut the fence and guided a dragline across the pasture to the spot Dad had selected to dig the canal for a sport fishing camp. During the next year I graded off the campsite and helped Bernie build ninety plywood rental boats. The camp was successful from the start; some days we rented all the boats, and on weekends I borrowed the commercial fishermen's boats and rented them out too. Between bailing the rain water out after each shower and renting boats, I mowed the grass and picked up the Coke bottles my customers threw on the ground. I didn't see any girls unless they were going fishing, and I put off enrolling at the university as each semester came and went. But eventually I grew tired of the camp and for the first time began to think seriously about what I wanted to do with my life. I finally applied to the university, even though Dad protested. He had a lot of money invested in my camp.

My entrance exam results reflected my lack of enthusiasm in high school, so I enrolled in several refresher courses offered to returning veterans. For the first time I could remember, I liked school. I decided I wanted to be an artist but delayed telling my folks.

Dad continued to buy land. When I returned from the army, he owned over a mile lying between the lake and the newly paved road to Gainesville, plus several parcels scattered east of the creek. The Glisson cows had changed too. They were of a much higher blood line and grazed on tender grasses in pastures behind secure fences. The orange groves, though small, were at peak production, and citrus prices were improving. The fish business, now nearly all catfish, continued to thrive. When I asked why he continued to buy land, Dad said it was because that was what he came to Cross Creek for. "I have accomplished what I set out to do," he said, "and as soon as I can get everything to where it is self-sustaining I plan for your mamma and me to rest and maybe build a new house in the pasture with a view of the lake."

In the fall of 1949 I finally got up the nerve to tell my dad I had decided to become an artist and had enrolled in the Ringling Art School in Sarasota. He took off his hat and traced the edge of the brim with his calloused fingers. "I'm disappointed. I thought you might want to take over here and be independent like me and your mamma or even be a doctor like the one straightened your feet." He stopped to watch a flight of white ibis glide over the grove. "I sure thought you would of wanted to look higher on the vine for sweeter grapes, but a pink-pencil pusher—damn!" He looked directly at me. "If that's what you want, luck be with you. Course you'll have to do it on your own. I won't help you." He put his hat back on and asked, "Are you sure that the fact that they draw naked women at them schools didn't have a lot to do with your decision?" I didn't answer.

Mrs. Rawlings thought I had made the right decision. She said, "Now, J.T., you go to the school and learn everything you can. And I'll stay here and fight with Tom. When you are accomplished you can paint this magnificent place for posterity."

Learning to draw and paint was the most exciting and rewarding experience I had ever known. I immersed myself in the art I knew so little about, coming home for only three days at Christmas and then rushing back to school.

I was surprised to learn from my mother that Dad had driven down and visited the school and spent some time in the gallery where some illustrations I had done of industrial machines were displayed. He told her later, "Maybe his art will amount to something after all." Apparently the heavy equipment had appealed to him. I was thankful he hadn't come the week before when I had exhibited a series of watercolors entitled "The Wildflowers of Myakka Park."

In April of 1950 I received a call from my brother, who had recently moved back to the Creek. "I'm calling from the hospital," Carlton said urgently. "Dad accidentally drank some tree poison this afternoon. The doctors said if you want to see him alive you better get here quick." I rented a small airplane, flew to Gainesville, landed on a dirt field without lights, and caught a ride to the hospital.

My brother met me when I arrived and said Dad had bought a chemical recommended by the university to kill trees where they needed thinning for pasture. He had purchased it in a gallon Coca-Cola jug without a label from a local farm supply. Carlton said he didn't know it was poison. He had a man working over in the pasture who was using the chemical in small quantities from the jug. Dad came over and saw it sitting on the ground by a tree. He thought it was the worker's water and decided to get a drink. When he tasted it he realized it was not water and tried to spit it out. He went into shock on the way to the hospital and almost died before he got there.

An efficient-looking doctor introduced himself. He spoke like an announcer reading a communiqué: "Your dad has ingested a lethal amount of poison and will not make it beyond some time early tomorrow morning. We almost lost him early this evening. He is all right now, but there is nothing we can do while the poison progresses through the kidneys and enters the bloodstream. When it reaches his heart, he will be gone. I have discussed his situation with him, and he knows what to expect."

Until I went to his room I had been acting on instinct. Dad was sitting up in the bed looking as normal as any healthy fifty-year-old, hundred-and-eighty-pound man could in a hospital gown. "This is the last place I ever expected to see you," I said.

His matter-of-fact answer brought the situation into perspective. "Son, I made a little mistake this afternoon, but I will be just as dead tomorrow as if I had made a big one. You should remember that; little mistakes can get you too." I tried to protest, and he waved my objection aside. "These doctors know their business, and they say I won't make it. If a fight would do any good, I would put up a hell of a good one." He changed the subject. "How did you get here so quick?" We talked about art school and what I planned to do.

He said, "Son, life is like taking a trip on the train. Once you get on, you might as well make the best of the trip and enjoy the ride, because when the conductor decides for you to get off, that is as far as you go. J.T., I'm gonna change something I taught you. You take my advice and have a good trip, enjoy it, and try not to miss anything."

The night was both inordinately long and cruelly short. All of us watched the sky turn pink in the east, and he was gone.

When we arrived back at the Creek, I was surprised that it was still there after such a large part of it had vanished before dawn. Neighbors and relatives gathered throughout the day. I had never been as lonely, even though the house and yard were filled with guests. Near sundown Mrs. Rawlings came to me and said, "You don't need to be here. Slip out the back door and come down and spend the night with me." Just as darkness enveloped the Creek, I followed her suggestion. Although it was near the middle of April, the weather was cool, and she had a fire in the living room fireplace. It was a time for remembering and soul searching. We talked about her youth and how she had come to the Creek. She reminisced about my dad and said, "He was one hell of a man." She was clearly angry that he was dead. I told her what he had said about the train, and she agreed. I told her that in retrospect, I wished I had put aside art school and spent that time with Dad at the Creek. We talked about her property at the Creek and the plans she had made for its future after she was dead.

My Uncle Joe from Georgia came down about midnight and slept in the bedroom on the north end of Mrs. Rawlings's house. It was four o'clock in the morning before my friend and I stopped talking and I joined my uncle.

I balanced the best I could on the edge of the bed, trying to keep from sliding into the giant chasm caused by his nearly three-hundred-pound body. He began to snore, vibrating the bed and floor. Moe, Mrs. Rawlings's pointer, sleeping in the next room with her, was alarmed by the snoring and began to bark. She yelled, "Get out, Moe!"

My uncle woke and rolled out of the bed, nearly turning it over. "What the hell is the matter with her?" he said. "She asked me to stay." I told him Mrs. Rawlings was talking to her dog, Moe. He said, "Hell, I thought she said *Joe*," and climbed back in and started snoring again. For the first time since I had received the call about my dad, I couldn't stop laughing.

❧ Three years later Mrs. Rawlings suffered a brain hemorrhage and died as suddenly as my dad had. She was fifty-seven. It was the end of an era. Although her writing will always preserve that time and place, the real people, too, are an essential element in nature, and no place is the same when they are gone.

Like most things at the Creek, a twist of circumstance was connected with her death. Her husband, Norton Baskin, told me she had instructed him that she was to be buried in the same little cemetery in Citra my dad had elected to be buried in. When the time came, however, Norton failed to communicate clearly with a Gainesville funeral home and discovered too late that the grave and the service were in the wrong cemetery. And that was only half the problem; she was also buried only a few yards from the grave site of her old friend and adversary, Zelma Cason. Norton considered having her body moved, but the press assumed the choice was intentional and dramatized the coincidence, taken with the notion that in life they had been friends and then enemies, and finally in death they had chosen to be near each other.

With my father no longer buying their fish, the fishermen drifted away, with the exceptions of Bernie Bass and the Bauknights. A freeze struck in 1957, wiping out the citrus groves. Bernie eventually became my only link to the old days. He reached every one of his three goals. All of his children finished high school and became good middle-class citizens. On a spur-of-the moment decision back when the Grand Old Opry was still in its original location, Bernie's son-in-law asked him if he wanted to go; they drove all night, arriving in Nashville in time to get good seats for the live performance. And one day I came around the curve approaching the new Bridge and met my old friend in a new, glittering, light-blue Chevrolet pickup truck. "It had less than two miles on it and the tire treads weren't dirty when I drove it out of the showroom," he told me. We walked around it, fondling the polished enamel paint and kicking the tires. He said, "They was a lot of things I could have done with the money, but if a man don't want much it don't seem right that he hadn't ought to get it."

Bernie is also gone now. He was killed in his pickup.

Today there are only scattered remnants of the place, time, and people that made the Creek so special. That Cross Creek lives as a fading memory among a handful of the last survivors. I often think of the Seventeen Sisters, those cabbage palmettos growing on a small mucky island out in Orange Lake near the mouth of the creek. On dark nights and in bad weather they stood silhouetted against the night sky, the landmark that guided us to the mouth of the creek. They were like the people and the landscape: strong, robust, apparently eternal. During the last half of this century I have been saddened to watch nature's natural order of attrition cause them to die one by one, until today there is only one left. It is the last survivor, old and diseased and standing alone, reeling under the wind and rain, clinging to a proud past that has long since slipped away.

Afterword

I ASK myself, has the Creek as I knew it stolen away like Seventeen Sisters, leaving an imperfect place that will remain lost forever, or is it lying dormant as it did after the big freeze in the 1890s, waiting for a new generation that will tend the soil and nurture the lakes?

Twenty years ago I purchased a house four-and-a-half miles from the Creek, on the west side of Orange Lake. The house and plant life are similar to those at the Creek, except there are no tall cabbage palmettos. I missed the stately monarchs and felt poorer without them. It is extremely rare that young palmettos can be successfully transplanted, and I would not enjoy a mature tree that had left a void in another landscape, so I resigned myself to living without their beauty and soft rustling. During the remodeling of our home I brought a load of fill dirt from the home place at Cross Creek to fill a depression adjoining the side entrance. I spread it, leveled the area, and planted ornamentals in the fresh soil.

Fifteen years later I discovered the delicate shoots of a cabbage palmetto had broken the surface of the ground, growing up from the Cross Creek soil. More than six years have passed since the infant tree broke into the Florida sunlight, and today its magnificent fronds stand higher than my head. When there is a breeze from the south I sit on the porch and listen to the soft rustling and remember Cross Creek. I am reminded of a comment my dad once made. "The Ol' Gal is obstinate and contrary and above all she does everything in her own time." I like to think there are seventeen cabbage palmetto seeds lying in the muck near the mouth of the Creek, waiting.

Index